"A long, strong hug; a love letter to love itself; an exploration of everything that is important, and why it's important, and why it's worth remembering that it is. Jeanne Marie writes with a directness, and a grace, and a keen honesty that few writers, even in their best moments, approach. This is not a book to read because of its broad implications or its tremendous political import; it is a book to read because it is a joy to read it, and in the process, purely by accident, you just might learn to see your own small world in a slightly brighter shade." —Wil Hylton, *GQ* columnist

"Laskas tells the twin stories of her mother's sudden paralysis and her own quest to adopt a baby from China. Serious domestic issues both, they're nonetheless treated with Laskas' sparkling sense of humor." —*Pittsburgh Magazine*

"Very enjoyable . . . I found the writing wonderful. I loved getting inside the author's head—[Laskas] writes just like an intelligent, caring, funny person thinks."
    —Will Shortz, *New York Times* crossword puzzle editor

FIFTY ACRES AND A POODLE

"Anyone who's toyed with the idea of moving to the country should read *Fifty Acres*. It's stunning, witty, sly—a wonderful surprise." —Katherine Russell Rich, author of *The Red Devil*

"Jeanne Marie Laskas is a formidable reporter and one damn fine writer." —*Esquire*

"Truly happy endings are rare, and to read about two extremely likable people making their dreams come (mostly) true means a pleasurable read indeed." —*Newsday*

"Humorous . . . This true-life tale charts a big-city girl's transformation to farm gal." —*People*

"The thinking woman's Erma Bombeck . . . Even the most entrenched urbanite will be charmed by this book."
    —Andrea Sachs, Time.com

THE
EXACT
SAME
MOON

*Fifty Acres
and a Family*

JEANNE MARIE LASKAS

BANTAM BOOKS

THE EXACT SAME MOON: FIFTY ACRES AND A FAMILY
A Bantam Book

PUBLISHING HISTORY
Bantam hardcover edition published November 2003
Bantam trade paperback edition / September 2004

Published by Bantam Dell
A Division of Random House, Inc.
New York, New York

Book design by Glen Edelstein

Library of Congress Catalog Card Number: 2003041795

ISBN 0-553-38149-0

Manufactured in the United States of America
Published simultaneously in Canada

BVG   10 9 8 7 6 5 4 3 2 1

For Anna and Sasha

*The names and other identifying details
of some characters have been changed to
protect individual privacy.*

I

HERE
AND
NOW

CHAPTER ONE

O kay, you go in first," I say to Alex, the husband.
He looks at me.

"I'm too shy," I say.

He lowers his head, glares at me through eyes that say,
"As if."

Ahem. I remind him that I wet my pants nearly every day
in kindergarten, so terrified was I of joining the new society
of little kids.

"Yeah, well, that was a long time ago," he says.

"Yeah, well, no one would let me go down the sliding
board," I say. I'm reaching up, trying to help tame his hair,
which has suffered some severe style damage underneath the
wool cap he just took off. "You have hat hair, honey," I say.

"Oh?"

"Just kind of all over the place."

"Oh." He does some smoothing. "Well, I imagine this is
a pretty forgiving crowd."

We're at our local Ramada Inn, stalled here at the entrance
to Conference Room A, where the third annual Equine
Clinic, sponsored by Agway, our feed and seed store, is about
to begin. We've never been to one of these seminars before.
There must be three hundred people crammed into Conference

Room A. That's more people than your mind might automatically conjure when you imagine a talk about "Pasture Management" and "Understanding Worms."

I'm not sure I'm up for this. I was really in the mood for something low-key, like an intimate little poetry reading—except with horse talk, instead of poems.

"I'm sort of missing Sears," I say to Alex.

"You're missing Sears?"

"In a way . . ."

Sears is right down the road. We were just in there looking at refrigerators. And the thing is, I had an epiphany, right there in Sears. Yes, I suppose you could call it an epiphany. In my mind I am still trying to process what happened.

Nothing really happened. Alex was busy flirting with Vicki, the sales associate, trying to get her to throw in some freebies with the Amana we were considering. And I was leaning on a Maytag. I was leaning back tapping the cold enamel surface, *clickety clack, clickety clack,* with my fingernails. And I got to thinking. I got to thinking how blank a mind can become in the home appliance department at Sears.

Yup.

Clickety clack. Clickety clack.

And so naturally I got to wondering if there was anything at all rattling around in my big, loose brain.

And all I could think of was this: *I am happy.*

I am really happy.

How could such a small thought seem so huge? And—who knew? Who knew you could find yourself feeling utterly satisfied, suddenly and infinitely at peace with every promise the love gods ever promised and broke and repromised and rebroke—that whole rocky journey to love, none of it mattered now, in that instant, in that burst of awareness that really should have been happening on a beautiful mountaintop, or at least on a tropical island, no, it was happening in the home appliance department of Sears.

Is this it? That's what I wondered. *Hey, this might be it.* This right here might be happily-ever-after. It might be as simple as this.

Clickety clack, clickety clack. The discovery settled a lot of doubt for me.

Because, and as you probably know, there is considerable evidence to support the notion that happily-ever-after doesn't exist at all. Oh, plenty of people will tell you all about this. They'll tell you that just because you happened to go into your bride stage—as I did two years ago, when I married Alex— just because you went waltzing through that garden in your satin ball gown, surrounded by swirling perfume, surrounded by your family and your friends and even Christine, your devoted hairdresser standing there armed with extra bobby pins in case of hair droops, no, it doesn't portend anything. In fact, just because the love of your life was waiting there, in his tux, in that gazebo waiting to promise your same promise, just because that whole day went perfectly, just perfectly, right down to the *clippity clop, clippity clop* of the mule you got for your love as a wedding present—I got him a mule, but a small one—just because all that happiness actually happened, don't be thinking the happiness thing will necessarily stick.

Happily-ever-after, it's sweet. Sweet in the way a flying saucer is sweet and sweet in the way an optical illusion is sweet. It's hope rising, then disappearing into the mist. This is the way anybody who ever tasted sour has learned to think.

It isn't a bad way to think, but it really is only one way to think. Anyone can fall into the habit. Anyone can look at the bloom of a Shasta daisy and say, "Well, that's not going to last."

Why get so far ahead of the story? Why not just: Be in

the story? That's what I was thinking. I was thinking that the key to the whole thing is living in the moment, which is where happily-ever-after is, if only for the moment.

The here-and-now. I was thinking: This is the answer to everything.

So here I am now, at a Ramada Inn—I am standing here longing for the here-and-now of an hour ago at Sears.

Which would be there-and-then.

See, that's not good.

Damn.

This is not as easy as it sounds.

Alex is still trying to mat down his poor hair. Quite a gymnastic feat, the way that hair keeps bouncing back. It's more salt than pepper these days. It looks good on him. I mean, when it's fixed right. Pushed back, full on the sides, curling up in the back. It's a look befitting his character as a psychologist with wisdom and distance. Plus, he got new glasses, kind of square, fashionably hip numbers that suggest sophistication. I don't think he looks a full fifteen years older than me. I really don't. I'm thirty-nine. In my mind I still look like a basketball player, right guard, with a blond pony-tail swishing across the number 25 on my back, and smooth skin and calves that say "athlete." But I do have some evidence to suggest that I look different now. For one thing, it costs me eighty-eight dollars every few months to keep this hair this blond, and now it's all layered and short, a cut designed to *lift* that face, yes, to draw attention to that *youthful* arch of those *youthful* eyebrows.

But I don't mind getting old. There are plenty of things about youth that I'm glad to be done with.

"You know, I just have one comment about your whole kindergarten problem," Alex is saying to me. (Speaking of which.) We're still outside Conference Room A. I don't know why he won't go in first. Sometimes we get into these little stand-offs, which are based on nothing more than a mutually stubborn urge to *win*. "Did it ever occur to you that your pants-wetting thing had nothing to do with shyness," he says, "that it was just about manipulating your poor mother?"

Inhale. Exhale. See, this right here is the problem with being married to a shrink. Number one, you get sidetracked a lot. And number two, for some reason he's always defending your mother.

"What, because she had to drive up and bring me dry underwear all the time?"

"Exactly. You had her at your command."

Inhale. Exhale. "Honey, it was about *survival*," I tell him. "It was about needing someone to rescue me from that awful, miserable place where, first of all, the teacher smelled like mothballs, and second of all, the one time I finally got the nerve to go into the bathroom, Judy Hampton tricked me into going into the *boys' room* and all the kids were waiting outside laughing."

Inhale. Exhale. Why are we even *talking* about this?

"Sorry," he says.

"Well, I'll remind you that my mom started sending me to school with dry underwear in my lunchbox—so that sort of blows your theory."

"You know what, I'm sorry I brought this up," he says, adding: "Did I bring this up?"

Inhale. Exhale. "What in the name of potty training do you suppose she was *thinking*? I mean—my *lunchbox*?"

Inhale, exhale, inhale.

"You know what, let's just drop it," Alex says.

And then he turns to go in first, which you have to admit is a gesture of something.

Conference Room A is packed, steamy. Whew, lots of

body heat in here. White and green Agway balloons float optimistically above people tucked nice and tight at long tables set with Agway mugs and pencils and notepads. The walls are done up science-fair style, with display after display intending to educate on such matters as hay and sweet feed and mineral supplements and horse hair conditioners.

Alex and I don't know a soul, as expected. The truth is, we've come to Equine Clinic only incidentally to learn about pasture management and worms. We're here to *participate* in something, to become a *part* of something. This has become a sort of new campaign for us. We have been cooped up together for two happily-ever-after years. Recently we noted that we were beginning to finish each other's sentences. Pretty soon we may start speaking our own language, like kids raised by wolves.

Cooped up together is a hazard of any happily-ever-after, I suppose, but people whose happily-ever-after happens to be set in the country, in the middle of nowhere, well, we are especially at risk.

Two years. It's been two years since we left Pittsburgh, the familiar land of taxis and traffic lights and espresso bars and steam vents, to come to these gentle hills, about forty miles south. Hills dotted with sheep, hills that seem to roll toward Heaven itself. It was a countryside that beckoned us unexpectedly. It was a countryside that shouted: "This is it! This is your dream come true! This is the setting where your own personal happily-ever-after will take place!" Of course, this is the sort of stuff you are apt to hear when you are in a certain stage of life. When we stumbled into this area, we were just getting on with the business of being in love, we were getting married, and so of course we were getting all swept up by the adventure, by the thrill of the gamble. Somehow, when the dust from all that sweeping finally settled, we found ourselves the proud and uneasy owners of a fifty-acre farm in Scenery Hill, Pennsylvania.

We knew nothing about farming, or country living. (I grew up in the suburbs, Alex in the city.) But that didn't matter. "How hard could it be?" That was our motto. Our new home has a lily pond, a chestnut grove, an Amish-built barn, and a funky old farmhouse with some fairly apparent self-esteem issues. We named the place Sweetwater Farm and settled in with our city dogs: Betty (mine), a happy mutt more or less in touch with her inner dog. And Marley (his), a huge, black, dazed and confused poodle. ("I am married to a man with a poodle. I am married to a *shrink* with a dazed and confused *poodle*"—sometimes it helps to practice just saying that.) Shortly after arriving here, we got a third dog that might act out the more rugged farm dog role, a boxy Lab we named Wilma. Then we got the wedding mule, Sassy, and her horse companion, Cricket. It mattered little that we knew nothing about mules or horses. It mattered so little, we ended up getting another horse, Maggie, and another mule, Skippy. We were in expansion mode, at least when it came to acreage and animals and our connection and commitment to each other. As for other actual human beings—well, we haven't moved too far on that front. We have our city friends who like to come down, and Alex has his two grown children, Amy and Peter, who live and work in New York and who visit. Alex's psychology practice is in Pittsburgh, and so he has those humans to interact with. As for me, I stay at home writing, so most of my days are just me and the animals. The risk of bonkers-going is, I'll admit, high.

I have found it somewhat difficult to gain entry into country-folk society. Not because people around here are unfriendly. Not at all. The main problem is you hardly ever see them up close. There are precious few opportunities for chance encounters when folks are all off in some field tending to a llama or training a horse or *clank-clank-clanking* on a stuck tractor part. Around here, neighbors are people who wave across the acres as your car goes by. I have come to appreciate the waving. I often think about how in the city people sharing the same sidewalk avoid eye contact, while out here, you're flagging each other down, flagging each other down as if to say, "Hey, over here! I'm a person! And you're a person! Why, we have something *in common!*"

So, Equine Clinic. We thought it would be a good idea to get to know some of the horse people around here, folks with whom we have at least something in common. It is, we are just now discovering, quite a large population. Either that, or maybe word is out that Agway is giving away free stuff.

We find seats way in the back. The men nearby are wearing cowboy hats. The women have fringe on their shirts. There are lots of big silver belt buckles. Alex is in his Eddie Bauer khakis and shirt, and I'm Little Miss Land's End here. "Think we're dressed too much like . . . clothing catalog people?" I ask Alex.

"I think we're okay," he says.

"Well, let's just relax now and enjoy this," I say.

"Right."

"It's all about being present in the moment," I say. "The here-and-now. That's what happily-ever-after is, you know, it's *living in the moment.*"

"Right-o."

"Because, if you think about it, if you aren't living in the moment, you risk missing out on happiness completely. Unless of course the moment isn't happy . . ."

"What about interrupting?" he says.

"Huh?"

"What about when people interrupt your moment?"

Right. But I'm not quite done. "Let me just go on record as saying that I'm *not* saying that the unhappy moments aren't worthy of living in, you know, those are every bit as vital, it's just—"

"Honey!" he says. He gives me big eyes. Big eyes that say: Your talking is causing me actual pain in my brain.

Ahem.

And for his information, I would also very much like to hear what the speaker up front has to say about inspecting a bale of hay. It's awfully hard to hear back here.

Suddenly the front of the room erupts into laughter.

"What did he say?" asks a woman near me.

"Timothy is the Slim-Fast of hays," someone closer up yells back.

Guffaws go around the back of the room. Alex and I look at each other. We are new at hay-humor. We laugh anyway, trying to fit in. It's weird the way fitting in can feel like the most important thing in the world sometimes.

I'm getting that kindergarten feeling again. This could be because two plump women behind me are setting up the refreshment table: cookies and juice. This could also be because the need to belong to a larger community is as natural to humans as it is to dogs and horses and coyotes and all the pack animals. Who do you think invented the whole family concept in the first place? It was probably the dogs and the horses and the coyotes.

Now the lecturer is saying something about how clover can make a horse slobber and alfalfa can give it bloat.

"Did he say 'get a goat'?" Alex whispers to me.

"I think he said 'bloat,' " I say.

"Get *bloat*?" he says.

A woman behind us snickers, leans forward, grabs Alex's shoulder. "I thought he was saying something about a mare's coat," she says.

We really can't hear. And an organ has suddenly started playing. The people near me are looking around. Where in tarnation is organ music coming from? The people in the front of the room seem oblivious to the music as the tune reveals itself: "Amazing Grace." It's coming from the other side of the partition. That would be Conference Room B of the Ramada Inn.

"Can you please speak up!" says one of the guys in a cowboy hat.

"Let us renew our lives by the spirit that is within us!" says a very loud voice coming from behind us.

We all look around at one another. What do you do in a situation like this? We are sitting in Conference Room A, but now all we can hear is what's going on in Conference Room B.

"I'm having some serious here-and-now interference," I say to Alex.

"Sir, we really need you to speak up!" the guy in the cowboy hat says to the lecturer in the front of the room.

"Fermentation in the hind-gut produces volatile fatty acids!" shouts the lecturer.

"Alleluia!" says Conference Room B.

"We need to maximize forage."

"In the name of Jesus!"

A guy in front of me is the first to crack up, slapping his palm on his knee. Oh, that feels good. That gives us all permission. Two ladies in fringed shirts let loose, followed by the men in hats, who remove their hats, shake their heads, and surrender to laughter.

"So anybody want juice?" I ask, and head over to the re-freshment table and begin serving drinks to these, my neigh-bors, wedged here as we are between this and that. I meet Alice and Jim. Nancy, Susan, and Hank. We learn little about pasture management, virtually nothing about worms. We swap horse pictures. We say, hey, let's get together sometime, in the way you do when you know you probably never will.

"Well, that was fun," I say to Alex as we head out toward the car. "Nothing wrong with a little stupid fun."

"Stupid fun is probably what happily-ever-after is all about," Alex says.

"Are you mocking me?"

"No. I actually sort of mean it."

"I'll have to think about that."

IT'S AN EASY DRIVE home, fifteen quick minutes down a highway threading through suburbs, then you exit at the brawny town of Eighty Four, where there's a truck stop and a couple of gas stations and the Eighty Four Lumber Company, and then industry fades and gives way to sheep and hills that appear covered in a patchwork quilt of brown, yellow, tan. Our tiny town, without so much as a stoplight or a drugstore, is the village that sits on the highest hill around, and so the name: Scenery Hill.

I love that name. I love living here. Driving around, you feel like you've entered a very good dream.

It's a gray March Sunday afternoon, and we're in the bright red Ford Explorer we got when we first moved out here. We feel okay about owning an SUV, really we do, even though it's fashionable nowadays to feel guilt and embarrass-ment and shame. As country-dwellers, we have some fairly legitimate four-wheel-drive needs, so really, we're okay with it. Then again, the fact that I'm even bringing this up proba-bly means I've got some SUV-owning issues. See, this is an-other problem with being married to a shrink. You're always on the lookout for *issues*. Pretty soon you have an *issue* about having *issues*. This is another reason I need to get out more.

The landscape out my window is now all knobs and val-leys, knobs and valleys, pasture rolling out like ribbons bil-lowing in the wind. This is the landscape we fell in love with. It always reminds me of the Cotswolds in England, where the villages are tucked comfortably inside the creases of the hills, and every cottage has lobelia blooming. Except here, instead of adorably cute cottage after adorably cute cottage, you do get the occasional double-wide thrown in. A double-wide is a mo-bile home that is, well, double the size of other mobile homes.

It's okay, though. I've learned to accept the occasional double-wide. What's not to accept? I mean, when you think about it, the real jump is not between people who live in adorable English cottages and people who live in double-wides. The real jump is between the dogs, horses, coyotes, and us, which is not even that huge a jump. We're still all just a scared bunch of pack animals. All of us huddled together, family after family, doing what we can do.

I'm so much more of a pack animal than I used to be. There was a while there when I gave up on family. Well, not gave up, exactly. I just decided it wasn't for me. I come from a huge family. Mom, Dad, two sisters and a brother, a million nieces and nephews, not to mention assorted spouses with their own families. They all live back east, most of them in the Philadelphia area. I love them. I mean, you can't not love my family. Not a bad seed in the bunch. Just a gang of overachievers applying the overachiever's work ethic to the happy-family objective.

You can't argue with that. You can't argue with a pack of

people that places its highest value on the pack itself. But still, there's a certain suffocation factor. It's not something you would even think to complain about. It would be like complaining that you have too many best friends. You expect, what, you expect sympathy?

I'm the youngest of my parents' four kids. The baby. So in a way I was the tail. The tail of a very mighty dragon. On the one hand, it's nice to have stuff already figured out for you. The dragon has plans for you, and your voyage to happiness is really just a matter of hanging on for the ride.

But I felt devoured. I didn't want everything already figured out for me. My religion, my political affiliation, my favorite flowers, and my taste in furniture. What would I pick if I had no one around me already doing the picking? The urge to know sent me running, finally. I was twenty-one when I moved from Philadelphia to the other side of the state, to Pittsburgh, five hours away, which might as well have been Alaska. It was just supposed to be a temporary thing. A graduate school thing. A figure-myself-out thing. But I discovered: alone. Alone! I bought a little house on the south side of Pittsburgh. I made a garden. I got a cat and I got a dog. That was it. That was perfect. That was my happily-ever-after. I loved *alone*. When you're alone, you have a chance to form your own actual thoughts. That was it! That was the life for me. Family, I figured, was something that was better placed five hours away. Family was there when you needed it. It was always waiting for you back east.

Then, in my thirties, came Alex. And love. And marriage, and a whole new happily-ever-after on a farm. With Alex, I am still able to be alone—except with another person. He doesn't devour me. And I do my best not to devour him. One thing we're good at is remembering that our relationship is made up of two separate individuals.

And so we are a family of two. We are a family of two living happily-ever-after on fifty acres in the middle of nowhere. And now we are starting to finish each other's sentences. We think we need to get out more. We want to be a part of something larger. There is something going on.

Have you ever noticed the ticking of your own kitchen clock? Imagine. This is important. Imagine what it would be like if your kitchen clock was starting to get so loud, you could actually feel it, and what it felt like was a bird pecking you on the head. That's how mine is. And see, that is not right. You shouldn't be able to hear the ticking of your own kitchen clock. That should not be a noise you even know about. The *tick-tock* in your kitchen should be drowned out by family noise.

This, anyway, is the way I see it. And this basically brings us up to date. I mean, this is the raw truth of my here and my now. It's not something I talk about much. I barely even mention it to Alex; I rarely allow myself to contemplate it. But the truth is, I am craving family noise. Craving it in a way that makes my teeth hurt, if only in those moments between sleep and wake, in those tiny blasts of consciousness you do your very best to ignore.

CHAPTER TWO

We live on a dirt road. It's a rosy-orange dirt that escorts you through a protective cover of woods, mostly walnut, maple, and cherry. Our driveway runs along the southern edge of our farm, where it hugs the pond, then climbs to the base of our small barn, cobbled together a century ago by Amish farmers who used no nails, just wooden pegs.

Here is our farm, our wondrous farm. And now here we are, pulling up our driveway, the proud owners of a new side-by-side refrigerator. We're feeling good about ordering that Amana. After two years of marriage, not to mention nearly a decade of friendship, we are just now discovering that neither of us has ever had a home appliance that can spit crushed ice.

"This is going to be great," I'm saying.

"Really great," Alex is saying.

When I fling open the car door, I'm greeted by Wilma, who is carrying her usual log. Wilma doesn't play stick; she plays log. "All right, girl, all right." With a heave-ho I hurl the log toward the old chicken coop. It lands with a crack, then a swish as it goes sailing over the ice that has accumulated on the driveway. Wilma goes skidding, her legs flailing like paddles on a paddleboat, right into a bank of snow. "Sorry, girl!" She returns happy as ever, the log firmly in her mouth, wagging her tail with that unique brand of dog joy that makes you content just knowing about it. If there is any actual living proof that happily-ever-after exists, it is Wilma. She is the embodiment of it. She is the Jesus of that church.

Alex climbs out of the car, looks around in the bitter March air. Snow is falling again, gently this time, winter's smooth, weary sigh. "Did we leave Betty and Marley in?" he asks.

"I guess so. I sure hope Marley didn't chew anything."

"Marley?"

See, he thinks Marley doesn't chew. He thinks Betty chews. But Betty would never chew. Well, this is the way it goes. He brought Marley with him into our little family, and I brought Betty, so naturally there are allegiances. And equally as naturally I suppose, Wilma is the one who ends up getting blamed for most everything.

We head toward the house, our oddly expanding house. You can track a lot of rural architectural styles by reading our house from left to right, room after room added on over the years, all of them headed east. It could use a central vision, our house. That would be the first thing you would want to do for it. You would want to make it so the dignified cedar siding on the east end had some *relationship* to the old aluminum siding out west. You would want to make it so there was a *reason* this house has six, yes, six front doors and not one back door. We should offer this house up as a contest for architecture students, that's what we should do. You solve this one, you get the job.

We bang our feet on the porch to knock the snow off our boots. Inside I'm greeted by Betty, who is dancing on her most delighted dog toes. I see no evidence of anything being chewed.

"Well, hello, girly girl," I say, reaching down to scratch Betty's head. "You been in here watching TV all day?" Betty's a dainty yellow mutt with bedroom eyes, a sensitive, excitable creature prone to barking feverishly at the sight of very tall men—and cops. I don't know why. I got her from the pound when she was just eight weeks old. Perhaps, in utero, she and her mother were involved in some criminal activity?

Marley comes bounding over. Alex smiles, pounds on his chest, inviting Marley to rest his front paws up there. Marley obliges. I'm telling you, it looks like the two are going to break into a tango when they do this. "Oh, Marley," Alex says. "What in God's name did you have for breakfast this morning?"

"Stinky dog breath?" I say.

"I still have some of those doggy breath mints in the drawer there," he says.

I reach into the kitchen junk drawer. "See how my life is?" I say. "A shrink with a bad-breath poodle. I am married to a shrink with a bad-breath poodle."

"It's terrible, your life," he says. "It's a tragedy."

"It is."

Whoops, there's the phone. The machine picks up on two rings, meaning there are messages waiting, which I'll have to remember to retrieve.

"Hello?"

"Um, yeah, hello," says a thick voice. "This is George calling. Your neighbor?"

"Hi!" I say, a little too cheerfully. (Hey, it's a *person*. I'm like a kid with a dead butterfly collection. "Here's one now!")

"Yeah, well," George says. "Mother and I were wondering if we could stop over to your place in about a half hour."

"Um, sure," I say, leaving out the rest of my response: *Um, why?* and *Mother?*

As an ex-city person, I'm not used to neighbors calling unless it's to complain.

"Why do you think they want to come over?" Alex asks, when I hang up and tell him.

"Something about the sheep we were supposed to get?"

"But he didn't say anything about sheep?"

"Nope, just that they wanted to stop over," I say. "Hey. Does George live with his mother?"

"Huh?"

"He said he's coming over with Mother."

"I'm pretty sure his mother is dead," Alex says.

We stop and think on this point.

Now, George. George is a sheep farmer. His property borders ours. We've really only spoken to him a few times. In fact, up until recently George was more your basic waving neighbor. Then one day last fall we ran into him at Scenery Hill Hardware. We got to talking. We told him we were looking to hire someone to help us at the farm, specifically with our grass-cutting situation. How in the name of alfalfa, we said, was a person supposed to find time to *mow* fifty acres?

George said, "Alfalfa?" Then he suggested we buy, or maybe it was borrow, some of his sheep to do the mowing for us. He made the point that nobody around here mows grass just for the sake of mowing. "Put your land to use," he said. The concept had never occurred to us. We bought a view. We bought a postcard. We hadn't really considered much beyond the looking at it.

"Sheep," George said. "Yeah, sheep would work good on your fields." Intrigued, we agreed we'd stop by his house to discuss details. We showed up one night with some peaches off our tree, just to be neighborly. We asked about maybe signing a contract, or was there insurance involved, or what, exactly, was required of this sheep transaction? George, a round man with an even rounder belly and a ring of tobacco juice around his mouth, just shrugged. He said, "I open the gate, you stand there and steer the sheep onto your place."

"Right . . ."

Soon his wife, Pat, appeared. I'd never even waved at her before. She was a tall woman with a square jaw and a tidy, thick mop of white hair. She had a tray of coffee and some German chocolate cake cut up. Pretty soon we were all eating cake and sipping coffee and looking at photos of their five daughters standing on navy ships.

The next time we saw George, he was dropping off a mineral feeder at our place and giving us a lecture about magnesium, and he told us he was dipping the sheep's feet in antifungal solution for us, and as soon as he was done with that, he'd send over 150 of them.

"How much is all this going to cost us?" I asked George, but he never managed to answer.

And so this, we figure, must be why George has asked to come over. He finally wants to deal with the financial matters.

We put the dogs in the basement, as we usually do when we know company is coming, so as to avoid the whole "Get down!" thing.

Soon enough George is rolling up in his navy-blue Chevy. And Pat is with him. We watch them negotiate the ice on the driveway, a situation for which I feel I should run out and apologize, but then I figure they must be pretty used to the terrain and conditions of driveways around here, seeing as George was born here and Pat has been here since she started having his babies, six in all.

"Well, hello!" George says when he finally reaches our porch. He looks different than I remember him. He looks . . . scrubbed. Or shaven? There is something considerably less scruffy about him. Well, I guess he's not always a farmer.

Come to think of it, he's also president of the local school board, and he's also a coal miner. So I guess he has a lot of looks.

"How do you do?" Pat says. She's wearing a nylon jacket with "Bentworth School District" printed underneath a picture of a Bearcat, the school mascot. She's carrying a white package with the words "ground beef" written on one side. "Our gift," she says.

"Our beef," George adds. (He has cattle, too.)

"Well, thanks," I say, as we all head inside. "Oh, this will go so nicely in our new, um—" See, I'm catching myself as I say this, but it's too late. ". . . in our new side-by-side refrigerator."

Whew. I am new at this.

Inside I take coats, offer coffee, offer pie. Pat makes herself comfortable on the couch, next to Stevie, one of our cats who does not so much as show a hint of interest in any of this, while George perches himself on the edge of a wooden chair. It's the kind of posture you'd expect of a man who has something on his mind.

So here we sit, four people with half-smiles on our faces, each of us anticipating something. Or nothing?

"Ahem," Pat says.

"Yeah, the dog man was out to our place," George says finally, folding his arms over his round belly. "He come over here, too?"

"Um, no," I say, at least I don't think so. "The dog man?"

"The warden," George says. "He's concerned about a bunch of dogs running around. I got a shot at one of them."

I feel my stomach sink. In this horrible split second I am putting two and two together.

"There's a Saint Bernard running around," George says.

"A Saint Bernard?"

"*A wild Saint Bernard,*" he says, punctuating each word with a bob of his head.

"Well, that's kind of . . . hard to believe," I say. I mean, that's sort of like saying there's a wild poodle running around. There are certain breeds that don't, you know, just run around.

Pat nods, shrugs.

"Well, I've never seen one either," George says. "But this, I'm telling you, it's a wild Saint Bernard. Then there's three black dogs with it. I got a shot off at the one, I think I hit it."

"Oh."

George says he lost six ewes to the teeth of dogs in the past week. Dogs are a menace to sheep farmers. Dogs will chase sheep to their deaths. It happens all the time, at least according to local legend. And this is the two and two I'm now putting together. Obviously, this is why George has asked to come over. Dogs are killing his sheep. We have dogs. George wants to shoot our dogs. He wants us to shoot our dogs?

I drop my gaze to the floor. "Well, that's awful," I murmur, about the ewes he lost. And I mean it. Of course I do. Poor lady sheep. And how in the world is he expecting to put sheep on our fields when he knows we have three dogs? Not that our dogs have ever shown even a tiny bit of interest in his sheep. And I walk them by George's field all the time, on our daily walks to the mailbox. I don't believe they've ever even *noticed* George's sheep. Wilma is too busy throwing one of her various happiness attacks. Betty is too busy thinking about not getting her dainty little feet dirty. And Marley? Well, Marley appears to have smoked way too much dope as a kid, as is evidenced by his slacker attitude toward anything except, perhaps, killing and devouring groundhogs, which is another whole horrible story I don't care to go into.

Alex is sitting there stabbing his fork in his piecrust. He

tosses me a glance. I can tell he knows what's about to happen, too. This man in our living room is about to ask us to, um, cancel our dogs.

I'm bracing myself. I'm preparing my response. I'll just tell him no. I will say, "No, and thank you very much, but we will not permit you to kill our dogs."

"I tell you about the electric fence?" George says, after a fairly long silence.

Um, no. And what does it have to do with shooting dogs?

Nothing, as it turns out. George is leaning back in his chair, way back, with his feet on the ottoman and his hands behind his head, and he's telling electric fence stories. The stories go on a long time before I finally catch on. Oh, *we are changing the subject.* George is not here about dogs at all. Pretty soon he's into a whole Great Moments of Almost Getting Electrocuted by the Electric Fence saga. He is one hell of a storyteller. He says once he was holding his fence-tester near a fence wire when a snake appeared and up and bit George's finger *and* the tester, uniting the snake, George, and the fence in an electrical current that could have lit up a shopping mall.

He also says kids make great fence-testers. "Yeah, I paid my kids a quarter per hit," he says.

"It's all true," Pat says.

Okay, then. Um. But this has nothing to do with the reason they've come over to our house, correct? What exactly is the purpose of this visit? And how exactly do you ask this? How do you turn to a person sitting in your home and say, "So why *are* you here?"

Alex attempts to steer the conversation back to sheep. He seems convinced this is a business meeting. He says, "George, about those sheep." He says, "How much are you charging?"

Well, that was blunt.

George laughs. "Oh, heavens," he says. "I should be pay-
ing *you* for all that alfalfa my girls are going to get to eat." He
says he's going to put his sheep on our fields in the spring, let
them eat away until fall, at which time he'll take them back.
"You don't want to winter sheep," he tells us. "It's a pain."

Right, then. So nothing is required of this transaction.
Absolutely nothing. But it doesn't seem as though he has
come to tell us this. This seems to be more of an underlying-
assumption type thing.

It goes on like this, until nearly ten o'clock. The evening
just goes on and on willy-nilly, never settling into theme or
form or reason. George has headed off into a fairly animated
lecture about hoof-and-mouth disease. Pat listens, as she has
listened all evening, and does not seem even a little bit bored.
Finally George turns to Pat and says, "Well, Mother, we don't
want to overstay our welcome." And Pat says, "Yes, George,
we better get you to bed," and George and Pat stand up, shake
our hands, and say, "Good night, now."

Then they are gone.

Alex and I clean up the pie plates and ask ourselves, now
what in the name of anti-fungal solution was that about?
Why did these people come over and entertain us with dog
and snake stories on a Sunday night?

We think of a few other neighbors who have, in the time
we've lived here, stopped by without much warning. These
are the few chance encounters we've thus far had. Most of
these people brought small gifts, a plant, a hat. They chatted
and left. Why did they do this, and why did we then never see
them again?

"Because we never visited them?" I suggest.

We are not used to a social fabric woven this way. We are
used to the other way around. In the city, hosting someone in

your home is an act of kindness, an invitation into the dance of friendship. In the country, visiting is. I am just coming to realize this. Out here, where there are more acres than people, people are like little treats. It's exciting to see them. They break up the monotony of green, brown, blue. And so a visit is a favor. Something that, in the dance of friendship, you are expected to return.

When we stopped by George's with our peaches last fall, we must have inadvertently started the dance. And George and Pat have just officially kept it going, with a pound of ground beef to seal the deal.

Standing at the dishwasher, Alex and I are coming to this conclusion at about the same time. "Oh!" we say, stacking our pie plates next to the silverware. George and Pat are our *friends*.

It feels like a revelation, sure as alfalfa.

Much of our time out here at the farm has been filled with small revelations like this, each in its own way oddly exhilarating. And baffling. It's as if you're repeatedly tripping over a loose board on your floor. Your feet go flying out from under you. You stand up, think: *What just happened?*

In this case: friends. Two friends just happened. Well, that's a nice moment to be in. Even though I suppose I am technically only in its echo.

As we get ready for bed, I try to explain to Alex what happened to me earlier today at Sears.

"Maybe I was making light of it earlier, but I'm serious. The happiness, it hit me. I was really happy. I mean, in that moment, entirely happy."

"That's wonderful," he says.

"It is."

"Your Maytag epiphany," he says.

"Something like that."

"It's good to stop and notice something like that," he says.

"It is. Because you don't get happy moments all the time. Most of the time you're flooded with all kinds of conflicting feelings."

"You mean feelings of being unhappy? Are you unhappy?"

"No more than anybody else."

"You're *unhappy*?"

"No, no, no!" I say. "I'm happy! I'm happy! Everyone has little sniggly things."

"Sniggly?"

"Is that not a word?"

"I'm pretty sure it's not."

"You know what I mean."

"I think so . . ."

"I'm happy," I say to Alex. "I'm madly in love with you. I often feel like the luckiest person alive to have this life."

"Me, too," he says.

"Plus we got a refrigerator that spits crushed ice."

"Happiness overload!" he says, climbing into bed. "Hey— who called?"

"Huh?"

"The answering machine. Did you check the messages?"

"You know what, I completely forgot."

It's blinking over on the bureau. I climb out of bed, push the button.

Beep.

"Ah, Jean Bean, it's your father." Well, that's weird. My father is not a phone kind of guy. *"It's about noon. Would you call me, please? It's about your mother. I'm afraid she's going to have to go to the hospital. She's having some trouble walking. I mean, she can't—walk."*

I look at Alex. My mother is a healthy seventy-five-year-old woman who has never had trouble walking.

"... I've called for an ambulance," my father says. "I've left word with your brother to meet me at the hospital. But I just wanted you to know what is going on."

Alex gets out of bed, comes over closer to the answering machine. We're both staring at it with our eyes scrunched up, trying to understand. There is another message.

Beep.

It's John, my brother. "I'm at the hospital with Dad," he says. "It's about two here. Where are you? Dad's fine. Mom is, we don't yet know much. There seems to be some paralysis."

What?

"... I'll call when I know more," my brother goes on. "Claire's on her way."

Beep.

Another message. It's Claire, my sister. "Dear?" she says. "Why aren't you answering? I really need to talk to you. Can you pick up please? Deeear, pick up!"

There is a long silence.

"Okay, well, it's about four o'clock," Claire says. "I'm with Johnny and Dad. Mom is, well, she is, you know what, you need to know she is paralyzed. But there is something going on with her breathing now. They are moving her to ICU. I will call you back."

What?

One more message.

Beep.

It's Kristin, my sister in New York. "What is going on? Did you talk to Johnny? Did you talk to Claire? Do you know what the hell is going on?"

CHAPTER THREE

Is this what labor feels like, from the baby's point of view? It's like, *come on* already. I'll never get out of here.

"Canceled," the woman at the US Airways counter says when I finally reach her, reach her like she's the only one who can rescue me from this situation, which she is. But no. "That flight is canceled due to fog," she says.

I can't believe this. I can't believe this! I am stuck in the Bradford airport, a tiny airport on the northwest border of Pennsylvania—the exact opposite direction from Philadelphia, where my mom is, where I'm trying to get to. It's now Tuesday, two full days after she went into the ICU, and I'm not there yet. I can't believe this. This is like one of those dreams where you're running and running and running but it turns out the whole time your feet have been carrying you backward.

I book myself on the two o'clock flight, leaving me four hours to kill in Bradford. Four hours to sit here and think about things, think about my mom, think about getting to my mom. This must be what labor feels like, from the baby's point of view, except, of course the baby is trying to get *away* from the mom and I'm trying to get *to* mine. But still. It's the stuck feeling.

My mother is paralyzed. Okay. My mother is paralyzed, and no one knows why. The story is, she woke up just like anybody wakes up, tried to get out of bed, and fell over. "John," she said to my father. "My legs don't work."

I come from a family of doctors. My brother, who is fifty-two, has a dermatology practice that grew out of my father's dermatology practice. My sister Claire, forty-one, is a pediatrician. My older sister Kristin, a forty-seven-year-old television producer, is the only one besides me who followed in my mother's English major path. Three of us, three of them. This is how my family is divided. And the three of us depend on the three of them when it comes to matters of aches and pains and itches.

When they wheeled my mom into the Emergency Room, none of the doctors in my family—nor, for that matter, any of the doctors at the Emergency Room—had the foggiest notion what was going on with my mother. Paralyzed. Her legs were paralyzed. As the day progressed, so did the paralysis. It was moving up her body. In just hours her torso, her fingers, her shoulders, her neck, her smile were losing contact with her brain. By nightfall, it appeared her lungs were shutting down, too. That's how she ended up in the ICU.

I have been receiving this information in bits and pieces, phone call by phone call, on my bright red cell phone programmed for no reason to ring with the Mexican Hat Dance song, *Dee dump, dee dump, dee dump, de diddly dump dee dump,* and which I'm carrying in my hand in case the song should suddenly play again.

I shuffle through the Bradford airport's so-called terminal—a room with a coffee shop attached. I plop my bags and miserable self into a booth. Alex is back at the farm. I told him it would be easier if I just went alone. For a week. Maybe more? Well, I had no idea how long I would need to be in Philadelphia with my mom. But Alex could take care of the farm, the dogs, the cats, the horses. I would have a thousand less things to worry about.

I should get coffee. No, I should get juice. I should get eggs and juice. I should get a sandwich. Is it lunchtime yet?

"Some fog," says an old man seated in the adjacent booth. He's got both his hands wrapped around a cup of coffee. He's wearing a US Airways cap and a work shirt with a patch that says "Mountain Pilot." "Ain't no airplanes leaving this airport today," he says with a smile.

Gee thanks, buddy. I smile at him anyway, as you do to strangers. "Well, fog burns off," I point out.

"In these mountains? With these ponds?" He laughs.

I smile again, thinking: *Why is this man torturing me?*

"Do you work here?" I ask.

"Naw," he says. "I'm just the mascot." He tells me he likes hanging out here. "It's better than a bar," he says. He tells me he has a small airplane in a hangar out back, and on clear days he likes to take people, "usually females," for rides. "But it's a small plane. So if a fat one comes along, I have to say I'm sorry."

"Right," I say.

"You might want to have a look at this," he says, handing me a computer printout he just got from a fellow pilot. It has a lot of Doppler radar lingo on it, and then: WARM FRONT IS WEDGED AGAINST THE WRN RIDGE OF THE MNTNS AND WILL MOVE LITTLE TODAY.

"Looks like you're stuck here," he tells me.

"Thanks," I tell him.

"Well, I try to be nice to a pretty girl once a day," he says, smiling. "Anyway, what else do I have to do?" He reaches over the plastic flowers separating our booths and extends his hand. He says his name is Mack. He confesses that he likes it when the fog rolls in. He gets to know people. He asks me what I'm doing here in Bradford.

"A conference," I say. "At the university." Which is all I feel like saying about it. See, I should have bagged the conference. It was the conference that kept me from just driving home to be with my mom as soon as I got the news. I should have canceled! I was going to cancel! But my sister Claire said, No. She said, Don't cancel. Don't panic. Just do what you have to do, come home when you can. She said my mom was stable. She'd given the same advice to Kristin, who had to clear things up at work before she could bolt.

So I figured, all right. You said you'd do the speech to kick off the conference, you agreed to it months ago, they have you in all the publicity material, your mom is stable, you have to do this conference. Even though the conference is four hours north of Pittsburgh. I mean, way the heck in the middle of nowhere. The other side of the universe from Philadelphia, where my mom is.

"What kind of conference?" Mack says.

"Just a . . . conference," I say. "It was yesterday. Today is, you know, today." Oh, brother. There's a statement. I'm not doing well. It's hard to be your normal self when you're walking around with big, awful news in your head. But what is there to say, anyway? Nothing except: Hey, never mind the stupid conference, my mom is sick! Completely healthy one day, my mother is now lying in an intensive care unit paralyzed up to her eyeballs—the good news is she can blink—struggling for every breath. And no one is exactly sure why.

And what about happily-ever-after? Whew. It sure can

get yanked out from underneath you. There is no holding on to happiness.

But then again, that's not exactly right. Happy moments don't vanish altogether. They just get . . . added to. Of course they do. Moments never exist in isolation. Moments are like music. The strings come in, then the brass, then some percussion. Moments never drown each other out unless you let them. Hey, it's your orchestra.

"Hey," says Mack, sitting across from me. "You want to come see my plane out back?"

"Thanks," I say, forcing a smile. "But I'm good."

"Aw, come on," he says. "I'm a harmless old man."

"You know what," I say, "I'm waiting for a phone call." I hold up my red phone as proof. He shrugs, looks away.

Aw. And now why do I feel guilty? I *am* waiting for a phone call. I've been waiting for phone calls for two straight days. My dad, who is sounding eerily calm about my mother's condition, is due any second with an update. I think all this reporting is helping him, like he's a foreign correspondent on the front line. He certainly has the deep resonant announcer voice for it.

At the moment there are three theories floating. Number one, my mom could have a collapsed disk in her neck. She's had neck pain for years, nothing serious, just discomfort. But perhaps the disk is now pinching her spinal cord? If so, she would likely need surgery—on her spinal cord. This option seems to be a very unpopular one.

The second theory is: brain tumor. This option is a lot less popular than even the first. There just isn't a whole lot to say past the words *brain tumor*.

The final guess is a rare disease called Guillain-Barré Syndrome, which at the moment is the diagnosis everyone is rooting for because, while we know almost nothing about it, the one thing we do know is that most people suffering from it eventually recover.

My dad is supposed to call any minute now. Why isn't he calling? Is that good news? Or is that bad news?

I'm trying to picture my mother paralyzed. It is an impossible image to invoke. I'm trying to picture my mother with arms that aren't able to move. They say she can't even move her fingertips. She can't smile.

But she can blink.

See, I can't picture any of this. Actually, at the moment I can't even picture my mother at all. Oh, I hate this. This used to happen to me, as a kid, when my parents took off on vacation together, leaving us kids in the gentle command of our Aunt Ag. I loved my Aunt Ag as much as anyone on earth, but somehow I'd end up missing my parents so much, I'd forget what they looked like. I'd absolutely lose the picture of them in my mind. I wonder now why I didn't just go get a photograph of them or something. Maybe I did. But I don't remember that. I remember only the blankness of forgetting.

Eventually, I could feel them. And this was usually the way back. I could feel my dad's hand on my cheek. He'd always put his hand on my cheek when I needed comfort. He had hands like clouds. Only warmer. And closer. Big and strong enough to ward off anything scary. He had hands that held you and made you feel like a flower.

I can feel his hands now. Oh, it's a cinch to conjure them. What I can't feel is my mother's arms. Well, that's weird. Because after feeling my dad's hands, I could usually feel my mother's arms. I could feel myself being held by her.

And now I can't. My mother is paralyzed, and I'm the one having trouble feeling.

There's my phone. *Dee dump, dee dump, dee dump.* Now

why do I have the Mexican Hat Dance song programmed in? A lot of the decisions you make when you're happy seem painfully stupid when you're sad.

"If you'll excuse me," I say to Mack, who's sitting here staring at me. He nods, climbs out of the booth, and saunters away.

"Hello?"

"Well, some good news this time," my dad says. "No evidence of tumor." I can hear the relief in his voice, or maybe that's a sound coming from inside my head. He says he should know any minute about the results of the MRI, which will give us the red or green light on the disk-collapse theory. I tell him about how I'm stuck at the Bradford airport, but I'm careful not to whine.

"Okay, sweetie," he says. "I'll give you a call after the meeting."

"Meeting?"

"She has a team. A neurologist, internist, a whole team. They're going to go over everything. I'll call you when I have some news."

"Good."

"Say some prayers," he says.

"I'm on it."

We hang up.

And here comes Mack again.

"You gonna come see my plane now?" he says.

"I'm waiting for another call," I say.

"You can't bring that phone with you?" he says. "Come on, you look like you could use something to take your mind off your troubles."

Well, that part's true.

"This'll work," he says. "Guaranteed."

There's something charming about the way his eyes meet

mine, then dart away. His skin is thick as a fisherman's, and the deep creases hold stories, you can count on that. I imagine myself out there looking at his plane. I imagine there's all of a sudden a miraculous break in the fog cover and Mack is able to start up his plane and whisk me on out of here. Hmm. This definitely could be what labor feels like, from the baby's point of view. It's like: How can I escape? You're open to anything.

"All right then," I say.

"You wait here, I'll pull my truck around."

Soon I am climbing into a blue Ford pickup with lots of airplane stickers on the dash, which I dutifully admire.

"You married?" Mack asks. "Not that it matters."

The way he says this—something in his tone. The pieces fall into place with a thud. "You're trying to *pick me up?*" I say. "Aw, jeez. Listen, I'm having a bad enough day as it is."

He shrugs, looks down.

"I didn't mean it that way—"

"It was worth a shot," he says. He tells me he's married. "Well, she died. Nine months ago." He opens his glove compartment and pulls out a small green photo album labeled "Claire."

"That's my mother's name," I say. And isn't that strange? I'm starting to wonder what bizarre forces are at work this day. "And my sister's, too."

He says she was fourteen when they met. They were married for fifty-one years. "Oh, I worshiped the ground she walked on. Everybody knew that."

I don't know what to say. How do you console a person you've just met? A lonely, if unreconstructed, old man who probably just needs a friend?

He pulls out another photo album. This one is red and

has no label. "Okay, now these here are a couple of girl-friends I've had in my life. This is my lady in New Jersey, and this here's my girl in Arizona. And then Betsy, she lives right here in town."

I look at him, confused.

"Oh, I stepped out on Claire all my life," he tells me. "She knew. But she never said a word about it." He keeps flipping through the girlfriends. He says Betsy rolls her own cigarettes and skins deer and fixes cars. "But see how feminine she is?"

I lean back, rest my elbow on the truck's window ledge and my fingers on my eyes. You know, all I really wanted to do today was go home and be with my mother. How did I get into all of this? Forget the whole birth-canal metaphor. Either that, or I definitely took a wrong turn.

Mack pulls his truck into the hangar and hops out to show me his yellow Cessna 150. He shows me how the flaps work and where the gas goes in. He opens the door, helps me settle into the cockpit. He says he loves machines. And adventure. "I like changes," he says. "It's why I drove a truck all my life. I can't stay in one place." His sons also drove trucks. "But both are dead," he says. The first one cancer, the second one suicide. "One day his wife told him his kids were not his own," he says, "and the next day he was dead."

I don't know quite what to say. Families are messy, that's what I want to say. Or, gee—and to think I've been craving family noise. Yeesh. Never mind. There's a lot to be said for living your life with just a bird pecking you on the head.

"Well, why did you cheat on Claire?" is what comes out.

He shrugs. "It was just a thing I did with my life."

My cell phone rings. *Dee dump, dee dump, dee dump, de diddly dump dee dump.* "There's my call. How do you open this door?" I find the lever. It reminds me of the way my old '73 Volkswagen Beetle door opened. Cute latch. Cute door. I step out of the plane. "Hello?" I clunk my head on the wing, clunk it good. "Aw! Ow! Awwwww!"

"Hello?" my dad says. "Are you okay? What happened?"

I have no idea in this world how to explain what just happened. "I'm fine, I'm fine," I say. "What's the word?"

"Her neck is fine," my dad says. "They just came in with the MRI results. No change at all from her last MRI a year ago. So I'm sure this is what they're thinking. They're thinking Gee-ann-bar-ray." He's careful in his pronunciation, as if he's been practicing.

"Oh Dad, that is so great," I say. "I mean, I think it's good news. Is it good news?"

"Well, I wouldn't say, you know, good," he says.

But of all our choices, wasn't this strange little disease the one we were rooting for? Shouldn't we be relieved to hear this diagnosis?

"We're learning more about it," he says. "We'll know a lot by the time you get home."

"Yeah, well, she could be all better by the time I get home," I say.

He doesn't laugh. He doesn't say anything at all for a moment.

"It's going to be a long haul, honey," he says, finally. "We still have a lot to get through."

"Not to mention the move," I say.

"Oh," he says. By the way he says that, I can tell he hasn't thought once about the move.

Whoops. Now, why did I have to bring this up? The last thing my dad needs to think about is the move.

For a long time, the move was front-page news. The move. The move. The *move*! This was all the family talked about. Oh, I must have a thousand hours of phone time logged in with my mom about the move.

"I can't think about the move," my dad says.

"No. I'm sorry. I don't even know why I brought that up."

"I can't think about it."

"No."

My parents have lived on the edge of Springton Lake, set back in a wooded cove, for nearly twenty-five years. This, you understand, was the land of my mother's dream. Her big happily-ever-after dream. She picked the spot and designed the house when she was in her early fifties, having nearly finished raising her kids and feeling quite ready to begin pursuing the things she had put off. I was in high school when we moved, and I remember seeing my mom become the picture of joy in that house. She decided to go back to art school, she got accepted at the exclusive Pennsylvania Academy of the Fine Arts, she took herself seriously as an artist for the first time in that house.

As a matter of fact, looking back, I can see she really was a model for me when I set about pursuing my dream of living on a farm. Looking back, I can see that Springton Lake was my mother's Sweetwater Farm.

The weird thing, though, was that just as my Sweetwater Farm dream was coming true, my mother's Springton Lake dream was coming to an end.

"Your father's talking about moving to the funny farm again," my mother said to me one day about a year ago on the phone.

"I really don't think you should call it the funny farm," I said.

"I just don't see myself living around a bunch of old people," she said.

I didn't either. I was not at all in favor of the funny farm, also known as Riddle Village, a brand-new retirement center just a few miles from the house on Springton Lake. My parents were by now well into their seventies, and my dad was more than ready to give up the daily cares of home ownership. My mother was not. She was in no way prepared to leave her dream house, her painting studio, her wildflower gardens, and all those millions of daylilies she had tucked so lovingly into the earth over the years.

Moving was a subject that was coming up a lot when I talked to my mom on the phone, a habit I'd long ago fallen into. For so many people my age, a mother is a touchstone. Something good happens in your life, you call your mother. Something bad happens, you call your mother. Your mother, the very person who sent you off to kindergarten with dry underwear in your lunchbox, she is a camera recording your life. It's nice to know she's there. It's comforting to know someone is interested in all of this. Actually, when you really think about it, it's fairly essential to your sanity that you have her there.

I hated when my mother got to talking about the funny farm. A retirement village? It screamed: OLD. It was a building that said: Your parents are on their way out. I'd never really thought of my parents as old until my dad got that stupid funny farm idea in his head. If you start imagining your parents as old, the next thing you know you're imagining them dead. I didn't even know how to imagine a world without parents.

One day last fall my mother called to tell me it was a done deal. They'd signed on the dotted line. "Funny farm here we come!" She tried so hard to appear happy about this. She said the apartment was huge. "And the food is great!" she said. "And the dining room is so elegant."

"Great, Mom," I said, even though what I wanted to say was: "I'm so sorry."

It was just a few weeks later that the For Sale sign went up on the house on Springton Lake. My mother couldn't even look at that sign. She got in the car and spent the day at the library. She went the next day, too, and the next. She grew increasingly withdrawn.

My parents' house sold within a month. Done deal. And then the minutes started ticking by. The move. The move. The *move*! It really has been like a time bomb we've been waiting to go off.

Who could have imagined that we'd have an entirely different explosion?

Now my mother is paralyzed. The movers are scheduled to arrive in just two weeks. No, my dad shouldn't be thinking about the move.

"It's just that, well, your mother is not exactly out of the woods here," my dad says to me on my little red phone. "And I don't want to scare you, but—"

"I understand," I say, even though I don't. Mack is craning his neck, trying to listen, trying to figure out what is going on. I give him a sneer. The kind of sneer you give to your best friend since seventh grade: "Quit it!"

"I'll talk to you later, Dad," I say. "I'll be there soon."

I hang up, turn to Mack, who is still sitting in his plane. I'm talking to him through my little window, which is closed but apparently doesn't block out sound. "Let's go in and check on my flight, okay?"

He looks at me, disappointed.

Oh, brother.

"I really like your airplane," I say.

"She's pretty, isn't she?"

"A real beauty," I say.

He drives me back to the terminal without incident. He stands with me in line. He seems to think I need company. I don't quite know how to tell him that I really, really don't.

"Canceled," the lady at the US Airways counter says. "All flights out of this airport are canceled due to fog."

"*All flights?*" I say to the woman. I mean, I didn't actually know they *did* that.

"All flights," she repeats.

I can't believe this!

The woman tells me that vans have been dispatched to drive passengers to either Buffalo or Pittsburgh, where there will be flights to take us all to our final destinations.

I didn't know they did that, either.

"Hey, how about I drive you myself?" Mack says. "I'll get you there faster."

I decline the offer. I'm sure he's quite harmless, but spending four hours alone in a truck with him, I don't know. Sometimes you have to set boundaries. There are people in this world who will move into your house if you don't set boundaries.

I plunk myself back down in the booth. The woman said it will take a few hours before the vans arrive. Fine. Fine. Fine. Sooner or later you just surrender. When you're stuck, you're stuck. This must be what a false labor feels like, from the baby's point of view. Contraction, contraction, then . . . nothing. Just more waiting. I wonder why I'm so stuck on this labor metaphor.

I lean back. I shut my eyes. I take a few deep breaths, sink into the moment. Eventually I feel it. I feel her. My mother. She was always so—bony. That's how it was. That's how it was to be in my mother's arms. I don't remember the kind of soft, mushy experience you imagine a baby feeling when you hold one. I don't know why my mom was bony. She's not an overly thin woman. Just a regular-sized woman. But she's not mushy. I mean, there is nothing mushy about my family in general. We're not kissy. We're not huggy. There's an emotional warmth, but not a physical one. It's like, sometimes you just want to wake up and be Italian. *Mamma mia!* Slobber, slobber. Sob, sob. Kiss, hug, slop, slop, slop. "I love you! I love you! *Mamma mia!*" See, I wouldn't mind a good dose of that in our family.

I think if I ever have a child, I'll work on becoming Italian. I'll be mushy and sloppy.

Well, that's funny. I mean, listen to that. "If I ever have a child." That child idea has been popping into my head a lot lately. It's strange. The idea comes into my head like the rumbling of a far-off thunderstorm. Then it vanishes.

Maybe it all goes back to being the baby of the family. That's your identity: baby. You cling to "baby" because, well, that's you. When the baby of the family imagines herself as a mom, it's always a far, far-off sort of thing. I'm the baby of our family. This is the way it has always been for me. But now I am, well, I am thirty-nine.

Hours pass before the vans arrive. Mack, who sticks right here by my side, has been entertaining me with flying stories. I still can't quite forgive him for cheating on Claire all those years. He follows me out to the curb. "Well, bye," he says. He asks if he could have a hug. I offer my hand instead. He shakes it. "I can't go without meeting people," he says. "It's why I come here."

"Right," I say.

"One last thing," he says. "I married the one I loved."

"Well, that's good."

"Oh, everybody knew that. But on the last night, you

know, it was a heart attack." He takes his hat off. His hair is wiry gray. His forehead has a crease on it from probably a lifetime of hats. "She had several before. I figured she would make it through again, I really did."

"I'm sorry," I say.

"And I never told her I loved her," he says.

"I'm really sorry."

"I should have told her," he says.

I nod, trying not to take sides, which really is quite impossible when you are face-to-face with one of the sides. "Maybe she knew," I say. "Oh, she had to know."

CROZER CHESTER MEDICAL CENTER is where my dad worked before he retired, where he served as chief of medicine, and it's the hospital with which my brother's practice is now affiliated. So there's a certain comfort zone here in this orange brick building clinging to the edge of Interstate 95. I worked here one summer when I was still in high school. I liked wearing the white nurse's uniform and the shoes. I liked strutting around the hospital in that get-up, feeling like a *medical* person, even though I wasn't one and knew I never would be. You learn some things about yourself early on. You learn if you are a person comfortable with seeing tubes sticking out of people's arms, or if you aren't. I swear even as a kid my sister Claire could see the arm-tube deal and she would want to run and help the person. I was more the runaway type from the get-go. Sick people scared me. Sick people still scare me. This isn't the most unique character flaw a person could have. But I think that many people, by the time they reach my age, have had some experience with sick people, so they get better at it. They start knowing what all the tubes are for; they have a familiarity with beds that go up and down; they no longer even notice the thick, sour hospital smell. I am not one of those people.

My mom is out of the ICU, reportedly in Room 109. I am trudging there. I see Claire first. Oh boy, she looks awful. Now see, Claire is bony. And when she's tired, she looks even bonier. She's got fiery red hair, borrowing from my maternal grandmother's Irish side, and a long, thin face from my grandfather's French. I got more of the total Lithuanian deal from my dad's one hundred percent Lithuanian side.

"Did you sleep here or something?" I ask Claire.

"Sleep?" she says. "Very funny. I just sent Dad and Kristin home. The nurses are changing her. We can go in in a minute. Did you hear about the septic tank?"

"Huh?"

"They have to dig the old septic tank out before they close on the house."

"Dig it out?"

"That's what the EPA guy said. Plus, they found radon. So they have to do a whole radon thing."

"Oh, jeez. Dad's not good at this sort of thing under the best of circumstances."

"Exactly," Claire says.

We're talking here leaning against the wall. A cinder block wall painted pink. I ask Claire to tell me everything she knows about this disease. This seems to brighten her mood. She gets comfort from using her brain. She tells me Guillain-Barré Syndrome, or GBS, can hit anybody, any age, for no reason that anyone can yet determine. One of her eighteen-month-old patients even contracted it. It often seems to come after a virus. "Remember Mom had that cold?" she says, as if determined to get to the bottom of this.

"Yeah, but . . . a cold? That was *a cold.*"

"There's also a theory that you can get it from eating partially cooked chicken," she says.

"Mom wouldn't eat partially cooked chicken," I say.

Claire tells me that in GBS the immune system suddenly goes haywire, and starts attacking the lining of the nerves, which deteriorate, so the nerves short out. "Kind of like if all the insulation came off an extension cord," she says, and then explains that in GBS the paralysis usually starts at the feet and moves up the body. "Do you remember Mom said she felt like her feet kept falling asleep last week?"

"Not really."

"Well, that must have been when it started. Some people, it happens really fast, some slower."

"I can't believe this."

"I know."

I'm tracing my finger along the ridges of the shiny cinder blocks. Pink? They painted this place *pink*? I feel like I'm stuck inside somebody's intestines.

"But the lining of the nerves grows back," Claire says. "So most people get, you know, better."

"How long does the getting better take?"

"A long time."

"How long is long?" I say.

"A year?"

"I can't believe this! This is the craziest thing I've ever heard of. You're fine one day and the next day you're totally paralyzed, checking out of life for a *year*?"

"I know," Claire says. "I know."

She tells me about my mother's breathing. As the paralysis creeps up the body, in many cases it strikes the muscles that enable you to breathe. This is what started happening with my mom. "They're hoping that it has stopped just short of that," Claire tells me. "If it doesn't, they'll have to intubate. Mom seems pretty determined to avoid that."

"That's a big deal, to intubate?" I ask.

"Well, if it's your throat they're putting the tube down . . ."

"Yeah."

"Yeah."

"So Mom knows all this is going on?" I ask.

"Oh, totally. Mentally she's just, you know, totally Mom."

I let out a rather enormous sigh, which Claire interprets with pinpoint accuracy.

"You're not good at this," she says.

"No."

"I'll go in with you. I'll stay."

"Yeah."

"Come on, let's go in."

See, I'm choking up. I'm doing the look-down thing. The hair-in-the-face thing. The bite-the-hell-out-of-your-lip thing to keep-yourself-from-crying thing.

Claire goes in first. I follow. I shake my head. I shake my brain loose. I have to look cheerful. My role in the family is: the cheerful one. Certainly with my mom. "Oh, thank God I had you," my mom has always said. "You would wake up in the morning and sing and play with your toes. Those others were terrible. Terrible! You were such a nice break." *Cheerful!* My job right now is to look cheerful. My mom shouldn't see some blubbering idiot. That would only make her feel worse. I am the cheerful one, so be cheerful, damn it!

It takes some doing, but I force my face into a smile and quicken my pace. "I made it!" I say to my mom, as I burst into her view. "Hey, I'm here! Oh, I've been stuck in the Bradford airport, you wouldn't *believe* that place. Hey, you know what! You look great! You really do!"

Her eyes are smiling. I think they really are. And she does

look good. I mean, for a paralyzed person. It's not like she was in a car accident and has bandages. She's just . . . lying down. Mostly she just looks like . . . my mom. My mom has a pleasantly round face, intelligent green eyes, and a jaw that often stays clenched, as if she's holding back, holding back telling you the history of everything you're talking about, because she's read about it, she's read a biography of all those characters you're mentioning; she often reads seven books a week.

That's the difference. Her jaw isn't clenched now. No, there is nothing holding that jaw in place. This lends a softness to her face I'm not used to. And she does look quite out of place in her pajamas, out in public like this. She's the type of woman who wears pantyhose and a skirt and a neat little blouse and a sweater vest to go to the grocery store or to sculpture class. She never even wears pants, unless it's to garden. She gets her chocolate-brown hair washed and set and styled every Friday, and she has a lot of faith in perms. In fact, this present perm is really holding up under the circumstances. She will be glad to know this. "Hey, your hair looks good!" I tell her.

She doesn't say anything.

I look at Claire.

"She's saving her breath," Claire says.

"Saving it?"

A nurse comes in. She's in white nurse pants and a colorful smock with cats all over it. This is so not the outfit I want to see on a nurse. I think back on my crisp white dress. And those white pantyhose. Damn. What's happening to the world?

"Okay, Claire!" the nurse says to my mother.

She's calling my mom by her first name? Oh, boy. And my mother isn't protesting. Oh, boy. Normally, my mother would not hesitate to rebuff the uncalled-for familiarity, remaining loyal, as she does, to the Victorian tradition in which she was raised. But she isn't protesting being called "Claire" by this stranger. She is saving her breath.

"It's three o'clock so we have to do this again, Claire," the nurse says, holding up a clear gizmo with a blue ball inside.

"She has to make the little ball reach fifteen hundred ml," my sister tells me. If she can do this, it means her lungs are still able to take in enough air.

The nurse pushes the button that makes the bed go into a sitting position. She holds the gadget up to my mother's mouth. My mother looks at it, closes her eyes. She is conjuring something. She opens her eyes, wraps her lips around the mouthpiece, breathes in, breathes in so hard her head and shoulders tremble, in, in, in, she's a soldier, she's an army defending her homeland, she's making the little blue ball jiggle past 1000, jiggle to 1200, jiggle, jiggle.

"Fifteen hundred, Claire!" the nurse says. "You did it! Good girl, Claire!"

My mother collapses. I'm standing here smiling. Smiling, I am, because this is my job. I'm saying, "Yay!" with my eyes. "Way to go, Mom!"

My mother is looking at me, exhausted, every inch of her exhausted from this fight that has barely even begun. I've never noticed this before, and maybe it is just in this moment, but my mother looks like a bird. A sparrow. A baby sparrow without feathers, and no mother to come to the rescue.

CHAPTER FOUR

I have a baby. A baby! My baby, as it turns out, is a peanut M&M. A green peanut M&M. Hmm. Well, that's okay. I love my baby. It doesn't even seem weird to have a baby that is a peanut M&M. But she is somewhat difficult to handle. She's so tiny. I'm trying to give her a bath. And I have out the infant tub. It's a regular-sized infant tub. I think: Why do they make these things so huge? I'm trying to figure out how to put my baby down so I can run the water. I think: Why don't they make some kind of little holders for babies? So I go get a coffee cup, which I am going to put my baby in.

But then—I drop her. I hear the plink, plunk, plink. She goes rolling under the radiator. I'm on my hands and knees, calling, "Baby? Baby? Where are you, my tiny little baby?"

I see her. I reach into the dust and muck and pull her out safely.

Hmm.

It appears her nose has fallen off.

WELL, IT'S A good thing there is so much to do. When there is a lot to do, there is no time to feel. Yes, yes, yes, this is exactly the way it should be. Everybody with a critically ill parent should have a house to pack up, a house holding twenty-five years of memories. And it should be a big house, a six-bedroom house with a huge attic and a vast basement, oh, it should hold about ninety million times more stuff than you could ever squish into a two-bedroom apartment at a retirement village. And you should have no idea what your parents want done with any of this stuff, your mother too ill to speak, and your father too terrified of losing her to care about earthly things. Yes, you should have to stand there in that giant house with your brother and sisters, and you should all be utterly immobilized, wondering what on earth to do with all of this stuff. And just for good measure you should have a guy with a backhoe in the backyard digging up the old septic tank and radon guys in the garage discussing ventilation.

Definitely.

You will have no chance to feel anything.

"You know what, I think the magnolia is about to bloom," Alex says. He's on the phone. He's still at the farm. I'm still here in Philly. It could be that I've been here a week, or it could be I've been here a month. I am not remotely sure. The phone is white. It's in my room, my old room, the room I got when I turned sixteen. The closet door still has the red, white, and blue sticker on it from our nation's bicentennial, the year of my high school graduation. Scrawled on the yellow wall next to me are phone numbers of friends I wish I could remember.

"The magnolia?" I say to Alex. "Oh, it's too early for that."

"Well, I'm looking at it right now, and it's ready to pop," he insists.

"It's *early*," I say.

"It's April," he says.

"April? Are you sure?"

"Definitely April," he says. "I just sent our taxes in."

"You did? All by yourself you did those horrible taxes?"

"I did."

"Wow, I love being married."

"Well, you married a good one," he says.

"Oh, I get the prize for having the best husband."

"No, no, no, I get the prize for *being* the best husband."

"Oh. Right. Okay."

"So you've already been to the hospital?" he asks. "You're not doing the afternoon shift today?"

"Claire and I switched," I say. "Just for today, though. I gotta tell you, I don't like the morning shift."

"No."

"Too many doctors coming in, poking at her."

"How was she?"

"Same. She didn't eat anything. Maybe like a half of one of those Ensure cans."

"Oh."

"And now her sodium level is way down again. She's pretty disheartened by that."

"It was staying steady there for a while."

"I don't know what happened. They get one thing fixed, and then the next thing goes kerplunk. And when the sodium is down, she's just wiped out. Wiped out. And just everything has shut down."

"I know."

"And who knew sodium could be such a big deal? Who knew people even *had* a sodium level?"

"I know."

"The neurologist was in, sticking little pins in her feet. No reaction. None."

"Well, they said it's going to be a while," he says.

"Yeah, well, I like my four-to-ten shift better. All the doctors are gone by then."

"Yeah."

Four to ten. That's been my main shift. We've divided our days this way. My mom really needs someone with her all the time, at least during waking hours. It's not enough for her that there is a nurse down the hall. She can't *call* the nurse. She can't push the call button. She can barely speak. She can't feed herself. She can't hold a spoon. She can't brush her teeth. She can't scratch her own nose. Maybe, in another family, they'd trust the nurses to do all of this. Maybe in another family they'd have to. But this is the way ours works. I've often thought that our last name should be Rally. We are the Rally Family. One of us is down, the whole clan comes in for the rescue. All for one and one for all. We have always been this way. I like it this way. It makes all the suffocation worth it. I remember as a kid when I first learned about people who were homeless. People down on their luck, living in the streets. I didn't get it. I literally could not comprehend. "But where are their *families*?" I would say. Hard luck just meant you had a lot of family around you all of a sudden. It took deliberate effort to imagine a life that worked any differently.

So with my mom sick, this is what we do. My dad arrives in the morning, sometimes as early as six, sometimes so early the guards ask him for ID. He goes in there in his suit with his little red bow tie, the uniform he always puts on before sunrise each day, he goes in there with his shock of bright white hair, silky smooth hair covering his big Lithuanian head, he goes in there, and he stands over my mom's bed, and he reads her prayers out of his little prayer book. He feeds her a poached egg, the one thing she can seem to stomach. Then he reads her love poems. The doctors doing their rounds have learned to wait outside until he finishes a verse.

Claire typically relieves my dad midmorning. A physical therapist before she became a physician, she spends much of her time ranting and raving and demanding that my mom receive proper care. Her point is: Every patient needs an advocate, and she's it. Claire is the Worry Sister, so this role comes naturally. She got the hospital to give my mom a special blow-up mattress, special boots, special pillows. She visits with the doctors as they make their rounds. She consults on every decision. Staying on top of all of this, she gives the rest of us tremendous peace of mind. It's funny how the Worry Sister can absorb so much of the family's worry.

Kristin, who like me has set up a little office with a laptop in my mom's room, usually relieves Claire around lunchtime. She brings in homemade soups and breads and tries to get my mother to eat. Kristin brushes my mother's hair. She holds her hand, tells her stories. Kristin is the Compassion Sister. Compassion takes courage—at least acting on it does. I wish I had Kristin's courage. I wish I could just sit at my mother's bedside the way Kristin does and say the reassuring things a critically ill person needs to hear. I wish I had the courage to hold my mom's hand and pray. Knowing that Kristin is there to take on this role, it takes the pressure off.

So then I show up at four o'clock, the Utterly Useless Sister. At least that's how I feel. I'm the baby. What else is there to say? I'm . . . the fool. At least that's how I feel. And out of my anxiety comes: entertainment. Oh, I'm good at entertainment. I work the TV. I've brought in a VCR for my mom, a CD player, and a tape player. I've coordinated a lot of buttons on a lot of remotes, and by now I've created a fairly sophisticated surround-sound system with the speakers I've placed around her room. I wish I had a better role, a more important one or a more dignified one.

My brother comes in during my shift, and several times throughout the day. He always brightens my mother's mood. He's the Crown Prince of the family who also happens to be the Maniac Brother with his prodigious enthusiasm for everything from growing flowers to eating a sandwich to watching a spider spin a web. He's a life force. He's my mother's first-born child and the apple of her eye; I never appreciated the extent of the admiration until now.

"So," I say to Alex on the phone. "Anything else new at the farm? Tell me everything. It really cheers me up."

"Well, let's see," he says. "Yesterday George and Pat invited us to a pancake breakfast at their church."

"Oh, that's sweet. Isn't that sweet? Did you tell them I'm away? Did you tell them what's going on?"

"I did. Pat sent over some stuffed peppers."

"Oh, that is so sweet! Isn't that sweet?"

"Yeah," he says. "But I'm lonely."

"I know. I'm sorry."

"I miss you," he says.

These are oddly soothing words. I can't imagine going through this ordeal without Alex out there somewhere, a guardian angel you can just dial up on the phone. He's coming here on Thursday, just a few days from now, to help with the move. He's going to bring a U-Haul. My sisters and brother have also ordered U-Hauls. We're going to park all those orange trucks out in the driveway and just . . . haul. Then on Saturday the movers will come and take the good stuff, the furniture and other items we've selected to appoint my parents' new apartment.

"I had a dream last night I had a baby," I tell Alex.

"Oh?"

"It was a green peanut M&M."

"Oh?"

"Which was not strange, in the context of the dream."

"Uh-huh."

"Well, I dropped it," I say.

"You dropped it?"

"But then I found it!"

Now he is silent.

"It was under the radiator."

"Uh-huh . . ."

"But the nose had fallen off."

A long silence. I'm waiting. Surely he will have some dream interpretation to offer up. He's a shrink. Surely he knows what the dream means.

"So what do you think it means?" I ask finally.

"Are you asking for my professional assessment of your dream?"

"Yes."

"Oh, that's an easy one," he says. "I can sum up what that dream says about you in two words."

"Okay."

He makes a big deal of clearing his throat, like some orator about to say something important. "The first word is *coo*," he says. "And the second word is *coo*."

"Cute."

"Thank you."

"But seriously. At first I thought it was a dream about some deep-seated need to have a baby," I tell Alex. "But I think that's too obvious."

"You have some deep-seated need to have a baby?"

"Um."

"Do you?"

My goodness! I have no idea. Shouldn't I have an answer? I don't have an actual yes or no answer. Do I? And why does this seem like an awfully personal question? My goodness. How rude.

"The dream," I say. "I really think it's about my mom. Because M&M's are her favorite candy, you know. At least in the milk chocolate family. As you know she's a dark chocolate person—"

"I really think you're stretching here—"

"No, the dream is about *her*," I insist. "She's reduced to a helpless little peanut M&M, and I'm . . . losing her. So I'm trying to rescue her."

"I don't know," Alex says.

More silence.

"Maybe you're just . . . lost right now," he says.

"Like a piece of runaway candy?"

"Well—"

"Well, I am."

"Anyone would be," he says.

"I guess. But the main thing I am is useless."

"Oh honey, all of this is normal. This is how people feel in a crisis."

"Like a peanut M&M underneath a radiator?"

"In a manner of speaking."

"Lost," I say.

"Lost," he says.

We don't say anything for a while.

"Tell me what else is going on at the farm," I say finally. "Tell me everything. It cheers me up to hear."

"Baby lambs," he says. "You should see all the lambs. All up and down Daniel's Run Road. All the hillsides are covered with lambs and their mamas. Quite a show, really. George must have over two hundred."

"Lambs," I say. "I can't believe I'm missing the magnolia and lamb season, too. How long does the lambing go on?"

"Awhile, I think. I'm not really sure."

"See, now we're out of our league."

"Yeah."

"Actually, I thought it was pretty impressive the way I said 'lambing.' "

"It was," he agrees.

"So what about George? He didn't bring any sheep over yet?"

"Nope."

"What do you think he's waiting for?"

"I have no idea. I don't even know how to ask. What's the protocol?"

There's a knock on my door. It's Kristin. "We're running out of green and yellow," she says, peeking in. "Can you go up to Thrift and get stickers?"

"Sure," I say, and I tell Alex I'll think about the lambing protocol, think about it and get back to him on that. We say good-bye. Kristin trudges in, throws herself on the twin bed next to me. She's got red hair like my sister Claire's, and round features like my dad's. She has a slight Asian flare to her green eyes, an exotic look that has always driven the boys wild. I'm glad she's able to be here. In addition to being the Compassion Sister, she's also the Write the Script Sister. Oh, she's a wonderful producer. She's gotten us organized. She's the one who came up with the sticker solution. I'm blue. Claire's yellow. Kristin is green. My brother is red. You take your stickers, and you walk around the house and you put a sticker on everything you want, even if there's already a sticker on it. (We've already put white stickers on the stuff that's going with my parents to the new apartment.) So if, say, a lamp ends up with two stickers on it, you talk about it and decide. So far this plan is working out beautifully. It's strange to think how worried my mom used to be about this deal of splitting stuff up. "Oh, I just don't want you kids fighting over things," she'd say. I don't think any of us could have predicted how much of a nonproblem it would turn into.

"Claire wants the piano," Kristin says. "Do you care?"

"Nope," I say. "So far the only things I care about are flowers and paintings."

All week I've been digging up daylilies and daffodils. I don't know if these really qualify as things you're supposed to move when you move out of a house, but these are what I'm moving.

My mother's garden. It was her passion. It was her therapy. It was her lime-green explosion of hope every spring and her wilted brown exercise in faith each fall. So of course I'm moving it. I'm taking as much of her garden with me as I can physically manage. I'll replant it at the farm. I am bound and determined to make sure those flowers get out alive.

Same with my mom's paintings. Long ago she said she wanted to throw away all of her practice canvases that have been stored in the basement. Practice canvases to her, maybe, but treasures to the rest of us one day. And I figure, hey, I have a barn. I'll take the paintings—perhaps a hundred canvases—and give them at least a temporary home in my barn. This way, if anyone else in the family ever wants them, they'll still be around.

"You're going to lose your light if you want to dig up any more flowers today," Kristin says.

"Yeah." I swing my weary legs off the bed. "What about the stickers? Can you wait a couple of hours?"

"Right now I'm aiming toward a nap," she says, pulling the green comforter up over her.

"Get it while you can."

I head downstairs, through this house so eerily adorned with white, green, yellow, blue, and red stickers. How ominous it all is. How I long to just get this move over with. I don't want some extended good-bye. I don't want to stand here and imagine Claire on these steps, Claire in her wedding dress, and me in a magenta bridesmaid gown next to her, and Kristin next to me, pinching me so I'll crack up when the photographer takes the picture, and my mom standing down there watching, saying, "I have beautiful girls! *Don't I have beautiful girls?* But you know what, they're so much more than their beauty. I mean, I have an interesting family! What an *interesting* family!" I don't want to stand here and imagine my mother pulling the photographer aside into her garden to brag about her children.

And I don't want to stand here and imagine my mother downstairs in her studio painting, and me upstairs writing, and the two of us meeting down here for tuna fish sandwiches, and iced tea, and the opportunity to commiserate over how the creative process, no matter what you're in the act of creating, dictates the degree to which you are able to stay your own personal sanity course.

No. Memories just take time. I have no time. And memories take feeling. Just say no to feeling! Let's just get this move over with.

I open the kitchen door and hear the *raaaack, raaaack* squeaking sound the hinges make. Now that is noteworthy. If you hold on to no other sound from a house you once lived in, you should hold on to the sound of the kitchen door.

It's funny. I have no idea what the sound of the kitchen clock is. I never knew that sound. I wonder if my mother came to know it when we all moved out.

But, *raaack, raaaack.* There. There's the door sound.

Raaack, raaaack. I think I've got it.

There's another sound following it. An echo in this house. *Clip* CLOP *clip* CLOP *clip.* The sound of my mother's determined heels over these wood floors. There's a sound that has surely become absorbed good and tight within these walls.

My sisters and I used to love to imitate my mother and her uniquely purposeful walk. *Clip* CLOP *clip* CLOP *clip* CLOP. The walk of a woman *going places,* stand back, move aside, she may just bowl you over. If my mother ever walks again, I wonder what new rhythm will make itself known. Then again, what sounds do footsteps make on wall-to-wall carpeting? The carpeting in the apartment at the retirement village is white. I don't see my mother being at home walking on a white carpet. I just don't. And that's the nicest image I can conjure. The more accurate one is probably her in a wheelchair on a white carpet.

Some of the doctors seem reluctant to promise that she'll ever walk again normally.

The whole situation, in the end, leaves me angry. I'm angry that my mother never got to say good-bye to her *clip* CLOP *clip* CLOP over these wood floors. I'm angry that the last time my mother got to see her dream, she was looking at it from the rear window of an ambulance.

Outside the side yard is all bright orange dirt. Clay in huge piles, courtesy of the backhoe. The sun is heading down, and so the water in the cove is still, smooth, asleep. The trees overhead are just getting a green glow around their edges, the faint foretelling fuzz of spring.

There should be some deer coming out for a drink any minute. I wonder how those deer are doing. I had such a complicated relationship with those deer. I used to chase them. Oh, I would run after them screaming like a crazy lady in curlers who just got her car stolen. Not because I wanted the deer to leave. Not really, anyway. I chased them so they would be afraid. It was the highest act of generosity, at least in my little adolescent mind. Don't befriend the deer! That's the worst thing you could do for them. The real act of love was to teach them to run. To fear. To never trust a human. Because the truth about humans was that humans were not trustworthy. Humans kill innocent creatures like deer. It was my singular duty—and sacrifice—to destroy their innocence so that they might survive.

I'd sort of forgotten about all of that. I wonder what happened to all of that. I wonder how the deer are doing. I don't suppose they've erected a monument to me, but you never know.

I head across the driveway, over toward the edge of the woods where the main population of daylilies are sticking their necks out of the earth, just peeping through as if to check the time.

Where did I leave off when I finished digging yesterday? I'm trying to remember.

There should be bookmarks for gardeners. I don't mean so you can find your plants. I mean so you can find your thoughts.

I was thinking about something yesterday. Something about the anger.

I take my shovel and place it about eight inches from the base of a plant. Ready. Aim. I hop and then, *stomp!* The earth opens with a crunch, like a big man cracking his knuckles. Well, that felt good. A little air in those joints. I'm able to free the roots of the plant with a gentle rocking motion. I lift the plant. A daylily. It could be the Hyperion variety, or maybe Happy Returns, or even Uncommon Love, I suppose. See, my mom would be able to tell you what kind of daylily it is. She would be able to tell you the botanical name, and what height to expect it to reach, and when. Not that my mom is a daylily expert or anything. Just a fan.

I think she's going to like it that I'm taking some daylilies. She'll be able to visit them at the farm. She can dig some up and give them to her friends.

Some of the doctors said that in a year, if all goes well, she could be ninety percent back to her normal self. Some say eighty. It would be a higher percentage, they said, if the attack on her nerves hadn't been so particularly brutal, if her nerves weren't so badly damaged.

If, if, if.

Why did this have to happen? Why is my mother paralyzed? Raw chicken? A stupid little cold? Oh, come on. Can't modern medicine do any better than that? I've read about an outbreak of GBS back in the late 1970s, when the U.S. government sponsored a campaign to get everyone vaccinated for the swine flu, which turned out not to be nearly the epidemic they'd imagined, no, it was the vaccine that wreaked havoc. They were able to link the swine flu vaccine to a huge rise in the number of cases of GBS.

So I guess that's a clue. But still. They should know more. Nobody should have to get this disease, but if they do, at least they should know why. There's a woman who visits my mom. Her name is Bobbie. She got GBS when she was thirty-two. Bobbie collapsed in her kitchen, the day before her daughter's first birthday. Normal one day, the next day she was on a ventilator, with a feeding tube in her, and her eyelids taped closed because her eyelid muscles had become paralyzed and she couldn't blink. She had a very severe case, was in the ICU for months. And she couldn't tell anyone about the pain. She had no way to communicate, could not even make a signal. The nerves that had shorted out were playing the most bizarre tricks: She had the sensation that she had two extra arms and two extra legs. She felt them as real as anything is real. And these extra arms and legs were twisted up underneath her. The pain. She had no way to communicate. The pain, the imprisonment, it drove her into full-blown psychotic episodes. She was losing her mind.

Two years later she's fully recovered; her daughter is three, and she's had another baby. She visits people like my mom, tells them it really is going to be over someday. Our whole family has come to think of Bobbie in saintly terms.

Okay, this is a whopper, this plant. A whopper! Ready. Aim. I place the shovel right in the center. Hop, *stomp*! And then again. Ready, aim, hop, *stomp*! And one more time. Whew. That felt good. I put one section back in the hole, the rest in the wheelbarrow to take home. The new owners will never notice the difference. No, of course they won't. And I won't even charge them for this service that I'm providing. This is a favor! These plants really do need to be divided if they're going to keep blooming.

Ready, aim, hop, *stomp*!

Ready, aim, hop, *stomp*!

Boy, is this therapeutic.

I'm thinking maybe the reason my mom got paralyzed was because she wasn't ready. She wasn't ready to leave her dream. Maybe this is the sort of thing that can happen when you get yanked out of your dream too soon. You end up frozen in time.

Ready, aim, hop, *stomp*!

Ready, aim, hop, *stomp*!

This is why I'm angry. I'm angry at my dad for yanking my mom out of her dream too soon. But then, I can't blame my dad for having his wants. You can't blame a man for being in a different life stage than a woman. Or vice versa.

I think of Alex and me, fifteen years apart. How long are we going to be in the same life stage? Are we even in it now? How long are any two people in the same life stage? What if one is speeding up, while one is slowing down? How do you possibly reconcile something as law-abiding as velocity?

When we were farm shopping a few years ago, Alex used to joke that I was a train. He would say "I see the train has left the station" as a way of surrendering to whatever scheme had taken hold of me. In that case, buying a farm. "Because," he would say, "when the train leaves the station, I know I have only three choices: I can get on board, I can get run over, or I can be left behind. But there is no stopping the train."

It was an interesting analogy, somewhat apt. And I hated that. I didn't want to be a train. I don't want to be a train! I don't want to yank Alex along on my dream. I want us to both be driving the train.

How do you do that? How do you do that without leaving one of you frozen in time, unable to so much as speak?

Here's an idea. Come to think of it, maybe the answer is pretty simple. It's all up to the train. If you are the train, well, then it's up to you to hold back. At a minimum, you have to make sure that your partner has a chance to build up steam for an idea. And if the steam doesn't come, well, drop it. You just have to drop your dream.

That's what I'll have to do. That is just the way I'll have to live.

I must control the train.

Ready, aim, hop, *stomp*!

I'll bet my mom lived a lifetime of controlling the train. I mean, talk about a *train*. I do come by this honestly. And now look. She's paralyzed.

Ready, aim, hop, *stomp*!

Okay, this might be a stupid example. But take, for example, my Chihuahua situation. Yeah, I have a Chihuahua situation.

The Chihuahua lives in a cage in a pet shop I pass on the way to and from the hospital. In the past week or so I've been stopping by to visit it, once, sometimes twice each day. There are no pets at my parents' house. Not one. And I guess I just kind of needed a fix. That's how it started. I was at the drugstore and saw the pet shop and stopped in.

I was drawn immediately to the Chihuahua in the middle cage, just next to a sweet little Border collie. He was a white Chihuahua, a puppy. He was the size of a healthy kitten. Could a dog this small really be considered . . . dog? His paws looked to be smaller than my fingertips. I asked the clerk if I could hold him. She said sure. And she opened the cage. And the so-called dog scampered right into my arms as if those arms were exactly what he had been waiting for. He was the most helpless little thing. I loved him more or less immediately. I told the clerk I would be back. I came back. I kept coming back. The shop owner said she didn't mind. When I went in yesterday, she just pointed to the cage, said, "Go ahead," and let me take the Chihuahua out. I nestled that dog into the cradle inside my elbow and took him over to visit the fish and the birds and the gerbils.

This is what we do, me and the Chihuahua. The Chihuahua makes me happy, and I'd like to think the dog gets some relief from its boring caged-in days.

But that's as far as our relationship goes. That's it. The point is, our relationship is *contained*. I have no intention of taking the Chihuahua home. Even the shop owner knows this. I'm just a visitor. A visitor who already has three dogs, thank you very much. A visitor who lives in a place that wouldn't be able to provide a good home for a Chihuahua anyway. The horses might trip over it or crush it. And then there is Betty, who would have a heart attack if I showed up with a dog that could out-princess her ten thousand times over.

But mostly—there is Alex. He loves animals, but he has a point when he says, "This is getting ridiculous." He started saying that way back at Maggie, horse number two. Nearly all of our pets have come into our lives aboard the train known as me. And I'm not going to do it anymore. I'm just not.

Ready, aim, hop, *stomp*!

Oh, that was a good one. Good Lord, this plant is approaching the size of a watermelon. When did my mom put these in here that they've had time to grow so large?

Ready, aim, hop, *stomp*!

I'm thinking about a promise I made. I'm thinking about my promise to control the train. Not a promise to Alex. In fact, he's always said that the good thing about my locomotion is it gets us places he never would otherwise get. So really, I made the promise to me. I made it when we got Skippy, mule number two, which was kind of my grand finale. I had no intention whatsoever of getting another mule when I got Skippy. I really did not. We already had Sassy, our wedding mule. How many mules does a woman need?

But what happened with Skippy, well, what happened was I saw an ad for a mule farm. Thirty mules at one farm! I couldn't imagine it. I just wanted to see it with my own eyes. I had grown to love mules. I had grown to love the mule *concept*. A mule is half horse and half donkey. The combination makes for a smart, strong-willed, sure-footed, and loving creature. But the main thing about mules is each mule is its own mule. Mules are sterile. There will never be progeny. This goes exactly against the more typical tradition of horse ownership, where bloodlines are everything. You get your papers from, say, the American Saddlebred Association, like those we have for Cricket, and you can trace your horse's ancestry back to the Middle Ages. Well, not really. But you get the point. Bloodlines dictate how much your horse costs, and bloodlines dictate how tall you walk when you talk about your horse, and bloodlines dictate how important you are when you show your horse—oh, your horse comes from a long line of famous horses!

In walks the mule. No bloodlines. Well, you'll have some people trying. You know, there is always Mister I Have a Quarterhorse Mix From Fancy Schmancy Mule Farm in Montana. But for the most part it's just: mule. A one-hundred-percent-in-charge-of-its-own-reputation mule. A mule unlike any mule before it and any mule after it. A creature that is here on this Earth on its own good time and for its own good reasons.

Well, after hearing about that mule farm, one day Alex and I took a drive just to see. Just to absorb the wonder. And while we were at the mule farm, standing there watching this sea of giant-eared animals, one of them seemed to stand out from the crowd. He was a light-colored Appaloosa mix, a bit smaller than the others, and my eyes went right to his. I swear that mule was looking right at me. That mule was staring at me! That mule was *picking me*! I asked the farmer about the mule. He said his name was Skippy. And I don't know what made me do it. How can you know? Suddenly I found myself calling out. "Skippy!" I called. "Skiiiippy! Mama's here!"

And the strangest thing—and Alex saw it, too—that mule shuffled this way and that until he had worked his way through the mule crowd and came toward me. It was like a movie! Like a peasant in a throng of peasants coming forth with some very important message. That mule walked right up to me, put his head on my shoulder, and snorted a huge snort of relief. Or so I interpreted the snort.

Skippy.

Yes, Skippy. Within a month Skippy was safe and sound in our barn.

I felt good about bringing Skippy home, but bad for Alex, who was looking a little bedraggled. One more animal to feed and clean up after. "Isn't this getting ridiculous?"

Yes, maybe it was. And so I got control of myself. This is why I am not even thinking of taking the Chihuahua home. I am not even allowing myself to imagine taking it home.

No, I am not.

No! Now, stop it. Stop it right now.

All right. One last daylily for today's haul.

Ready, aim, hop, *stomp!*

Ready, aim, hop, *stomp!*

Boy, is this therapeutic. Ready, aim, hop, *stomp!*

All right, then. I've got this wheelbarrow pretty much full. That didn't take long. See, if I just do one wheelbarrow a day for the next five days, I'll really have done something.

CHAPTER FIVE

Brushing your mother's teeth isn't so bad. You just have to pretend you're scrubbing a floor, or maybe a tile in your bathroom. Don't make eye contact, that's the main thing. If you look in her eyes, you will see her helplessness. If she looks in your eyes, she will see your heartache. It's best to avoid all of this, since your main objective here is the removal of tartar and the application of fluoride.

Tonight we're using Aquafresh Triple Protection. And a red toothbrush. It's a luminous, translucent red. The color of Jell-O, the color of cough drops. Back and forth, up, down.

It's May. Already it's May. The move is over. Alex has come and gone and come and gone a few times now. And I'm still here. I'm brushing my mother's teeth back and forth and up and down. I'm here, now. This is my here-and-now. I would do just about anything to return to my there-and-then. My new refrigerator. The ticking of my kitchen clock. All of it.

Kristin is coming to relieve me next week. We've changed the way our shifts work so as to open up the chance to return to some semblance of normal life. Now it's two weeks on and two weeks off. I've heard that the Red Cross does it this way when they send their disaster teams to hurricanes and floods.

They must have figured out that two weeks is a good amount of time.

Back and forth, up and down. Red. This is such a pretty red, this cough-drop red. But now I'm wondering why they call cough drops "cough drops." As if they're prepackaged little coughs you put in your mouth and then they go off, like little cough bombs, which of course they aren't, their job is to quiet the cough. Hmm. Cough Mufflers? Cough Terminators. Cough Quellers.

Hmm.

These are the sorts of thoughts you have when you are standing in a hospital room brushing your mother's teeth, doing your very best to avoid anything whatsoever to do with living in the moment. One thing about misery is, it has a way of making you give up doing what you think is good and right.

"You ready to spit?" I say to my mom, holding up a cup of water.

"Ready as I'll ever be," she garbles. She's able to talk now. And she's able to swish and rinse and spit. So we are making progress. The disease works in its own good time. You just wait for the lining of the nerves to grow back. Nothing to do but wait.

I hold the yellow half-moon bowl up to her neck, then tilt her head with my hand. The hair on the back of her head is flat and brittle. The perm is long gone. Tomorrow I should wash her hair. Washing your mother's hair isn't so bad. It just requires a lot of propping and towels and hoses. Kristin found some clever portable shower gizmo at one of those patient-care stores, so we can do the washing right here in her bed. Everything is easier if she doesn't have to be moved.

She spits. She takes another sip of water, swishes with

determination. She's gotten so skinny. Waiflike. She doesn't even look like my mother anymore. She has virtually no muscle tone, anywhere. She's my mother with all the air sucked out. She's the flat-tire version of my mother.

But all of this is fine. I mean, this is just tooth-brushing time. I'm telling you this is nothing compared with some of the things we do. Like in the daytime, when the physical therapists come in. Nice enough people. In fact, some of the cheeriest of the bunch around here. My mom seems genuinely pleased to see them each time. Then: the crane. You can see the panic wash over her face.

The crane is a nylon sling hanging from a big hook attached to a steel arm. They use it to get my mom out of bed and into a chair, where she is to sit for just a few minutes each day. This is how the muscles are invited back to life. "Come on, gang, get working!" The ones they're trying to awaken first are the muscles of the torso that enable her to sit upright. Muscles anyone has long since forgotten about. Muscles you first got to know way back when you were an infant in a crib wanting with every fiber of your being to . . . just . . . roll . . . over.

So this is what they do. They roll my mother to one side, tuck the nylon sling underneath her. They roll her on top of the sling. They hook the sling to the crane, push a button, and very slowly the crane lifts my mother out of the bed. For a few moments she hangs there in the air, hangs there like the tiny, helpless bird she has become. Hangs there chirping "Stop it! Stop this! Please don't do this to me!"

My mother.

It's all I can do to not run to her, throw my body underneath her to catch her in case she falls. Rock-a-bye, baby. When the bough breaks, the cradle must fall. Rock-a-bye, baby, my poor little baby.

My mother.

There really is nothing quite like seeing your own mother as helpless as an infant. There is nothing like it in the world or the universe or the galaxies beyond, I'm quite certain. There is nothing like suddenly being a thirty-nine-year-old woman with your first baby, and that baby is your mother.

She spits again. "Wonderful. Thank you. That does it," she says. She smacks her lips. "That was the highlight of my day."

"And we haven't even done Mister Washcloth yet," I say.

She rolls her eyes. She's grown sick of my Mister Washcloth routine. But she enjoys being sick of it. Hey, you do what you can.

I head into the bathroom, rinse off the toothbrush, find Mister Washcloth hanging on his rack. "Let's go, dude," I say. I turn on the warm water, immerse, wring, fold in half.

"Here comes Mister Washcloth," I say, returning.

"Oh, brother."

But I don't sing my Mister Washcloth song. *Hoobie Doobie Doo, Mister Washcloth Is Gonna Get You.* Enough is enough. I place the warm cloth on her forehead. "Ahh," she says, closing her eyes. "That feels nice."

I rub the cloth over her forehead and then, gently, over her eyelids. Then her cheeks. Now her chin. And behind her neck. "The highlight of your day," I say.

"Most definitely," she says, opening her eyes.

I see them.

Damn it.

I look away but it's too late.

Damn it.

Her eyes are small, deep set. In that way, they are far away. But that doesn't mean you can't see the helplessness. That doesn't mean you don't feel it in your heart like a punch.

My mother.

My heartache.

It's half her. It's half me. It's the two of us, stuck together in this room. It's everything I'm thinking when I think about her. It's wanting to save her. It's wanting her to save me. It's everything generous, and it's everything selfish. It's me, at seventy-five. It's coming down with some strange disease nobody ever heard of. It's being paralyzed and all alone. It's no one to come visit me. It's no kids to come in shifts. It's no one to wash my face, to brush my teeth.

What am I going to do? Why don't I have kids? Everyone needs kids.

Is this how moms are born? Is this *why* moms are born? Is it some howling of the heart, the fear of having nothing, no one, when disaster strikes?

I don't think so. See, I really don't think so. I don't think the reason people go have babies is just so they might have some company when they get old. No, there's a lot more to it than that.

I wonder why my thoughts keep leading me here, to thoughts of babies. I keep trying to convince myself that I have no interest in going here. And yet I keep getting pulled here.

Then again, I was the one craving family noise. I was the one getting pecked on the head by a bird in the form of a noisy kitchen clock. Not that the feeling of a bird pecking you on the head is the easiest sign to interpret.

But still.

I keep hearing that conversation I had with Alex after my peanut M&M dream.

"You have some deep-seated need to have a baby?"

"Um."

"Do you?"

My goodness! I had no idea. Shouldn't I have had an answer?

Hell, I do have an answer. An answer that flattens me with fear. Why should that be such a scary answer?

And now. The more I stand here caring for my mother, the more of her helplessness I see, the more mother I seem to become. And the more mother I become, the more I notice that I have no child. No child except this one, my mother.

It isn't right. I'm telling you, it's completely inside out and backward. But heartache isn't a puzzle to figure out. Nor is heartache a monster you have absolutely no control over.

Well, some heartache is. Grief is. When someone dies, you have grief. You have a void you can't fill. But when someone isn't born yet, what you have isn't exactly grief. What you have is a void to fill.

A void I've only recently met. A void that seems far too complicated to even think about.

A void.

Avoid! Oh, Alex would love that one. That's just his sort of wordplay.

Now, I wonder what he would do with this baby idea. I think he wouldn't do. That's what I think.

"You want to watch *The King and I*?" I say to my mother.

"Oh, I don't think—"

"Come on, it's a happy movie," I say. I put Mister Washcloth back in the bathroom for the night and get my canvas bag.

"Here," I say. "Let's just watch it together."

"I really don't think—"

I put the movie in.

I sit in the gray vinyl chair, prop my feet on the jazzy red hazardous waste can. Pretty flimsy for a hazardous waste can, if you ask me. I watch as Deborah Kerr goes swaying and singing and twirling in that giant hoopskirt. My mother says nothing. Nothing until Yul Brynner claps his hands and the children go running obediently away and he folds his arms and Deborah Kerr looks at him like he's the biggest grouch on earth.

"He's so mean!" my mother says.

"Well, not mean exactly—"

"He's so mean!" she says. "Why is he so mean! Oh, turn it off! Turn it off!"

"Mom, it's Yul Brynner. It's *The King and I*. He's going to get nice later, you know that."

"Please, turn this off! I'm begging you, turn it off!"

Okay, but jeez. "Mom, it's a movie. It's a *story* with a happy ending. You can't have happily-ever-after unless it's set against a little tension."

"I can't take conflict," she says. "I just can't take it."

"I know."

"I told you I just can't take conflict."

"I know—but I thought *The King and I* was, you know, it's not really conflict."

"He's mean."

"Right . . ."

"Well, I can't take it."

This, I want you to know, is not my mother talking. This person in this bed they call my mother is not really my mother. This whole conflict issue seems to have come out of nowhere. Yesterday she couldn't take the rerun of *The Mary Tyler Moore Show* I brought in because Mr. Grant was chewing out Ted Baxter, which was, to her, too much conflict.

Fine. So I figured: a musical. Tomorrow I'll bring in a musical. I really thought *The King and I* would be benign. I am striking out day after day with the entertainment here.

I rewind *The King and I*. I reach in my bag for my ace in the hole: *Swing Time* starring Ginger Rogers and Fred Astaire.

I figure: singing and dancing. Just some happy singing and dancing. These movies got a lot of people through World War II.

My mother watches the opening dance with the blankest of stares.

"You don't see dancing like *that* anymore," I say, because this is what people say when they watch these movies.

She looks at me with the most impatient glare.

"Inane," she says.

"Excuse me?"

"This is utterly inane."

Okay, then. I let out the biggest sigh I can muster and hold the bridge of my nose. I just need a . . . moment.

"I'm sorry," my mother says. "I just can't seem to—take anything."

"I know."

She's depressed. Of course she is depressed. Who wouldn't be depressed? Look at Bobbie; she had psychotic episodes. She nearly lost her mind. Everybody with GBS goes, to some degree, bonkers. It's in all the literature. If depression is the manifestation of a loss of control, well then, here you have the ultimate case study. A person trapped in her own body. A person with virtually no choices. A prisoner who never even got her day in court. One day you're running around free, and then, bam—your body betrays you, and you can no longer brush your own teeth.

This is a depression that makes perfect sense. But I've never seen my mother depressed before. So I really don't know this woman.

"I'm sorry I didn't like any of the shows." She's watching me pack them all up.

"Well, they're all going back in the bag," I say forcefully. I'm losing patience. Losing patience, I am.

"I'm not really a TV watcher," she says.

"I know."

She'd read, but she can't turn the pages. Plus, her eyes aren't working right. Her hearing goes in and out, too. My mother's body has turned into an extremely complicated rocket ship where all systems are definitely not Go.

"How about I put something in the CD player?" I say. "I brought *The Marriage of Figaro* back in." It's her favorite opera.

"That's okay," she says. "I'd rather not."

"You're just going to lie here and stare at the ceiling?"

"I'll be fine," she says.

"I don't know if that's so good for you, Mom," I say.

"Well, maybe it will work tonight."

"Maybe what will work?"

"Prayer."

"Well, but—"

"Maybe it will work," she says.

"You're not going to be able to pray your way out of this," I say as gently as I can. "You do know that. You're not going to wake up and suddenly be over this."

"That's not what I mean."

I look at her. She's staring at the ceiling, her eyes are welling up, her chin is quivering.

"I can't pray," she says.

"Oh, I didn't—"

"It just doesn't work. I haven't been able to pray."

I stand here wondering what to say.

"You're angry at God?" I say finally.

She shakes her head no.

"It would be normal," I say. "You know, it would be normal to think 'Why *me*?' "

She shakes her head no again. "That's not it," she says. "Why *not* me? Why should I be spared from suffering?"

"Because you're my mom," I say.

"So it's 'Why *you?*' "

"There we go."

She manages a smile.

But it fades.

"I'm just . . . cut off," she says, then. "I try to pray, but it's just blank."

My mother is more than simply a "religious person." My mother, we have always said, has a direct line to The Man.

"I'll tell you," she says. "It's like losing your best friend." The tears are coming in fuller now, pushing the pool over the edge.

I wish Kristin were here. She would know what to say. Oh, this whole thing is a disaster. My mother's having a crisis of faith, and I'm bringing in Mary Tyler Moore reruns?

"Let me tell you something," she says. "This is the worst paralysis you can have."

"This?"

"Not being able to pray."

"Oh."

She closes her eyes. The tears come trickling down.

"I wish I knew what to say," I say.

She shakes her head no.

"It's my own battle," she says.

"I know, but—"

"Don't take it on," she says. "Really. It's useless."

"No, that's me."

She opens her eyes, looks at me.

"I know all about useless," I say. "Useless is my middle name."

She clearly has no idea what I'm talking about.

"And let me tell you, uselessness is the most disgraceful form of anguish," I say.

"Just plain anguish is plenty enough to bear," she says.

"Right."

"Right."

She smiles. Something is funny? "Hold my hand," she says. Oh, we are so not the hand-holding type. I do it anyway. Of course I do. Sometimes you have no choice but to reach through fear. It's a small, bony hand. It's a baby bird's claw.

"You're my rock," she says. "Thank you for being my rock."

I have no idea what she is talking about.

"You're just—my rock," she says.

A rock. A firm foundation for her to stand on. An unmovable, reliable presence. How wonderful. How useful.

The reassurance, it boosts me right into the sky. I throw my shoulders back, raise my chin. She looks at me. She sees something new now. Oh, she sees what she has just done. She did what all good mothers are good at. She gave her aching kid some comfort.

"Well, thank you," I say. "That was good medicine." I tell her she's a good mom. I tell her that her motherhood muscles seem to be working just fine.

AFTERWARD I STOP to visit the Chihuahua.

He's in his metal cage, chewing a rubber mouse. I see that his neighbor, the Border collie, is gone. Hmm. But the husky below is still here.

A *mouse*? Hey, why did they give him a mouse to chew on? That's a cat toy. He is a dog! *He is a dog!* And why is no one buying this dog? Two months have gone by, and no one is buying this poor little dog.

He sees me. His big brown eyes bug out. Well, his eyes are always sort of bugged out. But still, he knows me by now. I open the cage, and he scampers, falls into my arms.

"Okay, buddy. I'm here."

He nuzzles my chin, reaches his head frantically toward my ear. His body is warm and strong and panicked.

"Okay, it's okay. Everything is okay."

Everything is, yes, okay. Everything is just as okay as it was yesterday. Okay, okay, okay. These days are blending together. Spring is in full bloom. Pretty soon summer's going to take over. Okay, okay, okay. I wonder how the farm is. On my last trip home the sheep came. That was exciting. One day we woke up, and there were all these little puffballs over the back hill. "Sheep!" I said to Alex. "Sheep!" We stood there awhile and watched them from our window. I loved what they did to the hill. Like if this were a painting you were doing, a lush landscape, and suddenly you got it in your head to add some action. Sheep! It makes the painting come alive with stories. That's the way I was looking at it. Alex was having a more literal reaction. Alex was seeing: lawn mowers. Lawn mowers that don't mind going up and down a steep hill, and as a bonus they fertilize while they go. Ten acres, straight up, or straight down, depending on your vantage point. The first few times Alex mowed that hill, he didn't admit to being afraid. But I could tell. For instance, he didn't complain when I made him take the cell phone with him in case of an emergency.

It's a guy thing, I suppose. He was trying to take the idea of driving a big machine down the side of a cliff in stride. Then one day he was over at George's, and there were some other farmers there. And all the farmers were filled with admiration for Alex. "So you're the guy," they said. "So you're the guy who mowed that hill." Lifetime farmers, not a one of them said he'd ever have the nerve to drive a tractor down that hill. "It's not a hill for people," one said. "At least not if you're figuring on living long."

After that, Alex got more and more interested in the idea of George's sheep. He started aggressively pursuing George's sheep offer. We'd had a particularly wet spring, so the grass was growing early and fast. So you can imagine Alex's relief when we saw the sheep that morning.

"Sheep," I said to Betty and Marley and Wilma. "Now you dogs go outside and you ignore those sheep."

I let them out, closed my eyes, and hoped. They went and stood by the fence—an electric fence. They stood by that fence for the better part of the day, staring at the sheep. And that was it. Within a day the sheep faded into the background of their doggy consciousness.

"See, I told you," I said to Alex.

"Well, you told George," he says.

"Yeah."

I miss Alex. I miss Betty and Skippy and all the animals. I miss normal days. I miss waking up and feeling good about sheep.

I miss the me I used to be. The me before the void. Last time I was home I didn't have the void. Well, I had it but it wasn't formed. You know, it's easier to complain about the loud ticking of your kitchen clock. It's . . . easier. This is one thing I can say for sure: Vague longing in the form of a bird pecking on your head is a lot easier than walking smack into a brick wall. Whew. I should get that one framed and put on a magnet to hang on our new refrigerator.

Impossible. This is an impossible situation. There is no

way Alex is going to go for the idea of us having a baby. And there is no way I can live without Alex. And there is no way I can live with the void.

I wonder if the void is the reason I've been visiting the Chihuahua. Maybe the Chihuahua is my surrogate baby.

Well, this is just getting more and more pathetic.

But I do think: I'm a mom. I think some moms are born way before the kid comes along. Of course, plenty of kids come along way, way before the mom is born. Moms are born. That's the thing. Moms are born. As a mom, I think, I am just being born.

This, I tell you, is a most startling discovery.

It's not that I've never thought about wanting a baby. Nor have I ever had anything against babies. As a kid, I had dolls. I had a doll that burped. I easily imagined myself a mom. I thought babies were swell. Not that I had ever touched a real live baby. I didn't do that until I was sixteen years old. I met her at the airport. Gate 10 at Philadelphia International Airport. We had signs and balloons. I saw her, in Eileen's arms. My brother's wife. Their first baby. Alyson. I saw her tiny bald head from across the crowded gate. Alyson. I saw her! I burst into tears. The tears were coming from some new place, some place in my chest I'd never even heard about before. I stood there crying, biting my thumb, folded into a tile wall. They came near me. They held her up to me. I was to be her god-mother. Here, hold her, they said, don't you want to hold your goddaughter?

No, I didn't. I was too busy holding on to consciousness. Was this what fainting felt like? Was this the instant of warn-ing you got?

But I didn't faint. Instead, I reached out. I reached through. I reached through terror and awe and love, and I touched her. I touched the baby. I touched her forehead. It was warm and soft and moist. It was nothing so spectacular, and yet it might as well have been God. Maybe it was.

Alyson became the center of my world. And then, a year and a half later, my nephew John arrived. My brother went on to have four kids in all, and my stated goal was to be the favorite aunt, the number-one aunt, oh, I would maintain that status even if it meant ten more hours of playing Play-Doh Fuzzy Pumper, a toy beauty salon, you pushed the lever and watched the Play-Doh come squirting in strings out of the heads of the bald lady and the bald man, neither of them, miraculously, bald anymore. It was fun being the favorite aunt.

But—my own baby? That had always been something way, way far off. I had too much to do. I had too much me, me, me to get right, to get on track, to polish and protect. There was no room for another. In fact, just about the time most people are thinking about having babies, I was headed in the other direction. I was discovering alone. I was all about *subtraction,* not addition. Was something wrong with me?

Me, me, me. How tiresome it now seems.

The Chihuahua fits in the crook of my arm. God, I love this little dog. His ears, I swear his ears are twice the size of his head. They stick straight up, tall and strong and so paper thin, the light comes through them, making them pink. I scratch the spot between his ears. He likes that. He also likes it when I scratch his chin bone, either side is good.

"It's okay, Chihuahua," I say. He smells like cedar chips. Not a bad smell for a pet shop dog. He's trembling. He's doing a little quiver dance. He's probably picking up the beat of my heart. My heart is pounding like crazy. *Thump-thump, boom. Thump-thump, boom.* My heart is pounding the way it pounded when I saw my name on the list of the high school freshman basketball team—holy hell, it's there! It's there!—

and I had to pretend that this was merely a very nice thing to see, yes, very nice, but certainly not the single most exciting event to happen in the history of my life. Which it was. But you don't go acting like that. You are in *high school*. You wait until you can get somewhere. You wait until you can get home and tell your mom, or your cat, or your favorite tree outside, you wait and wait and wait all the way through fifth period and all the way on the bus ride home, all the way down your street until your feet reach the place, under your favorite willow tree, that one place where you can explode, up, down, up, down, leaping for joy.

That is exactly the way my heart is pounding now. *Thump-thump, boom. Thump-thump, boom.* I have a secret inside. I have a revelation sure as hell. Hey, Chihuahua! *A baby.* A mom! I am a mom! But of course a Chihuahua in a pet shop isn't the place for a thirty-nine-year-old woman to take something like this. Especially not a thirty-nine-year-old woman who thinks of herself as a mom but who doesn't have an actual baby and who is at once thrilled about her new self and miserable about the fact that it is, after all, merely virtual.

"You want to go see the gerbils?" I say to the Chihuahua.

He doesn't protest, so we head over.

I wonder if Alex will give me credit for not bringing this Chihuahua home. For not even *suggesting* bringing the Chihuahua home. Does that earn me extra credit that I can put toward maybe getting a baby?

Oh, brother. We are now sliding well past pathetic.

But—Alex doesn't want a baby. I'm certain of that. He's already done fatherhood. He raised Amy and Peter as a single dad. He has fatherhood medals out the wazoo. He thinks he's too old to do it all over again. He's fifty-four, forgodsakes. There is no way.

There has to be a way.

What if there is no way?

Okay, now he's snoring. I have never imagined the sound of a Chihuahua snoring. It's the highest pitch. Sweet little dog. When I put him back in his cage, he wakes up with a start. I tell him good night, now. I tell him the store is going to close soon so I have to go. He cocks his head to one side, cocks it like a puppy on a poster in a little girl's bedroom. Oh, come on. "I am going to turn around now and not look back," I say to him. "Do you understand?"

I take four steps. I look back. Oh, jeez. Those are the most pathetic eyes. Okay, one last pat. "But this is it," I say, opening the cage. "I *mean* it." I bring him into my arms. He's shaking. He must be so terrified of going back in that cage. I can't blame him. A taste of freedom must be the worst thing to dangle in front of a prisoner serving life. The shaking, it's a jet-propulsion kind of shaking. The shaking, it thrusts him up, over my shoulder, and then down to the floor. He lands on his feet. He does not look back. He goes zooming toward the gerbils, past the gerbils, his feet clicking and clacking past the fish and the birds and around to the gerbils again. "The Chihuahua!" I am yelling. "Hey, anybody! *The Chihuahua is loose!*"

II

EGGS

CHAPTER SIX

It's a hot Saturday in July. We were just about to head out for a walk, but the phone rang—someone needing something from Alex—and then George showed up. I don't really mind the interruptions; I don't much care what happens. I'm just glad to be home, back to normal, back where happily-ever-after was reportedly last seen.

From my spot at the kitchen table I can see Marley and Wilma lying like walruses on the porch, their chests rising and falling with the rhythm of sleep. Betty is here with me, curled up in a ball between my feet. And George, he's leaning on the kitchen counter, arms folded. He's waiting for Alex to get off the phone, waiting for him like a kid eager for his buddy to come out and play. That's the thing. Alex and George have become pals. A shrink and a sheep farmer. It's not the most natural combination. It's something to see. They'll hang out for hours at his barn or our barn. They do tractor-talk. They do livestock-talk. They do hay-humor, and I suppose they share plenty of beef-and-poultry-gossip. I don't really know what they do. I just know that it's usually George doing the talking and Alex doing the laughing and nodding and chin-scratching. It really is something to see. It makes me happy to see it. Except I am getting a tiny bit worried that Alex is going to start chewing tobacco.

"Anyway," George is saying to me, "as far as that goes, you could say a drought is better than a flood!" He's laughing. Oh, he's been going on for quite some time here about how he's absolutely convinced we're heading into a drought, which isn't funny at all, of course—but somehow the idea of drought has led him into a riff of flood stories, including the one he's just finishing about two of his lady sheep thinking they were on dry land, but actually they had stepped into his canoe, and eventually the water rose and got so high the canoe got loose, and there was his neighbor calling to say, "Your sheep just went floating by. . . ."

"Oh, golly . . ." he's saying, wiping his eyes with the back of his fist, his laughter fading.

Then he says, "I'll bet you're happy we're heading into a drought."

"Well—"

"I mean, I'll bet you curse every time it rains, what with that basement of yours."

"Actually—"

"Matter of fact, I'll bet you're cursing the guy who put in that basement of yours."

Um. Not really. But should I be?

See, another story is coming. Probably a big one, from the sound of the way George is setting it up. Oh, I know the signs by now. Question after assumption after question. It's the rhythm that sucks you in. It's like a vacuum cleaner turning on. This is almost always how the stories start.

George is smiling. His gaze has moved to the floor. He's nodding, staring at that floor as if searching for the exact plot points he will now put forth.

I sit patiently, as you do waiting for a movie to start. I should have popcorn. Here comes the feature presentation, folks. Actually, this time I feel a bit more like a zoologist waiting for

the antelopes to make love. You know, I'm sitting here thinking I should make a little study of George's storytelling. How
does he do it? And where did he learn the craft? Is there some
sort of tall-tale trade school here in Scenery Hill? Sometimes
I think so. Sometimes I really do. George is one of the best,
but George is only one of the story machines roaming this
land. There is, for example, also Billy, the bulldozer driver,
the man who cleared our fields and rebuilt our barn and who
also found us our wedding mule. Like George, Billy has a story
for every visit and then some. But with Billy—well, with Billy,
it got so his tales were so tall, so full of swagger, I stopped be-
lieving them. I'll never forget the day he was over here telling
me that he was drinking horse medicine. Hell, it had worked
on his horse's tumor, so why not his? He said he had quit going to his doctor for his cancer because the horse elixir was all
he needed. I sighed. I said, "Okay, Billy." I really figured that
was it for Billy. His stories had gotten the best of him. You
can't tall-tale your way out of a tumor. But now it's three
years later, and Billy is healthier than ever. So I don't know.

Anyway, George. You never know where George is going to take you. I wish Alex would get off the phone. He's
going to miss the show. George has gotten himself good and
comfortable, his legs opened like a soldier at ease. His T-shirt
clings to his belly, clings like plastic wrap. "Old man Collins,"
George says. "Yeah, Red Collins. He's who lived here when I
was a boy, and he's the man who conceived of your basement."

Is that a fact? George has already told me plenty of stories
about Red Collins and his wife Marie, but that doesn't stop
him from introducing his main characters properly.

"Now, old Red, he had a wife," George goes on. "Marie
was her name. Marie didn't want a basement. She liked the
house the way it was."

"You mean the basement was put in after our house was already built?" I ask, to clarify.

"That's exactly true," George says. "And the way Red was, he could have dug it with his bare hands. Because Red was huge. Over seven foot tall, feet as big as tennis rackets. People throughout the valley said they could feel the earth shake just from Red walking. He played for the Steelers, you know. Red could tackle a guy with just his hip. He could just pitch his hip and send guys sailing twenty yards."

Now, literal-minded people might think it's a mistake to exaggerate while telling a story. They think, Oh, I'll lose my credibility. This, according to the George method, is incorrect. A good storyteller knows that exaggeration is key and that exaggeration is worthless unless it's extreme exaggeration, and that it doesn't work unless you, as the storyteller, begin to actually and truthfully ninety-nine percent believe in it.

"But the basement?" George says. "I'm serious. Red could have dug it with his bare hands, his hands were so huge. You see my hand?" He stops, holds up his hand. "My hand is like as big as a catcher's mitt. It's why I can shear three sheep in under fifty-five seconds. But Red's hand? His was three times the size of this hand of mine."

He holds his hands higher so I can fully examine their monumental massiveness. But these are really just a prop. A prop enabling him to insert into his story a good, prolonged silence, which is the best tension-builder God ever invented.

"Now, old Red was tough," George goes on, shaking his head as though he can hardly believe it himself, so he'll understand if you don't. "Grown men were afraid of him. He would kill a pig with just his hands. He would hang it up for slaughter, and do you know what he would do next?"

No, I really, really don't.

"He would tilt his head back and drink the blood pouring out of that pig."

Note the delivery here. Because George doesn't say, "HE WOULD TILT HIS HEAD BACK AND DRINK THE BLOOD POURING OUT OF THAT PIG!!!!" No, George just lets the pig-blood fact pour out of him like, well, blood out of a freshly slaughtered pig. This right here is a crucial key device and most certainly requires a lot of practice.

But the really interesting thing I have to note is that, technically, George hasn't even started his story; up till now it's all character development, and yet I'm not sitting here wishing he would move on, I'm not saying "Uh-huh" a lot, nor am I saying "So what happened next?" rushing the story along. A storyteller who hears these sorts of responses should definitely take the hint and be merciful on his audience and say "Never mind" and maybe just go make dinner or something.

Instead, and here's the real magic, I'm hardly here, at all. I'm actually years and miles away from George. I'm here with Red and Marie. I'm trying to figure out what Marie sees in Red. I'm trying to find a nice way of asking Red and Marie why they put all this dreadful paneling up in this house. George is going on and on, and I'm here daydreaming, loving George for bringing me where he has brought me. This is what impresses me. What is a story if not a legitimate, sanctioned escape from the here-and-now? A new here-and-now to climb into, like the basket of a hot-air balloon. A free vacation! If I learned nothing else from my time at my mother's bedside, I learned that living your entire life in the here-and-now isn't a worthwhile goal at all. The trick is learning how to *find* it so you can be in it, leave it, come back to it at will. The trick is in the recognition, and the muscle of choice.

"So old Red, he did want a basement," George is saying, making his voice low and thunderous, like drums announcing the important part of a song. "And sweet Marie, she refused him again and again. She said, 'Red, we don't need a basement.' Red stewed on this point for many years. One day he waited until Marie went off to work. He said, 'Well, good-bye, Mother.' And he ran. He ran and he ran. He ran four miles up to the coal mine. And there he retrieved for himself seventeen sticks of dynamite."

George stops, looks me in the eye, gives me the time and space to *imagine* what happened next. Because time and space are what the imagination feeds off of. Time and space, I tell you, are the actual Kibbles'n Bits of the imagination.

"So old Red," says George. "He stuck those seventeen sticks of dynamite here and there, all around this house we are standing in today. He then ignited the dynamite." George throws his arms high in the air, makes his eyes as wide as Rhode Island. "BOOOOM!" he shouts, in such a way as to shake the lampshades.

"So that explains the stream in your basement," he says, bringing the story all the way around, because the circle is the storyteller's infinite and everlasting most sincere responsibility. "Red blasted through a seam of limestone that was holding back a few springs. It's a wet basement, as I understand it."

"It is," I agree.

George looks down at his shoes. Then he glances past my shoulder, says, "If you could please ask Alex to meet me down at the barn, I have some sheep to check on."

In other words, "The end." Because even if this story is true, we are teetering right on the tippy-tippy edge of believability, which of course is the most vital and exciting place for a story to sit. A lot of people have trouble leaving a story here. A lot of people would go on and on about what happened to Red when Marie came home, and what happened to Marie when she discovered the foundation of her life . . . missing, and some would even go into a big explanation of basement construction fundamentals. This would be a violation. This would be like a light going on in a rocket ship flashing ABORT ABORT ABORT and the rocket ship doing a nosedive into the bottomless sea.

so, normalcy. my life back at the farm. Betty and Marley and Cricket and Sassy and Skippy and Maggie and all the gang. A whole brood of healthy, happy creatures. And my garden full of slugs. And work in my dusty office. And my satellite dish. And laundry drying in the cellar. And broccoli steaming on the stove. And the *tick-tock* of my kitchen clock that somehow doesn't seem nearly as loud as it once did.

Everything looks so different when you return home. The things you used to complain about seem to hardly bother you at all. And the things you were thinking about while you were away seem almost adorably funny or at least irrelevant. Right now it seems like years since I stood in a pet shop with a Chihuahua running loose. A Chihuahua running loose that I came to understand as something in me running loose, yes, something in me that was now unleashed and there was no containing it.

The Chihuahua was, of course, contained that night. He was put right back in his cage. A few weeks later, when I went for one of my regular visits, he was gone. The clerk said an old man had come in with his son. The son had been trying for months to get his lonely old dad to agree to get a dog. But the right dog never seemed to materialize. Not until the old man met the Chihuahua. The clerk gave me the old man's phone number. I sat down to make the call, I really did. I wanted to tell the old man how much I loved the Chihuahua; I wanted to hear something in his voice that would tell me that he too loved the Chihuahua; I wanted him to put the phone up to the Chihuahua's giant pink ear so I could say, "Hey Chihuahua! I'm so happy for you!"

But then I decided it really was best to let it go.

As for my mom, well, things are slowly improving. She can sit up on her own. We all gathered around and applauded the first time she did that. She's moved well through the acute phase of the disease, which means she's out of danger and doesn't need the medical attention she once did. But she's not nearly strong enough for the rigors of a rehab hospital. When she's ready for it, she'll need months in such a facility. And so for now she's living on the fifth floor of Riddle Village, in a special nursing-home section of the retirement village where we moved my dad three months ago. Just four stories up from the new apartment. A mere elevator ride away. My dad is able to wheel my mom around the place, even down to their apartment; he shows her where all her stuff is, gets her opinion on where to move lamps and pictures. My sisters and brother and I are somewhat dumbfounded to see how this has worked out; if my parents still lived back at the old house at Springton Lake, there would be no way they'd get this time near each other. My mother would likely be spending these transitional months in a nursing home with virtually no connection to a place she would be able to think of as "home."

"Can you believe this?" my mom said to me the other day on the phone. "Can you believe that I'm now *relieved* that your dad brought me to the funny farm?"

I told her that now, more than ever, she would need to stop referring to the place as a funny farm.

"All right," she said. "You're right."

Her mood has improved considerably, thanks
to finally getting out of the hell that Room 109
represent, but thanks in larger part to her priest an.
The priest did a miraculous thing. He taught her a prayer she
could say: "I will be faithful." He said she didn't need to pray
any more than that. Just work on that one. She told me that
that one simple prayer provided a kind of tether to God. And
thus came grace.

It must have seemed ironic, or at least strange to my
mom, that Alex would turn out to be yet another trusted
guide. He is, after all, Jewish. To a Catholic, especially a de-
vout one, this can mean you are on the other side of a very
important fence. It can mean *What is the matter with you* that
you haven't chosen to live over here?" It can mean "You can't
possibly understand me."

I don't know what exactly transpired between my mom
and Alex. His visits to her hospital bed became more frequent
when her depression began to deepen; she rapidly progressed
to full-blown panic attacks. He would hold her hand, sit right
next to her bed, close to her ear. "Just listen to my voice," he
would say, and then nod in my direction so I might give them
privacy. I'd leave the room, wait for the door to open again.
Sometimes it would take an hour. Somehow each time Alex
was able to bring my mother's mind back. I'd go in, and she'd
be laughing, she'd be joking about having a bad hair day or
expounding on the virtue of patience.

He also taught the rest of us how to deal with her panic
attacks so that we weren't inadvertently making them worse.
He explained how, if you try to talk someone who is terrified
out of the thing they are afraid of, it just reinforces their be-
lief that the thing exists. So we learned to redirect her
thoughts rather than challenge them. And she learned to tell

us to go away so that she might close her eyes and employ one of the tricks Alex had taught her.

I really don't know what the tricks were, or how Alex taught them to her. I only know that when it's your time to be sucked into madness, you're very lucky if you have someone with the courage to sit with you—really sit with you—on the edge of that pool. That person is the reason you can let go, plunge, get it over with.

My mom and Alex now have a date. She's vowed to be well enough to dance at Christmas. She's reserved the first dance for him.

SO, NORMALCY. MY life back on the farm. Alex and George. They're down at the barn, and last I checked they were all involved in some anti-fungal campaign with the sheep feet. The morning is long gone, and so, it appears, is my husband.

I'm sitting on the porch. Oh, good. I can see Alex starting to say good-bye to George. Sometimes it takes a long time to say good-bye to George. George has one foot in the door of his navy-blue pickup, the rest of him out. Alex is nodding, scratching his chin, nodding. Finally, a laugh. George always leaves you laughing. He drives off, finally. And Alex comes up to the house.

"Did he tell you about drought?" he asks.

"And the sheep canoeing by?"

"Yep."

"Yep."

"George. You ready for our walk?" he says. He's wearing khaki shorts and a T-shirt advertising Canada.

"Oh, you still want to go?"

"I think we should. While we have our nerve up."

"All right. But let's put the dogs in. We don't want to be showing up with three maniac dogs jumping and slobbering."

"They're not *that* bad," he says.

"I know, but—"

"No, you're right," he says.

"What?"

"I said, 'You're *right,* dear.' "

I smile, raise my chin like a famous movie star. We both have a thing about being right, Alex and I, and feel it's important to stop and notice whenever one of us gets to be it.

"Ta dum!" he says.

"Thank you."

"I'll put the dogs in," he says.

Our walk today isn't really a pleasure walk. Or it's only incidentally for pleasure. We're going to visit the old lady who lives down the road. We've never met her. We don't even know her name. Everyone around here just calls her "the old lady." As in "Stay away from the old lady. She's wacky." And "Stay off the old lady's land." And "Don't even make eye contact with the old lady if you happen to see her out in her yard."

Ordinarily we would heed the advice, but as it happens, we need the old lady. She owns a piece of land we want. Just a small chunk, a few acres at most, a narrow strip that abuts ours. It's an utterly useless piece of marshland—except to us. Owning this piece would give us the room we need to one day build up the dam that forms our pond. It's something we've talked about doing ever since we moved here. Build up the dam, and the pond could be raised a good six feet— which translates to a pond that grows from one acre to about six. A giant pond! Oh, we have dancing visions of canoes in our heads. And a sandy beach with willows hanging down.

The pond project is probably years off. But we've been

advised to ask the old lady now. She's probably on her last legs. And her heirs are reputed to be even crankier than she is.

And so it is with some trepidation that Alex and I head down the driveway, dogless. We make a right onto our dirt road.

The dirt is reddish brown, and it's so dry we can hear our feet crunching over it. The towering hardwoods are in full splendor, providing a cool tunnel of shade. "Hey, girls," Alex says to the neighbor's cows as we pass. He always does this, sort of tips an imaginary hat to them. One answers with a pause in her cud chewing and a glance in our direction; the rest keep their heads down, their tails swishing. At a time like this you appreciate that your neighbor has chosen to breed Holsteins; nothing says "cow" like the black and white kind, and nothing says "farm" like the sight of a cow set against the greenest grass—with a crooked red barn in the background.

Perfect. Picture perfect. And here I am now, right in the middle of the picture.

Well, this is happily-ever-after if ever I did see it. Oh, it's here all right. Of course it is! I mean, if there's a problem, you can't blame the picture and you can't blame happily-ever-after.

If there's a problem, it's . . . me. All this new stuff inside me. The void. This newly discovered mother in me. She's really mucking things up, no matter how hard I try to get rid of her.

Ever since I got back here to the farm, I've been trying to get rid of her. And the way I've gone about getting rid of her has been to hold her in. In. In. In. This, oddly, is just the immediate impulse you have when you are trying to get rid of something. You hold it in. You think if you just don't talk about the thing, if you just ignore the thing, it will go away.

Well, I am here to report, live from the Land of Holding

Everything In, that it doesn't work. I've tried every which way to make this motherhood thing go away. I've tried deciding that it was utter nonsense. *A baby?* Oh, forgodsakes. The idea had, after all, hit me when I was away from home. Not in my normal life. It hit me when I was in a heightened state of horribleness, dealing with a paralyzed mother, for heaven's sake.

And everything looks so different when you're home. Everything! Who doesn't know this one? There you are, off on vacation, far away from home, you're sitting on some beautiful beach drinking a fruity drink, and you get this giant urge to change your life; you vow to quit your job and start a new life. Yes! Because the truth is you've always wanted to open a cooking school or something—yes, a cooking school! Yes, as soon as you get home you will get right on that!

And then you get home, back to your real bed and your real dust under your real couch, and you think, *Cooking school?* And you go back to work, and your old job really isn't all that bad, and the routine of your days lulls you back to a kind of comfortable, if slightly fitful, sleep.

That's what I've been thinking about the whole baby deal. I've been thinking: That's so silly. Now get back to the real world.

The problem, of course, is that what I have inside me isn't some harebrained scheme to start a cooking school. No, I am changed. Like it or not, I'm a mom now: a mom who happens to have no kid.

"I have something to ask you," I say to Alex as we walk. Just that abruptly, I say it.

"Well, I'm not afraid of her, if that's what you're thinking," he says.

Um, no. That's not what I was thinking. What is he talking about?

"I mean, it's not like the old lady is going to pull out a pistol and start shooting us," he says.

Oh, the old lady. A pistol? Our brainwaves are way out of alignment here.

"Actually, my guess is she's more the sawed-off-shotgun type," he says.

"Right."

"But we'll just go in there, tell her our business, ask her to think about it, and walk out. It won't take more than a minute. How bad can it be?"

"Right."

Our feet are crunching even louder now, our pace quickening with entirely separate types of determination.

"Well, what I had to ask you wasn't about the old lady," I say.

"No?"

"No."

Something in my tone, I guess I've got his attention.

"It's important?" he says.

"I think so."

"You're mad at me?"

"Nope."

And then everything falls out of me like rain.

"Now, I know this might not be something you want," I say, pointing my finger like a teacher. "In fact, I'm pretty sure it's not something you want, and that's okay, because I'm not saying it's something we have to do, I'm really, really not, it's just if we don't *talk* about it, then I'm all alone with it, and that's not fair to you or to me or to the relationship, and so really my first goal here is to protect our relationship that we worked so hard for and I think is pretty good, don't you think it's pretty good?"

"Yeah . . ."

A chipmunk comes darting out from the brush and scurries across.

"Okay, then." I take a breath.

"Okay . . ."

I bite my lip for a moment. "Well," I say, finally. "I feel better already. Whew. It's never good to hold things in. Let that be a lesson. Out! Out! Out!"

"Right," he says. "But—the question?"

"Oh." And, damn. "Well, it's important that you understand where this is coming from. Okay?" I'm trying to think of where to start. "It's just that, well, the wind is blowing," I say. "The wind is blowing really hard. And I know my wind is not the same as your wind, and there can never really be an *our* wind, not in any relationship, not really, anyway."

"There can't?"

"There can?"

"I'm really not sure what we're talking about so I'm reluctant to take a stand."

Oh, for heaven's sake. See, this is why it's bad to have an imaginary conversation with your husband for months on end. He's so far behind you. I run through the events of last spring in my mind. I grab his arm. "Look," I say. "I want to remind you that I did *not* bring that Chihuahua home."

"Oh my God, this is about getting a Chihuahua?"

"No, the Chihuahua has nothing to do with it."

"Okay, then. So we're not getting a Chihuahua."

"No."

"Well, that's . . . good."

We walk in silence. Oh, we're really making headway now.

"I just want you to know that this is not a case of the train leaving the station," I say. "I am totally in control of the train."

"I can tell."

"And I am not going to stand here trying to convince you to do something you don't want to do, I've already come to peace with that, but I'm in a bit of a quandary here because I have this hole in my heart and I really don't know how to go about filling it."

"You want to tell me what you're talking about?" he says. He pulls a maple leaf off a tree, hands it to me. He knows I like deveining maple leaves.

"Okay," I say. "I'll tell you what it is. It's . . . the old lady. The cranky old lady in the big horrible house who no one will make eye contact with. That's me someday, you know."

"It is?"

"You'll be dead and gone and I'll be all alone out here and I'll turn into a mean old witch without a name."

"Wow," he says. "So, um, you want to make sure I don't die before you?"

"That's not—"

"I can't really promise, but I can certainly do my best."

"That's not really—"

"You're afraid of being left alone?"

"Partly." I messed up the maple leaf and lost the minor veins; now all I have is the big one that runs down the middle. I tie it in a loop, slip my finger through.

"You have a lot of family," Alex says.

"Yes, I do. And so do you. But what about us?"

"It's *our* family," he points out.

"I know."

"We have a huge family. We have half of suburban Philadelphia related to us. And my kids in New York. And the Israelis. And jeez, all the babes in Pittsburgh. And now George and Pat and—"

"I know, but—"

"You want more family?"

"I do."

"Oh."

There are no sounds at all now, nothing but the foot crunch and a distant cowbell.

I hand him my maple leaf vein ring. He slips it on the tip of his pinky.

"I've been thinking about this for months now," I say. "Ever since my mom got sick, and I know you don't want a kid, I know you already did that, so I've been trying to figure out what to do with this hole in my heart, and for a while it was going away, but now it's just getting bigger and I don't want to be a train that's left the station, and I certainly don't want you to have to live out your retirement years with some cranky teenager in the house, and I don't want you to have the stress of, you know, car seats and McDonald's Happy Meals, but I would happily do all of that part, I really would, but I know that's not enough, I really do, but I don't have much else to offer."

"Do I get to participate in this conversation?"

I don't answer.

"You know," he says, "it sounds like you've been having this conversation with me for the past six months, except I haven't had a chance to talk."

"Yeah. I knew you would think that. See, that's what I mean. I already know what you think."

"No, you don't," he says. "Hell, I don't even know what I think."

"You don't?"

"I don't."

I pull down three more maple leaves.

"So you want, like, a baby?" he says.

"In a word."

"Well, I was wondering if you might."

"You were?"

"Of course. Why wouldn't you want a baby? You're a natural mom."

"I am."

"You're a mom to your friends. You're a mom to all our animals. You've been a wonderful mom to your own mom."

"That's the one that got to me. That's the one that got me all twisted up with this."

"You think it's twisted?" he asks.

"You don't?"

"I think it's pretty normal."

"You do?"

"Why wouldn't wanting a baby be normal?"

"Well, you don't go marrying someone fifteen years older who's already raised two kids and who you know is quite past the kid-raising thing and then just walk around thinking about having a kid."

"Well, it sounds to me like you do."

"Well, it's stupid," I say.

"It's not stupid," he says.

"Well, what is it then?"

"It's something to think about."

"Can you tell me what you think about it?"

He looks down at his feet. He looks over at the cows again. He looks down at his feet again. "I have a lot of thoughts," he says. "Not the least of which is, you don't go marrying someone fifteen years younger who's a born mom and who hasn't had kids and just walk around thinking the kid thing isn't going to become an issue."

"Issue," I say. "We have an *issue*." A real issue. Not just an

SUV issue. *Issue.* What a horrible word. A word that sits heavy in my stomach.

The air is beginning to get moist now, humidity moving in. Suddenly the bugs seem a lot more eager for their bug meals. We wave our hands over our heads, swatting. See, it would be good to have a tail like a cow. Or at least ears that flicked. I hand Alex one of my maple leaves to use.

"Well, I'll be honest," he tells me. "It's not something I want."

"I know."

"I never wanted kids. In fact, that was the one thing I was sure I didn't want to be: a dad."

"You told me."

"And yet raising Peter and Amy is the thing I'm proudest about in my life. It's the one thing I think I was good at."

"I know."

"So it's not about wanting," he says.

We talk about wanting. We talk about how the wanting in life might just be the smallest piece of the whole happiness equation. Either way you look at it. If you think about people who go through life wanting the next thing, and the next, and each time they get what they want, they want what's next. There's no happiness in that. There's no life in that. There's just the tease.

"Then if you look at it the other way," Alex says. "Me with Peter and Amy. Or me with this farm. How does anybody know what they want before they have it? I never in my wildest dreams wanted to live on a farm. And now look at me. I love living here."

"Maybe you're just adaptable."

"Or maybe just a chump."

"No." I tell him I think adaptable people just have to

make sure they're surrounded by people who won't take advantage of them. "I don't ever want to take advantage of you."

"You don't," he says.

Well, we're making some headway.

One foot in front of the other, that's how it goes when you walk.

The old lady's house is now looming just over Alex's left shoulder. "Let's get this over with," he says, nodding in its direction. We'll continue our conversation later. He needs some time to think, to catch up. Right now I'm relieved that I'm not alone with the subject anymore.

But—"issue."

THE HOUSE IS a Wedgwood-blue Victorian towered over by a row of shaggy Norway spruces. There's a cardboard sign tacked to the back door: "NO Trespassing. NO Solicitors."

I elbow Alex.

He knocks.

"Who are you?" we hear. A thin voice, but a loud one. "Who is there?"

I elbow Alex again.

"We're neighbors," he shouts, in a tone suggesting that we come in peace. "We live down the road. The second pond down?"

"The frogs?" she says. "The place with all the frogs? You're the new people in the place with the frogs?"

"Um, we have frogs," I say, and now the screen door is swinging open. The old lady is in a light blue housecoat with butterflies on the collar, and bare feet. Her hair is the whitest silky white, tied loosely back. She might be tall if she stood all the way up; as it is, her back is bent round as a turtle shell.

We can see that there are two other women in the room, and a teenager. All three are sitting around a gleaming mahogany table, set with formal china.

"Oh, we didn't mean to interrupt your supper," I say.

"Come in," the old lady says. "It's really nice of you. I'm surprised. People don't do this anymore."

Right. Um. Do what?

"When I was a girl, everyone new introduced themselves to the neighbors." Her voice is high, like the sound of a violin barely in tune. "You don't see it anymore, not hardly."

Right. And do we need to mention that this is not why we've come? Yes, we need to clear this misunderstanding up immediately.

"You must be good people," she says. "Sit down. This is lemonade. This is lasagna. I made pie. We'll have that later. What are your names? Where did you move from? What nationality are you?" In a matter of seconds, we skip all the way up to religious affiliation.

"Jewish," Alex says.

"Catholic," I say.

She looks up at Alex. "Land's sake. I don't believe I've ever had one in my house. Well, welcome. You don't look any different."

The two women smile politely. They have identical black bobs. The girl watches intently, as if she has no problem following anything.

"A Catholic," the old lady says to me, looking me up, then down. "Well, it's none of my damn business."

I'm not quite sure what is happening here. First of all, the lady is not living up to her reputation. She isn't the sawed-off-shotgun type. I'm not sure what type she is. But she's certainly a force. In fact, it's hard to believe the world hasn't heard more from her. The women at the table, who we soon learn are her daughters who live a few towns over—the teenager is her granddaughter—bring us chairs and lemonade. It all happens so fast, as if a great vortex of welcome has swept us up.

It feels great. And it feels awful. Great in that we are being welcomed like honored guests. Awful in that we are imposters. We are not who they think we are. We're here on business. We are not, technically, country people. We are not, let's face it, George and Pat. We are not people with *time* for random neighbor visits. We are normal busy Americans with cars and TVs and errands and phone calls to make and appointments to keep. And—neighbors? We come from the city. We come from a place where neighbors are just people to keep the peace with. People you talk to only when you need something. People outside the place you call home.

Around here neighbors are something altogether different. Neighbors are people you just automatically pull up a chair for. It's been strange for us to have been invited this way into virtually every neighbor's home. It is especially strange to have been invited this way into the home of the notorious "old lady." And why hasn't she been embraced by the other neighbors? What secrets does she hold? What secrets do they hold?

"Tomatoes," the old lady says. "I have tomatoes growing. You need tomatoes, you come here." Her daughters nod. She says the sauce in her lasagna is her own. The apples in the pie are from her own orchard. She asks if we'd like to see pictures of the family, the cousins who still live in the Old Country. We look at the pictures. We laugh. We write down our phone number in case the old lady ever needs anything.

"And would you like to see the graveyard out back?" says Lisa, the teenager. "There are stones from the eighteen hundreds." She says the Weaver family is buried there. "The people who settled this land."

Eventually, as if everyone in this room had this whole thing planned in advance, we end up following Lisa out the back door, past the apple orchard, and through an overgrown hay field. Lisa's a slim girl with dark, happy eyes. She's giving us a history lesson. She says she loves history. She asks what we know about the Whiskey Rebellion. "Everyone thinks of it as a lesson in taxation," she says, "but if you ask me, it was a much bigger lesson in political deal-making."

Well, then.

She asks if we have a favorite war, says her current favorite is the Revolutionary War. "But the Civil War is a *very* close second."

Okay, then.

She has sandals on. Pink sandals with the thinnest soles. I'm so impressed with the way she walks through the field, into and out of the briars, with just those sandals. Alex and I have on our "hiking boots." We know they are "hiking boots" because it said so right in the Eddie Bauer store, it said "hiking boots." We bought the most rugged-looking ones they had. Wasn't this what country people wore?

Actually, no. Country people don't need a lot of outerwear. They have thick skin. They have calluses built up. They have a *hide*. Not only that, but country people are interesting. Country people are intelligent. Country people *read books*. It feels like a revelation—not the discovery of country people but the discovery of my own biases. It's not every day your whole perspective changes just by seeing a girl's feet.

When we get to the graveyard, we find that it's a tiny plot surrounded by a rusted and broken iron fence. Inside the fence there are about ten thin stone markers leaning left and right. Lisa yanks at the crowding weeds and helps us read the words nearly washed away by a century of wind and rain. She tells us which Weaver was married to which, and whose child was whose, and she speculates about the whereabouts of others. "I love history," she says again. "I first started loving it because I figured it was *finite,*" she says. She flashes a knowing smile as if to suggest we all start out with this sort of thought. "I thought, well, this is a subject you can learn every single thing about because everything has already *happened.*"

Alex is making some interested mumbling noises, encouraging her. She's using a stick to scrape some moss off the marker of Adam Weaver, 1833 to 1889. Her brown hair is pulled behind her ears, her face long and serious.

"But the more I learn, the more I realize that's not true," she says. "There's *so much* that has already happened, I don't know if I'll ever catch up."

She looks at me, cocks her head, as if to give me a chance to catch up.

"But that just makes me love history even *more,*" she says, throwing down the stick, standing up. "Do you have a favorite explorer?"

I look at Alex. His face is as blank as my mind.

"*Don't* say Magellan," Lisa says.

"No way," Alex says.

We follow Lisa back to the house and listen to her doubts about Ferdinand Magellan, and all I can think is how this is not your average member of the Britney Spears generation. How does a country kid skilled in walking with flimsy sandals through briars get such a curious mind? Why do we think people who grow up in cities are the only ones with a lot going on upstairs? If I have a kid, I hope she is as interesting as Lisa.

When we get back to the old lady's house, we thank Lisa for all she has taught us. We turn to say good-bye to the old lady, to thank her for the meal. She's throwing stale bread over the porch railing for the birds. Alex elbows me. Right. And whoops. We've been here for two hours already—we're becoming part of the family, practically—and we have not yet gotten to our business. We have not yet addressed the real reason for our visit. The land. We need to clear this up. We need to just say, hey, we came for a reason, actually, we wanted to ask you something.

Or do we? I like the people we've been mistaken for: friendly folks who came with nothing more on their minds than a little goodwill. Couldn't we be those people instead?

Alex elbows me again. Right. Come clean. The land. Well, why doesn't *he* say it, then?

One more elbow. Ouch. Right in my rib. *"What?"*

"Don't say anything about the land," he whispers. "Okay?"

And so we don't. We can't bring ourselves to do it. We don't want to bring ourselves to do it. We become, at least during this one July afternoon, the people we've been mistaken for. We become country people.

When we start to say our good-byes, the old lady says, "No." She says, "You will stay here on this porch and eat ice cream." Both her daughters are already loading their cars. They have, apparently, been excused. We say good-bye to them, and to Lisa, and wave as they make their way down the driveway. The old lady hands us our bowls. The ice cream is, technically, orange sherbet. She reaches down between the railings of the porch and plucks some fresh mint. She puts a sprig in each of our bowls. She tells us about her daughters. She tells us she doesn't actually get along that great with them anymore, but she's trying to maintain what she can. *"I'm trying!"* she says, thumping her fist on her knee.

I look at Alex.

He's stirring his sherbet quickly, as if trying to busy himself.

"So what do you do?" she asks Alex. "What's your job?" He talks briefly about being a psychologist and how he came to specialize with the bereft, especially those mourning the loss of parents.

"Oh," the old lady says wistfully. "Well, dear, when you lose your parents, you lose your past," she says, as if she's already figured this one out. She takes a soft breath. "But when you lose a child?" She looks at us, pausing as if to give us time to fill in the blank. "When you lose a child, you lose your future."

Alex and I both nod as if understanding, which neither of us really can.

"My youngest daughter," she says. "Lily was her name. I named her after the lily of the valley growing right under that maple tree," she says, pointing. "We were soul mates. We did everything together. You know how you have one person like that, one person in all your life?"

I raise my eyebrows with recognition, tilt my head toward Alex, the person like that in my life. I'm feeling instantly lucky. And instantly full of dread for what she is about to say.

Evening is settling in. The crickets are out in full blast, and the lightning bugs have begun to dance. The old lady begins checking her fingernails, then throws Alex a glance. "Maybe you knew my daughter?" she says. "She was a psychologist."

Alex smiles politely.

"Well, there was a fire," she says. "She was thirty-six years old, and there was a fire that took hold in her house." She says it happened at night, while her daughter lay sleeping. The fire burned her house to the ground. "With my daughter in it," she says. "Nothing but ashes left."

She sits here on the porch with the orange sherbet melting on her lap. She says it's been nearly ten years. "I'm very sorry to burden you with this," she says. "I just thought you should know." She puts her hand up to her eyes, squeezes them shut. "I don't know," she says. "Maybe I didn't tell it right."

"It's a powerful story," I say awkwardly. I don't think the storytelling is foremost on her mind.

"Well, I am not the same person I used to be," she says. "I'm not nice to people. I'm not—"

"Oh, that's not true—" Alex says.

"Listen to me!" she shouts. *"Listen!"*

We listen.

"You don't lose your soul mate in a puff of smoke"—she opens her eyes, looking up as if she can see that smoke—"and stay the same person." Her voice is trailing off into a kind of moan. "Don't you see what I've turned into?" she demands. "Don't you *see*?"

ON THE WALK home, through the darkness, we don't say a whole lot.

At one point I say maybe we should look at how much fire insurance we have.

Alex says loneliness insurance might be a better investment.

We wonder where to get some.

We agree that having kids really isn't it.

CHAPTER SEVEN

Those sumac trees are weeds. There is really no polite way to say it. The poor things. Tall and leggy with pointy leaves that look like knives sticking out. A child could draw a more convincing tree.

The only thing is, every year I watch them. Because they're the first to go. While the maples and oaks and other hardwoods are out there basking in the summer sun, basking as if there is no tomorrow, as if this is summer and summer is here to stay, the sumacs get the slightest tinge of crimson red. They're the ones that say, "Hey, it's gonna happen. It's gonna be over."

No, not just summer.

Me.

I don't know. Am I being melodramatic? Well, what do you expect? It's the first of September. In twenty-one days I turn forty. Twenty-one puny days.

Forty.

Forty!

I've started to design my headstone. Yeah. Something simple, I think. Maybe just an ivy design etched around the edges. Then inside the border it should say something like "Whew. That was *complicated*." Or maybe "Why does life have to be so *complicated*?" The main thing is I want italics on the word *complicated,* so as to connote protest. Because I don't want complicated. *I never wanted complicated.* If, as I was being born, I got to stand in the cafeteria line choosing the menu of characteristics that would define my life, I would not have chosen even one spoonful of complicated. I would have chosen . . . *happy.* I would have chosen *amusing.* I would have chosen *honest* and *clean* and *dignified.* Then for dessert I would have chosen a dollop or so of *adventure.* And I would have walked out and felt glad.

Instead—*complicated.*

So why did I marry a shrink? There's a reasonable question. A shrink-spouse would, you might imagine, just complicate things. A shrink-spouse would be the worst kind to have if, say, you were forced to wrestle through an "issue" such as: He's turning fifty-five and he doesn't want kids, and you're turning forty and you desperately want kids, and now what in tarnation are the two of you going to do?

You would think, oh, I have a headache just imagining how those conversations went. You would think the two of us might have spent night after sleepless night *processing* this complicated matter, and *re*-processing it, and taking *responsibility* for our feelings, and *owning* our emotions, and *locating* our true selves, and *honoring* each other's fears, and doing all that sort of complicated talking that leaves the average person needing to run and hide and curl up and watch reruns of *Gomer Pyle.*

But, no. This is not what happened, and this is not the complication I am talking about. What happened was, we took more walks. Walks to the old lady's house, just to say hello, to bring her some of our corn and some of our peppers and some of our friendship. Walks to George's to say "How about this drought, huh?" (He was right.) Walks to the mailbox with Betty and Marley and Wilma. Walks on the ridge with Skippy and Maggie in tow, or Cricket and Sassy. It seems as though we've walked away much of this summer.

I did not, by the way, wear my hiking boots on our walks. Oh, no. I got a pair of flimsy fluorescent-green sandals at Wal-Mart. They have a big pink flower motif on the soles. I am still wearing these sandals everywhere. Alex hasn't quite gone to this extreme, but I have noticed him caring a lot less about his feet.

Walking in flimsy sandals, visiting neighbors, telling stories. This is the way of the country. This is the way we did it.

We told stories to each other. We told stories of every person we could think of who'd decided to raise a child later in life. We couldn't think of one person who regretted the decision. And that went for plenty of second-time-around dads, some of them older than Alex.

We told enough of these stories that pretty soon we could see a more or less predictable plot. It really was the same story, over and over again:

A man and a woman talk about having a child. The child in question, when it is still just a question, is simply that: a question. An abstract notion. And there is no connecting with an abstract notion. An abstract notion is one hundred percent imagination. You can turn it into anything you want. If you are a person who wants a child, you probably turn the abstract notion into a cute little bundle of joy running up to you with nothing but kisses and hugs on her itty-bitty mind. If you are a person who does not want a child, you probably turn it into a howling goo-coated creature in a car seat that won't stop kicking you in the kidneys.

Each figment of each imagination is as valid as the other, in that both are born somewhere along the continuum of desire and fear. That is, neither of them is born in the world known as the real one. The here-and-now.

Enter actual child.

What happens when the actual child is born—that real-world creature with more or less ten fingers and ten toes—is, love takes over. Of course it does. This is not the complicated part. This is virtually instantaneous. Because this is just what love does. Love is like gravity. It really has no choice but to pull.

This is why people, no matter what their age, tend to end up wondering what in the world they were thinking when they suspected they might regret having this child. How, you wonder, could you even have thought that? When little Sammy or Mary or Tiffany or Jamal is here, in your arms, the abstract notion has vanished. In its place is Sammy or Mary or Tiffany or Jamal. Love has taken over.

It was the same story, over and over again. It wasn't so hard to figure that we were living it, too.

And yet if we were living it, then our answer was already made. This lent an inevitability that sat uncomfortably on both of our shoulders, and so for a while we fought it.

I thought about love. If having a kid was about the transforming power of love, well then, let's look at love. Any relationship will teach you that love often means sacrifice. Love almost always means sacrifice. When a man loves a woman, he wants to make her happy. When a woman loves a man, she wants to make him happy. You sacrifice in order to make life better for the other. Sometimes you feel you'll do just about anything. This is why, for instance, a loving husband might be inclined to drop a big wad of cash on a wife's birthday present (read: sapphires?). But I digress.

As Alex and I took our walks and told our stories, I kept asking myself, in private, this question: What sacrifice is too great? I mean, if bringing a child into our lives has even the potential of making Alex's life miserable, I shouldn't do it, right? If he thinks he's too old, if he really, and quite reasonably, would rather not spend his retirement years dealing with the inevitable storm of adolescent angst headed our way were we to have a child now, then I shouldn't do it, right? That's a sacrifice I should make.

And yet.

That sacrifice?

Really?

That's what I kept asking myself. What sacrifice is too great?

But then one day while we were walking, Alex was the one, he was the one who brought up the word.

"It's not like it would be some huge sacrifice," he said.

"No?"

"It's not like I have some big retirement plan I'd have to cancel," he said. "All I've ever done is work. What else am I going to do? Buy an RV and drive around the country? Take up golf? Canasta?"

"I hadn't thought of it that way," I said.

We were on the ridge overlooking George's sheep. Kind of a sacred spot, really. This was where we walked on our very first trip to this farm, the day we discovered it, the day we discovered the view that made us both fall head over heels in love with this place. We promised, back then, to put a gazebo up here. The gazebo is still, at this time, an abstract notion.

"So it's not like I'd be sacrificing anything, really," Alex said.

"Well, you'd be sacrificing freedom," I told him. "Any parent sacrifices freedom."

"Yeah."

"And in your case, you'd be sacrificing the freedom that retirement represents. You'd be giving that up, and in its place you'd have . . . algebra homework."

"Yeah."

"And working on science projects, you know, a volcano you spend all night helping your kid create and then at three in the morning you flick the switch and the damn thing doesn't spit the lava."

He thought for a moment on that. He said: "Well, if I imagine my so-called retirement years—if the choice is between troubleshooting a volcano and sitting in a chair with nothing more to do than watch *Magnum, P.I.* reruns, I've got to go with the volcano."

"Yeah."

"I'm telling you, I could get into this."

"You don't think maybe you're trying to talk yourself into something?"

"I think it might be fun to raise a kid with someone who actually *likes* me," he said. His relationship with his children's mother had never been easy.

"Well, I do like you," I said.

He smiled.

"So that's what it comes down to?" I said. "Boy, this was a lot easier than I thought."

He just . . . smiled.

"Look," he said. "We have to make sure you get to be a mom. That's just—that's what we have to do."

"Well, I think—"

"Think about it. What if you live out the rest of your life regretting that you never got to be a mom—"

"It's not an easy thought."

"No. And for me it's an impossible thought."

"Impossible?"

"Well, let's try to imagine it. Here I am watching you live out the rest of your life regretting that you never got to be a mom—and it's because of *me*? I couldn't live with myself. You know what, I couldn't."

"It wouldn't be *because* of you—"

"It would be like you were a dancer, but because of me you never got a chance to dance. You know? What the hell is that?"

"It wouldn't be because of you—"

"Or you were a singer, and I'm holding my hand over your mouth—"

"Wow."

"And I can't be that. I won't be that. I'm *not* that."

"No, you're not."

"So it's an impossible thought," he said. "You know, Sherlock Holmes had it right. He said if you eliminate the impossible, what you're left with, however improbable, is the truth."

"The truth," I said.

"The truth," he said.

"How about that Sherlock?"

"Underestimated."

"Well, doesn't this put you in a sort of dilemma?" I asked. "You don't want a kid, but it's impossible for you not to have one. Doesn't that make you trapped?"

"I don't feel trapped. I feel like this must be what's next."

"Okay, then."

"Okay, then."

And that really was that. We stood at the gazebo spot and looked out over these now-familiar hills, hills that always remind me of the jolly beer-bellies of men, we stood there, and we let go of the impossible. It was miraculously simple, but a miracle all the same.

Then, on the walk home, Alex put his arm around me. "One thing," he said. "If you get to have a kid, shouldn't I get to have a pool table?"

"A pool table," I said, pausing to consider. "All right. In

fact, for the rest of our lives you get everything you could possibly want."

"Good," he said.

"Good," I said.

"I want to be in the NBA," he said.

"I'll see what I can do."

"Not a benchwarmer," he said. "I want to *start*."

I imagined him in a pair of snazzy, shiny shorts, with tattoos all over his arms, dribbling his bad self up to the kneecaps of Shaquille O'Neal. "You need to think about that one, okay? I just want you to think about it."

SO THIS BRINGS us back to the present. This brings us here, to the first of September, three weeks before my fortieth birthday, the sumacs, and the design decisions concerning my headstone.

Forty?

Oh, come on. This is getting ridiculous.

Forty.

Forty is a number that says, "No more denying it, sister." Forty is a number that says, "You are *so* not a baby anymore." Then again, maybe this makes forty a very good age to have a baby. I don't know; things have gotten complicated.

"It's not that I'm angry at God," I'm saying to Alex. We're in the car. We are country people now, and so we are doing what country people do on a Friday night in September. We are heading to our county fair. We have, neither of us, ever been to a county fair. We are not entirely sure what happens at one.

"I mean, it's not like I'm walking around crying 'Why *me*?' " I say.

"Right."

"I mean, why *not* me?" I say, borrowing, as I do, from my mom. "Why should I be spared from suffering?"

"Right."

"So it really is not that I'm angry at God."

"Well, it's not like you're one to yell at God even if you were angry," Alex says. "You're more the type to give the silent treatment."

"I guess—but I don't mean it as a treatment."

"No."

"When things get complicated, I just like some time to . . . think."

"Things have gotten complicated," Alex says.

"Yeah."

The complications came almost immediately after we found ourselves agreeing yes to the kid and to the pool table and to the NBA contract. Yes! Yes! Yes! The world was full of possibilities. We were somewhat giddy, joining together in a life of renewed commitment. A life in which each looked out for the other's needs. It wasn't so much a turning point in our relationship as an affirmation. Like a lot of couples, we've talked the talk: "I want you to be happy." And: "I'm happy if you're happy." All of that essential happily-ever-after talk. But now it was time to walk the walk, one foot in front of the other.

The complications came, as complications do, with reality. Making a baby. Was I even capable? That was the first question. There was, of course, the "old eggs" issue that so many of my friends in their forties had found to be a fairly serious obstacle. There was my sister Kristin, who met with exactly that obstacle, but eventually overcame it with the miracle now known as Katie. But there was also my sister Claire, who had no such problem and with relative ease produced Peter and Matthew and Elizabeth. And both my sisters were older when they became parents. So maybe I had Claire's genes instead of Kristin's. I doubted it. I seriously doubted it. Because there was also a memory, a lingering memory of a short gynecologist with a long braid down her back telling me, when I was about sixteen, that I would one day likely have "a lot of trouble" getting pregnant. I do not remember the reason, if I ever even knew it. To a teenage girl in Catholic school who wondered if sex before marriage really did equal a free pass to hell—but who knew that getting pregnant before marriage definitely equaled a free pass to hell right here on earth—this "trouble" seemed rather convenient, or something that might, at least, come in handy someday.

I never wanted to become pregnant in my twenties or thirties, and so I never had occasion to follow up on the long-braid lady's prediction. My checkups were always uneventful.

There was another possible complication. There was the story of one of my "old egg" friends who had spent six years undergoing infertility treatments, not to mention about a hundred thousand dollars on in-vitro fertilization attempts, only to discover that the problem, all along, had been in her husband's body, not hers. The doctors, all male, had simply never bothered to check.

Alex had reason to worry about a similar outcome for us, and so in the end we decided to save ourselves a lot of guesswork and get us both checked out. So we did. A week ago all the test results were in.

The results, in layman's terms: Fat chance.

Actually, the one doctor said, "You really have only three choices: divine intervention, scientific intervention, or a combination of both."

And see, I am not at all opposed to divine intervention. I am just not quite sure how to call it up. In the last week I have spent a good bit of time talking to God. And really, the only thing I'm hearing is: "You're going to have to help me out here." And: "I don't see how I can do this without some human intervention." We're talking hormone shots, test tubes, petri dishes, the whole deal.

But I am not entirely sure this is God's voice I'm hearing. I am not even close to sure. And neither is Alex. We are not the fertility clinic *type*. We are, or we like to believe ourselves to be, of the wind. If this is so—if we are not the sort of people who believe in trying to yank and pull and push life to *behave* a certain way—then we are certainly not the sort of people who believe in trying to force life to *happen*.

People are, I know, all over the map on this one. There are people who think nothing of shopping for human eggs on the Internet, people willing to spend tens of thousands of dollars for eggs harvested from women with degrees from prestigious colleges, or women with long legs, or women with especially good hair. There are people who think nothing more of this than simply "Cool!" And then there are people who think nothing less of this than simply "Sin."

"It's just not that simple," I say to Alex.

"No, it's not," he says.

"Does it strike you as arrogant?" I say.

"Arrogant?" he says.

"Something like that."

I'm not even sure what I mean. I lean back in my seat, rest my feet on the dashboard, admire my fluorescent-green sandals while feeling the reassuring vibration of the smooth Ford Explorer engine.

I don't know. The idea of in-vitro fertilization. The idea that we humans think so much of our special selves that we can go about procreating when nature is standing there saying "Whoa." Are we even listening? How can you be listening when you're so busy saying "Whatever" and "Out of my way" and "I want what I want, and you're not gonna stop me." It seems to me we should at least listen first.

The procedure the doctors suggested for Alex and me is to take one of my aging eggs, and one of Alex's possibly reluctant sperms, and to physically inject that sperm into that egg, and to then see what might happen in the petri dish. If the two happen to agree to stick together and make an embryo, the doctors would then put that embryo in me and see if it might grow. Kind of like when you order sea monkeys in the mail.

"Arrogant . . . ," Alex repeats, still trying this on. He turns right at the BP station. There's a giant chicken on the roof of the restaurant next door.

"You know," I say, "forcing that little sperm to go somewhere it doesn't necessarily want to go."

"Honey, men don't like anything about them called 'little,' least of all things having to do with this particular function."

"Sorry. How about 'that cute rascal sperm'?"

"*Cute?* How about 'big manly hunkatomic-power sperm.' "

"Right. And as I was saying. The arrogance. The arrogance of forcing that big manly hunkatomic-power sperm to go somewhere it doesn't necessarily want to go. And forcing that beautiful little angel princess egg to accept something it may have no interest in accepting."

"Kind of like genetic breaking and entering," he says.

"Something like that." Outside my window I see two pizza parlors rolling by and a church in between with a sign that says "Jesus needs no extra toppings."

"Or sort of like sea monkeys," I say.

"Huh?"

"Did you ever grow sea monkeys when you were a kid?"

"Um. No, I never did that."

"Me neither. What the heck were they?"

"I have no idea. Something in the shrimp family?"

I tell him the forced embryo idea reminds me of sea monkeys. "Just one of those things other kids did."

"Yeah."

"Oh, I don't know."

"Me neither."

"Oh, what-*ever*."

"I hear you."

"Grrr."

"Ugh."

"I hear you."

We have easier things to talk about. For example: adoption. No matter which way we decide to go with the sea monkey idea, we're both set on adoption. That decision took all of about three seconds.

"How about adoption?"

"Well, that's a good idea."

"Okay, then."

Something like that. Barely even a conversation, really. I got an instant picture of some nurse handing me a baby, and there I was standing there saying, "Well hi, Baby! It's about time we found each other."

Something like that. I know, for some people it's a lot more complicated. I have friends who really *needed* to be pregnant, who needed to feel a baby growing inside of them. I know of plenty of people who need to grow a baby that looks like them, sounds like them, has their grandmother's hair. I know of people whose paths toward adoption are circuitous and painful. I know of people who arrive at adoption only after years of infertility treatments, followed by periods of grieving, and then adoption comes as some sort of consolation prize. Most of these people—this is the way this story so often seems to go—end up wondering, after adopting, why in the world they waited so long. More than that, they wonder how this child could ever have been thought of as a consolation prize. The child, it seems, went from abstract notion to actual child, and so of course love took over.

This whole thing is about love.

I hear of people making the "leap" to adoption, as if having needed some sort of fuel to propel them there. I am aware of no such leap for me. If indeed I once leaped, it must have happened a long time ago. In an airport, perhaps. Gate 10 at Philadelphia International Airport. A baby. The first baby I ever touched. My niece Alyson. It was love that buckled my knees. It was an utterly unexpected and supersize punch of love that sent me flying into that tile wall. That this baby—the source and the carrier and the patron and the object of that love—was coming into our family via adoption . . . well, that really was quite beside the point. The love was so . . . loud. Adoption? Adoption was about as significant as the style of car seat the baby happened to be in. A baby! A *person!* A new actual member of our family! Adoption? Adoption was, apparently, one of the vehicles babies took in order to get to you. I suppose I grew into adulthood with that notion hardwired into me somewhere.

And now, as I think of my life with Alex, as I think of a family we might create, the child I can imagine most clearly is the one we would adopt. There might be one that we create out of our own bodies. But the adopted one, that one is obvious.

I'm a mom who needs a baby. And somewhere out there, there's a baby who needs a mom.

It's so . . . simple.

And I trust simple. The truth, I have always found, is in

the simple answers. The truth is never complicated. Lying—
and denying—is what takes up all your time.

This gives me an idea. An idea for my gravestone design.
Maybe inside the ivy border I'll have it say "Why does life
have to be so *complicated*?" up top, but then underneath I'll
answer it: "It doesn't."

Hmm.

The other thing I could do is have my gravestone ask the
question, and then have Alex's next to mine answering it.

Hmm. He always gets the good lines.

"Have you given any thought to your gravestone?" I ask
him.

"Excuse me?"

"Like what design you want, or what you want it to say?"

He looks at me. "You're giving me whiplash," he says. "I
thought we were talking about sea monkeys, although I wasn't
quite clear on why we were talking about them either."

"Sorry—but what do you think? You don't want some
kind of, like, big monument or something, do you?"

"Um. Well, actually, I always thought I'd get cremated
and be sprinkled somewhere."

"Oh, that won't work. That won't work at all."

He looks at me. He looks at me like maybe I'm traveling
too close to the tippy-tippy edge of loo-loo land.

"Sorry," I say. "I didn't mean to get into that. I was just
thinking about adoption."

"And that led you to me being dead and needing a gravestone?"

"Well, not in a bad way. In a good way, actually." I'm
pushing in the pink flowers on my sandals. They're so spongy.

"Uh-huh," he says.

"We should definitely go to that meeting about adopting
from China," I say.

"I thought we already decided we would." He's the one who spotted the ad for the meeting in the newspaper. He's the one who suggested we go. Maybe I'm just now deciding he was right. We've also decided to look into domestic adoption, as well as adopting from Russia and Guatemala. But something about the idea of China . . . I don't know. I have no explanation. The idea of China has become a kind of pleasant bell ringing in my ear. Come to think of it, I haven't heard the ticking of my kitchen clock for some time. Not since this adoption talk started.

Well, we're here, anyway. This is it. This is our county fair! Beyond the trees you can see the Ferris wheel spinning and the arms and legs of other rides reaching like spiders into the clouds.

We pull into a parking lot, which is really a cornfield with all the stalks mostly cut down.

"Hey, look at that," Alex says, pointing to a sign. "It appears we're on time for the School Bus Demolition Derby."

"Oh . . . goody. . . ."

So we go. We pay our five dollars to get into the fair, we get the back of our hands stamped with red cows to show our legitimacy as county-fair-goers. Soon we are sitting in the grandstand, the aluminum kind with pleated benches and crimped walkways, hot when you touch them and first sit down. We're eating popcorn and nachos, looking down at nine school buses parked in a circle, revving their engines, ready to, um, bash.

This can certainly take your mind off things.

There are teenagers in front of us, teenagers with cigarettes and tattoos, and kids with painted faces to our right, and here and there are women with tired eyes leaning back on their men. There is, we have learned, a goat show we can go to later. And a swine-breeding lecture. A lamb carcass class and a milk-chugging contest. There are snow cones and funnel cakes, and there is Helga, a headless woman ("Still ALIVE!").

There are triangular flags hanging everywhere, blue and red and yellow flags snapping in the muggy breeze, announcing that this is the two hundredth anniversary of the Washington County Fair. An old woman behind me is telling her grandson that she hasn't seen it this crowded since she was a girl, when the fair was the one event that everyone, young and old, worked toward all year long. Farmers would shine up their tractors to show off, kids would fatten their pigs, and moms would try yet again to win a prize for their pies. And it still goes on like this, two hundred years after it began. It still goes on.

"Tradition," I say to Alex. "That's what this fair is about." We decide that we love our county fair and this is what we love about it. This isn't like Disneyland or some other prefab fun fest where no one really belongs. This is a place where everyone belongs.

Except, well . . . us.

We are still newcomers. That's the truth of it. No matter how much we're learning about sandals, and outerwear, and storytelling, the fact of the matter is we are newcomers. It can take years to convert a city-person into a country-person. It can take generations to fully convert a familial line.

We look down at the buses, each spray-painted with the howling urgencies of youth: AMY! DONNA! WHIZ KID. 2002 RULES! Five of the buses rumble onto the muddy field and form a circle, back ends to back ends. "Five, four, three, two, one!" the announcer shouts, and all five buses fly in reverse until BAM!

"Ahhh!" shouts the crowd. The buses zoom forward, slam backward again, zig and zag. BAM! "What a hit!" says the announcer. BAM! FOOM! "There went a front end, folks, there went a front end!" SMASH, *hisssssss*. "They're popping and crackling, folks. Smokin' and steamin', but at least they're moving, folks!" BAM! "There went a fender or something, folks. I'm not sure what it was. But by golly, we're still moving, folks!"

"Can-dee! Can-dee! Can-dee!" the crowd chants.

I turn around and look up at the crowd. Arms are flailing against the hazy autumn sky. People are on their feet—tattooed teenagers, painted-faced kids, and tired-eyed women alike. And every face, young and old, has a smile on it. I turn back around and look at Alex. His face is . . . different. He has a ruffled brow. He seems to be wearing the same thought I am thinking: Why? *What is the point?*

These are the questions of newcomers.

BAM! Okay, there went an electrical system. You can smell it. Two of the buses are declared dead. Another is lurching like a bug drowning in bug spray. The crowd is hollering: "Smash 'em! Can-dee! Let's go, Fort Cherry! Bust 'em up, Bentworth!"

"Bentworth?" I say to Alex. "Isn't that our school district?"

"I think it is," he says.

"That's our school!" I say. And instantly I see things I couldn't see before. This isn't just buses bashing into one another. This is school against school, team against team, us against them. Belonging is, after all, about joining. Belonging involves an act of will on the part of the potential belong-ee. And Bentworth, the blue bus with all the pink swirls on it and the lime-green tires, is still bashin' with the best of 'em.

"We're alive!" I say to Alex, grabbing his arm and shaking it like a pom-pom. "We-are-alive! GO BENTWORTH!"

A woman nearby seems pleased. She is also a Bentworth fan. She tells us that Bentworth has the only female driver in the competition. Her name is Candy.

"Can-dee! Can-dee! Can-*dee!*" shouts the crowd.

"Can-*dee!*" Alex shouts, pumping his fist in the air.

Our bus is clearly the best. Oh, we are swellin' with pride, we are. But now we can't really see the buses, on account of all the steam and smoke. Engines are coughing. The bashing is just noise, steam, sputtering. "I think only one bus is alive, folks," says the announcer. "Can anyone see? Uh-oh. . . . What? Okay, folks, we have a winner. The one bus that will go to the finals! It's . . . it's, what is it? It's Trinity!"

"Trinity!" I say to Alex. "But they *suck!*" He shakes his head, sits, looks down.

We don't stay for the finals. Too depressing. Besides, our lips are wrinkled from all the salt on all the nachos and popcorn. We get Cokes and head over to Helga, the headless woman. The sticky-sweet air is cooling off a bit. The fairground lights have blinked on, and an army of eager bugs cavorts in their glow. We each pay a dollar, walk into the darkness with a group of others. We gaze at a seated person who has a black shroud where the head should be. A plastic breathing tube is attached to the neck. "NO SMOKING," reads a sign. "OXYGEN IN USE."

"Helga sure has huge hands," says a fellow onlooker.

"Yeah, and I've never seen ankles that big on a woman," says another.

Soon we are joined in consensus. "We got rooked!" All of us. Together. Bonded in the darkness of disillusionment.

The headless woman is a *man.*

LATER, AFTER WE leave the lights of the county fair behind us, we drive home and get bombarded by the moon. An enormous full moon. A moon that demands that you stop and take notice. It's hanging over our pond like a giant lost polka dot.

We're standing in the driveway with our heads bent back, admiring this amazing fact of country life: You could do needlepoint under the light of a moon like this.

"China," Alex says. "Can you believe the people in China see the same moon that we see?"

China, I think. China is a place you dug to as a kid. I have little other association with China.

"I mean, isn't it strange?" he says. "The exact same moon."

"I can't say that I thoroughly believe it," I say.

"That's what I mean."

CHAPTER EIGHT

I have a baby. A baby! My baby, as it turns out, is not a peanut M&M. She's a lot bigger than a peanut M&M, although roughly the same shape. You can't tell if she has arms or legs. She's just an oblong there, on a bench, with two eyes moving back and forth. She's wrapped in a blanket, swaddled up tight. She's on this bench, in a park, watching children play on the monkey bars. The children run around her, singing songs and enjoying the afternoon sun. That's the thing. The children don't notice her. The children are too busy being children. My baby's waiting for someone to notice her.

I wake up wondering where I am. She's my baby. So where am I? I wake up wondering how you can have a dream you're not in. A dream, in fact, about your own absence.

But I keep having the dream. The setting changes. Sometimes the baby is on a beach. Sometimes she's in a toy store. She's always a she. She's always swaddled, and her eyes are always going back and forth, back and forth, like that cat clock you see sometimes. She's looking for me. And I'm not there.

I don't think you should be able to have a dream like this. This kind of dream should defy the laws of dream logic.

*   *   *

HERE, ANYWAY, IS the thing I probably should have mentioned about my birthday: It's the same as Alex's. September 22. Yep. That's us.

I know. I should have mentioned this. Yeah, yeah. This is cosmic. Well, sure it is. Well, in the beginning it was. One of those sweet astrological convergences you discover during those tender dating days. *"We have the same birthday?!"* That first year we took a trip to the mountains together, said "Our birthday!" and had a toast to the gods of coincidence. Then I gave Alex his present: a violin. Quite a present, if I do say so myself. He got me something equally wonderful, but the sad thing is I can't remember what.

The second year I spent weeks in used-camera shops looking for the exact model of the exact vintage Nikon that I knew he dreamed about. I found it forty miles from my home. I found the case that went with it, forty miles in the other direction. He got me something equally amazing, but the sad thing is I can't remember what.

See what I'm getting at? Isn't this *sad*? Tomorrow! Tomorrow is it. Tomorrow is my birthday. And look at me: I am standing here in this bedroom, wrapping his present, feeling positively flush with joy in anticipation of the moment when I give him this present. Tomorrow is my birthday, and I am totally out of the spirit of receiving. I am all about *giving*.

This is so wrong.

A birthday should be me, me, me. Not him, him, him. My birthday should be my own personal Day of Receiving. The Day of Me. On your birthday you have permission to be the person you have spent your every posttoddler day suppressing. "Hey, everybody! Look at me! I am the center of the universe! Now give me stuff."

Instead—and here is the really sad part—I don't care what he gets me. I am too excited about what I got him.

I got him a pair of cowboy boots. His first ever. Is there a better present for a man? Other than a violin and a vintage Nikon and, okay, a pool table, which will be coming some-day. These boots are authentic Justin cowboy boots. I mean, these are *cowboy* boots. Dark brown. Lots of tooling. Leather soles. Big chunky heel. Oh, he'll be able to wear these babies over to George's barn and scratch and spit with pride. I'm standing here in the bedroom wrapping them in paper with little red cowboys all over it, and I can smell that new-leather smell right through the box.

The phone rings.

"Hello?" I say, speaking through a piece of Scotch tape.

"Oh, hi, hon, it's Caroline." Our postmaster. Postmistress? "I have something up here for you," she says. "A big flat thing Debbie doesn't think she can fit in your mailbox." Debbie is our mail lady. Caroline and Debbie account for fifty percent of our postal employees. The other half are Vivian and Kathy.

A present? A big flat birthday present? I tell Caroline I'll be right up. I finish wrapping, hide the box under the bed. Alex is in the kitchen filling salt shakers. Now, how can he be filling salt shakers? It's birthday eve, for heaven's sake. Shouldn't he be . . . wrapping?

"A present!" I say. "Caroline just called to say there's a big flat birthday present waiting up at the post office."

"Yours or mine?" he says.

"Oh, it must be mine," I say, even though I have nothing but blind hope to support the prediction. I am, however, some-what delighted to find the spirit of receiving starting to fill me.

I grab my keys, ask Betty if she wants to ride in the car with me. She could use an outing. She could definitely use some head-out-the-window ear-flapping time.

The Scenery Hill Post Office occupies a small room separated by a partition from Scenery Hill Hardware. The sign out front proudly announces our ZIP Code: 15360. This sign was hand-carved by Jim, a taxidermist who lives four doors down. Caroline started at the post office over twenty years ago as a cleaning lady, worked her way up. She is more than just a postmaster. She's the person in Scenery Hill you go to if you need to understand anything. Caroline can tell you when Kenny the grocer is coming back from his fishing trip, or who has a car to sell, or who last saw your dog running down Needmore Road. We got our plumber through Caroline, and also a snowplow.

"How are you, dear?" Caroline says, the moment I walk in the door. "Oh, hi, Betty," she says, looking down. "Nice to see you."

"She needed an outing," I say.

"She's filling out," Caroline says.

"It's nice of you not to use the F-word," I say.

"Fat?" she says.

"Well, it *was* nice of you," I say.

"Oh, Betty, you are *not* fat!" Caroline says.

"Say thank you, Betty," I say, half-expecting to hear it. I tell Caroline that neither Betty nor I think she's fat, either. "It's just that she used to be so skinny, and now that she isn't skinny, well, some of my friends from the city say she looks fat."

"City people," Caroline says, shrugging. She's a slight woman, about fifty, with short red hair and a nervousness about her. "Look, I have something to tell you," she says, turning serious. "And look, I'm sorry."

Uh-oh. Something about my package? She broke my birthday present?

"We're moving," Caroline says, after a big inhale. She

looks down, runs her finger along a groove in the counter. "It's all my dumb fault."

Moving? I'm not sure if she's talking about the post office or perhaps her family. "I'm . . . sorry," I say.

"You know, I have been asking for a new post office," she says. "For *years*."

No, I didn't know that. Caroline tells me she's long complained about the work conditions to her bosses at the central office. And who could blame her? How was a person supposed to work like this? The space heaters barely keep up in winter. There's never enough light. And the sorting space problem is just getting worse: The daily stack of incoming 15360 mail has grown in the past few years from ten feet to more than forty.

"Like I told my husband," Caroline says. "I said, 'I asked for a new post office, but I meant one right here in town.' "

"They're moving the post office out of town?"

"Up by the Frosty Kiss," she says. "That new building?"

"Ew."

"Yeah. Like I told them, I said, *'What are you doing?'* I said, 'A post office should be *in town*.' "

The Frosty Kiss is about a mile away. Not really that far, actually. But technically well on the outskirts of downtown Scenery Hill, such as it is.

"I told them a post office should be a *gathering* place, like a hardware store," she says.

"Right," I say.

Our existing post office is definitely a Scenery Hill hot spot, especially in the mornings, when folks meander in and catch up on gossip with Debbie and Kathy as they sort.

"I told them a post office should be a *strolling-up-to* place," she says. "Or else *what is the point*?"

"Exactly," I say.

"But why would they listen to me?"

"They should listen to you," I say. After all these years hasn't she earned the right to express her post office philosophy? "But, look," I say. "Caroline, most people have cars. The post office can still be a gathering place."

"It's not the same," she says. "I saw the plans. Everything is regulation this and regulation that."

"Oh."

"There's a *wall*," she says. "A huge *wall*."

"A wall?"

"Between the public and Debbie and Kathy's mail-sorting area. That's it. No socializing. My sorters will hereby be *anonymous* mail-sorters." She shakes her head, disgusted. "Like I told my husband, I said, 'They're taking the personal out of the post office.' "

"It's not right," I say.

"It's certainly not," she agrees. "And what about Sammy? Oh jeez, if only they knew what went on around here. Then again, I'd probably get fired."

"Oh, Sammy—" I say.

Sammy is the mentally retarded man who lives a few doors down. He has depended on Caroline and the post office to give structure to his days since he was a boy. He comes in each morning, usually dressed in his bright orange hunter's jacket—in summer as well as winter—and Caroline gives him things to do. Post a sign on the bulletin board maybe, or make sure the pens on the counter are lined up right. Caroline takes care of Sammy. She takes his laundry home and washes it and irons it, even though her husband says this is well beyond the call of duty for a postmaster.

"Well, it's my dumb fault," she says again. "I don't have

anyone else to blame. I should have shut my mouth and been happy with what I have."

She reaches on a shelf for my mail. "Here you go, dear."

"This?" I say. "This is my package?"

"Did I lead you to believe it was something exciting?"

"No—" I look down. The big flat envelope says: "Happy Birthday from your friends at Dish Network."

Oh.

Apparently, I have just been inducted into ClubDISH, the Preferred Members Club.

I have two words to say to that. Yip. Ee.

Did they have to make this envelope so big? Did they have to make it a trip-to-the-post-office envelope?

For my birthday I see here that Dish Network, the provider who brings TV from outer space into my house via the twelve-inch platter perched on our roof, is giving me a certificate for an entire free Dish Network system, including installation, that I might give to a friend. So let me get this straight. I get to *give* somebody something for my birthday. Hmm. I wonder if these marketing people know they've hit a raw nerve here.

"I'll see you later, Caroline," I say.

"Hey, in case I don't see you tomorrow: Happy birthday! And tell Alex, too!"

Well, that's weird. I don't remember ever telling anyone around here about our birthday collision. Sometimes I wonder if Debbie reads my mail.

"Thanks," I say. "Do you know when moving day is?"

"They haven't told us. Last I heard, they were getting bids on the new sign."

"Bids?"

"It has to be *regulation*," she says.

"Regulation!" I say.

She gives me an army salute.

"Ten-four!" I say, because I can't think of any army talk.

"Bye-bye, Betty," she says. "And I think you look great. Nothing wrong with being a fuller-figure gal. . . ."

When I get home, I give Alex the mail. "Happy birthday from your friends at Dish Network," I tell him.

He's hunched over a ham sandwich. He flips through the mail and takes a surprising interest in ClubDISH, the Preferred Members Club.

"George," he says. "Why don't we give this to George?"

"Oh, I don't know about that." George and Pat don't strike me at all as the TV type. Or I don't want them to be the TV type. There are some people you want to keep nice and settled in your romanticized image of peach pie making and sheep shearing and beef slaughtering.

"Guess what, the post office is moving," I tell him. "Up by the Frosty Kiss."

"That new building?"

"Yep. Caroline just told me. She's upset."

"Modernization is not something Scenery Hill is ready for."

"No."

"Me neither."

"No. But we still have the hardware store to go to."

"If the new Home Depot in Washington doesn't put it out of business."

"Yeah."

"Listen—I don't think you should give George the Dish Network coupon," I say. "I don't want to be responsible. You know? I'll be the person who infected the area with TV."

"You don't think that's maybe a little . . . grandiose?"

"Hey, it's my birthday," I say.

"Yeah. Well, almost."

"You have to admit it's kind of a rotten birthday present from our friends at Dish Network."

"The gift of giving," he says. He's finishing his sandwich, eyeing some Oreos.

"Whatever."

"Speaking of which, are you ready for your present?"

I look at him. Has he lost his mind?

"I thought we could start early this year."

"Have you lost your mind?"

Presents on birthday eve? No. We have a ritual. We "surprise" each other by having our presents waiting at the bottom of the bed so that presents are the first thing we each see on the morning of September 22. It's a little bit tricky to pull this off. "Okay, well, good night, I'm just gonna stay up and read a little bit," one of us will say. And the other will pretend to be asleep, waiting for the first to finish reading and go to sleep, so he or she can sneak the presents out and onto the bed. Each year we seem to hope that the other has forgotten all about this, or in any case we want to be the clever one who remembers. And so inevitably we end up bumping into each other in the hallway in the middle of the night, presents in hand.

Alex is sitting here dipping his Oreos in milk. "Why don't you just go put my present on the bottom of the bed now," he says. "And I'll pretend I don't know."

"You really want your present now?"

"Why not?"

"It's September *twenty-first?*"

"It's September twenty-second in China," he says.

True. And ever since we got this China idea in our heads, there seem to be a lot of new dimensions to consider.

"And we're going to be out most of tomorrow, so I thought—"

"All right," I say. "It's *your* present. You can have it now if you want. But don't blame me if you walk around tomorrow feeling naked and horrible."

"Naked and horrible?"

"You know what I mean." I head into the bedroom, pull the box out from under the bed, perch it atop the down comforter.

"Okay, ready!" I call to him.

He prances into the room.

"Happy birthday!" I yell, flinging my arms like a magician toward the box.

"Back at ya, birthday girl," he says, because this is what he always says.

He touches the box, nods as if to show preliminary approval. "Love the paper," he says. He unwraps. He sees the "Justin Boots" logo on the box. His eyes get as big as Utah. He opens the box. He sees the boots through the tissue paper. His eyes grow to the size of Montana. He looks at me, the boots, me. He seems afraid to actually touch those boots.

"Oh, I'm not worthy . . . ," he says. He peels the tissue paper back carefully, like it's an ancient map he'll need to read later. He looks at the boots, me, the boots. "I have just two words to say," he says finally. "Yee," he says. "And HAAAAAA!"

A few good marveling minutes later, he turns to me. "Doesn't that pillow of yours look lopsided? Huh? What? Could there be something *under* that pillow?"

I reach under. I pull out a silk pouch, green with yellow fringe. I shake the pouch, and a pair of sapphire earrings falls out like stars.

"Happy birthday," he says.

"Back at ya, birthday boy," I say, because this is what I always say.

OKAY NOW. AND please forgive me. But here's the thing about the meeting about adopting from China. The thing I probably should have mentioned. The meeting is scheduled for September 22. Yep. The birthday.

Yeah, yeah, yeah, yeah. There is a reason I didn't mention this. There is a reason I have not made too much of this in my head. Because when one is thinking about certain things like babies, there is a tendency to make too much of certain other things. There is a tendency to look for *signs*. Signs in every cloud in the sky and the position of every rubber band on your desk and the pattern of every other date on your calendar—most especially the birthday you happen to share with your soul mate and husband.

And I don't believe in signs. Or I don't believe in making decisions based on signs. I think whenever you find yourself making a decision based on signs, well, that decision was really already made. The signs are really just signs of how clever you are at inventing the validation you need.

And this decision is anything but made. We're looking into the China adoption program, but we're looking at a lot of other ways of building a family, too.

Where am I, and why am I not there to grab hold of that baby? This seems to be my driving question. If I'm a mom who needs a baby, and if there's a baby out there who needs a mom—a lost little girl on a bench with desperate eyes—well then, it's my responsibility to look, to do whatever I have to do to find her.

And yet I'm the one missing from that dream. So who really is finding whom?

Alex and I have talked about becoming foster parents. Maybe that's where the girl is, maybe she's bouncing through the U.S. foster care system. It certainly makes sense to go looking there. In the foster care system you have a whole population of kids who need moms and dads. So why not enter the system, take in a foster child—most of them are older children—with the hope of one day adopting? We've gone to a few meetings. We've learned that before we would even be considered as adoptive parents of a foster child, we'd have to take classes. We'd have to become versed in RAD, re-active attachment disorder, and PTSD, post-traumatic stress disorder, and FAS, fetal alcohol syndrome, and countless other conditions that some of these children suffer. We are game to do this. As a psychologist, Alex thinks he might bring special skills to a troubled child. As a new parent, I think: um. I think: I was hoping to maybe learn how to do the diaper thing first. Is this really the way for a new mom to jump out of the gate? I don't feel qualified to meet the com-plicated demands of a child who has suffered through so much so young. On the other hand, who does? These are the kids with perhaps the shortest supply of potential parents. That alone makes me want to jump in.

And maybe I will someday. I would like to, in theory. And in theory I would like to get some actual mom experi-ence under my belt.

In theory.

Theory is really all you have to go on, and theory is really just a puzzle your head does to stay occupied while your heart does all the work.

These are impossible decisions.

Who knows what the pull is? This is a maze. Adoption versus sea monkeys versus foster care versus international adoption versus domestic adoption versus foster care versus sea monkeys versus China versus Guatemala versus Russia versus domestic versus international versus sea monkeys. It's a bewildering maze to walk through. You make a right, hit a wall, or maybe just get scared because that alley is too dark. So you turn around, find another fork in the road, and make a left. That path keeps you moving, moving, and moving, until you hear a song playing somewhere, or you smell a smell that pulls you left, then right, then left again. It's the way you do the maze. There are probably a million ways to do it. You can't say that the way another person did it was wrong or right. The most you can say is that your way is . . . yours.

There are practical considerations. There is: twenty thousand dollars. That's the approximate cost of adopting a baby, whether it be a domestic adoption or an international one. Twenty thousand dollars. Interestingly, twenty thousand dollars is also about what it costs for one IVF cycle at the fertility clinic. One sea monkey chance. This, at least when I first did the math, was convenient. Because there was no way. At least not right now. There was no way Alex and I could come up with much more than twenty thousand dollars. We certainly couldn't come up with double that. So we couldn't do both. We couldn't do adoption and IVF.

This really was convenient. This was some real-world evidence to help support our decision to not bother with the fertility clinic. If I had twenty thousand dollars to spend on becoming a mom, I would do the sure thing, not the bet. Why would I gamble?

But then I did a stupid thing. Not that stupid, really. I called my health insurance company, just to find out what the deal was. In a few states, insurance companies are required to pay for infertility treatments, but in most states, like Pennsylvania, they are not. And most health insurance companies don't offer much, if any, coverage when it comes to infertility treatments. Did mine?

As it turns out: yes. The lady on the phone said my policy would cover one IVF cycle. The whole thing—free.

Was this a *sign*? Was God answering my prayers for guidance through . . . managed care? "Hey, here you go. Here's the one little boost I need to make this thing happen."

But of course, it wasn't a sign, because the decision was far from made. No, this was just one more fork in the road.

THE CHURCH HOSTING the meeting about adopting from China—the meeting that happens to be on my birthday and Alex's birthday, a coincidence that holds no, absolutely no significance—is inches off the highway, with hardly any clearance from the road. It's a big old orange-brick church with two matching steeples with copper tops. It must have been terrible when they announced the plans for this highway; I can just picture the old folks at some spaghetti dinner or bingo night railing at the city planners.

Alex is looking for a place to park. He's wearing his cowboy boots, which apparently are squishing his toes quite severely— a pain he says he is enduring in the name of all cowboys with squished toes throughout time.

I'm wearing my earrings, which are not squishing my ears, not even a little. I'm loving these earrings. I'm loving this birthday.

I'm eager about the meeting. I'm drawn almost instinctively to the idea of international adoption. I'm drawn to the romance, I suppose. To the sheer adventure of it all. I have friends, Vince and Chris, who adopted from Guatemala, and another friend, Lynn, whose baby came from Bolivia. I remember so clearly the day six years ago when Lynn stepped off the plane with baby Sam in her arms. I wouldn't have missed that moment for the world. Lynn, who is single, had traveled with her social worker. They looked utterly bedraggled by the journey. And yet Lynn had a lightness to her step. I mean, she bounced. And Lynn isn't the sort of person to . . . bounce. But now she wasn't just Lynn. She was: Lynn and Sam. It seemed she really did have a whole new center to her universe.

Carmela, Vince and Chris's daughter, came next. She was accepted into the fold as simply and as automatically as Sam. These were our friends, and these were their kids. You couldn't see anything else. Adoption, among our friends, was a nonissue. Race, among our friends, was a nonissue. Maybe I'm just lucky to have such a large group of friends who are this way. Friends who think souls are souls no matter what the packaging and no matter what the transport that brought them into a parent's world. Then again, maybe this is one of the reasons I've chosen the friends I've chosen. Like minds. Like hearts.

So certainly one of the reasons I'm drawn to international adoption is because these are the models I have. I have no one in our immediate circle of friends who has adopted domestically. I have, of course, my brother and sister-in-law who adopted Alyson. But that was a 1970s-style adoption. Things have changed a lot since then. And I'm not talking about the sensationalized headlines of domestic adoptions gone wrong—of birth-mothers who change their minds at the last minute, sometimes after the child has been in the home and hearts of his new parents for months. No, leaving all that madness aside, when I look at adoption in this country now, I have a difficult time finding a place for me.

"Open adoption" is the current trend. In an open adoption, a birth-mother has the ability and perhaps even the legal right to stay involved in the life of the child. The arrangements vary widely. For many families, it's little more than a matter of the adoptive mom and the birth-mom swapping holiday cards—if even that—and of the adoptive parents keeping in touch with the birth-mother should access ever be needed for the psychological or medical welfare of the child. There's certainly a lot to be said for this arrangement. It has got to be better than the very old days when adoption wasn't talked about, when kids weren't actually told that they were adopted, when the thing was to *pretend,* and the child's file was closed, end of story. The child would never, not even as an adult, have the right to discover the identity of his or her birth-parents.

But now it appears the pendulum has swung the other way. Now there are some families who have their child's birth-mother over for regular Sunday dinners. Now there are birth-mothers and birth-fathers and birth-grandparents and birth-aunts and birth-sisters coming to the child's birthday parties. Now there are birth-mothers who have arranged for formalized visitation rights, days when they can come take the kid to the movies or the mall.

Maybe that's a nice thing. I don't know. I do wonder how a child understands having all these parents in his or her life. Sometimes I think of open adoption the same way I think of the "open marriage" experiments back in the 1970s. Interesting concept, but did anyone make it work? Did anyone, in the end, *want* it to work? Boundaries are a rather necessary component to human well-being. Would you want to live in a house without any walls at all?

But the thing that keeps me from pursuing domestic adoption is more basic than all of this. It's the competition. It's the way it's done now. You don't just sign up with an adoption agency and wait your turn. You have to *put yourself out there,* as you would to try to land a job or a role in a play. You have to snag yourself a birth-mother, find a pregnant teenager who *likes* you well enough to allow you to raise her child. (In some states she can request that you pay her college tuition, rent on her apartment, and numerous other expenses.) I've read of couples making fancy brochures, advertising themselves to birth-mothers in the hopes of winning the so-called first prize of adoption: the increasingly rare white infant.

Competition? An ad campaign? A first prize? In the end, it's just not the call I'm trying to answer.

If a whole lot of moms are lined up outside the door, requesting interviews from one baby lucky enough to have so many willing moms, I say, "Let the moms in!" I say, "Good luck, moms!" Why would I get in there and muddy things up? I've got a baby to find. My baby. Where is she?

If I were to adopt a baby domestically, it would probably be an African-American infant. That would feel right. Those are the babies in this country with precious few moms lined up outside the door. One of those might indeed be the child I am searching for or the one searching for me. Alex and I have tried the idea out on some people. We live in a rural area. And in America *rural* is hardly a word you associate with diversity. And so we said, for instance, to Billy, we said, "What if we adopted a child of African-American descent? How would that child be received by this community?"

"I wouldn't do that to a kid," Billy said. "That child would have a hell of a time in school around here. Why would you *do* that to a kid?"

Talk about the ugly side of living in the country. Talk about the bleakest of truths. In this way, neither Alex nor I will ever become country people. There is racism out here. Plenty of it. You can pretend all you like that it's not here, you can go about your days refusing to believe that these beautiful hills contain pockets of ugliness, but in the end you have no choice but to face it.

We tried the idea about adopting an African-American infant on the old lady one day. She said, "A child is a child." She said, "What the hell difference does the color make?" That was comforting. That was such good news. Then one day when we were visiting the old lady, her son and daughter-in-law stopped over. I was surprised to find that her daughter-in-law is black. A soft woman with an easy smile and gentle brown skin. I wondered, for a moment, if this was one of the secrets. I wondered if this was one of the reasons people shunned the old lady. I hoped not. I prayed not.

I wondered about some of the small-minded ways of country people. I tried to be sympathetic. I tried to remember that ignorance is quite different from evil. I thought about the need to educate. I thought about taking a stance and taking on the responsibility for change. I thought, well, this is what I must do. I must adopt an African-American baby and show them. I must *teach* them. I must convert them all.

Then I thought: a child. This is a child we're talking about. A child is not an example, not a teaching tool, not a political symbol, not a catalyst, not a vehicle, not a mechanism. A child is a *child*.

I thought: If and when I finally make it through this maze and get to my baby, get to the girl on the bench with the eyes looking for me, and if she turns out to have a skin color declaring a heritage that my neighbors can't accept, well, I suppose we'll move.

"OKAY, YOU GO in first," I say to Alex, when we get to the door of the room where the meeting about adopting from China is being held.

He looks at me.

"I'm too shy," I say.

"Oh . . . my . . . God," he says, grabbing the bridge of his nose.

"Kindergarten?" I remind him. "Lunchbox? Underwear in lunchbox?"

Alex lets out a big, audible sigh. He turns to go in first, then stops. He brings his arm around me, yanks, so when we go in, it's more together than him first or me first. Oh, I'm sure we look like one lovey-dovey couple entering this meeting about becoming parents.

We have to wade through a lot of legs to get to two open middle seats. I hate middle seats. There are about seventy-five people here to learn about adopting from China. See, I hate sitting next to strangers. I lean in to Alex on the right, so as to maximize my personal space on the left.

There's a child up front. A little girl, maybe about two, Asian. She has pigtails. She has on light blue corduroy overalls. She's coloring. She has a juice box next to her.

I think: Is she available? Does she need a mom?

Hmm. Perhaps I'm a little too open to this idea?

As it turns out, she has a mom. Her mom goes up to her, helps her gather her crayons and papers, carries her to the back of the room. The talk is about to begin, and the little girl and her mother are apparently a later part of the program.

A man of about forty stands up, greets the crowd. He has a gentle face, a thin beard, slim shoulders; he could be a physics professor. He tells us that he and his wife started this adoption agency five years ago, after adopting their own child from China.

He tells us about China. He tells us about the babies in China, perhaps hundreds of thousands of them, who need

moms and dads. Infants found in front of shops, on pave-
ments outside hospitals, at tollbooths on highways, anywhere
you can imagine. Infants, almost all of them girls, who end
up in state-run institutions—the tragic result of a government policy to control a population explosion that has reached
dire proportions.

China's so-called "one child policy" was instituted in 1979.
It's a complex system that requires a woman to fill out an application form in order to obtain permission to have a baby.
And in most cases she is allowed only one. If she gets pregnant without permission, she could be forced to have an abor-
tion, pay steep fines, and she could lose her job and home.

Cultural biases dating back to the time of Confucius
place a value on boys over girls in China. In rural areas boys
are needed to help with the farm. As men, they are the ones
who care for elderly parents; in marriage, a woman becomes
part of her husband's family and must leave her own behind.
And so in China, if you can only have one child, there is
every reason to want a boy rather than a girl.

So each day mothers in China are making the most difficult choice imaginable. They are leaving their baby girls at
train stations, on the steps of government office buildings, at
open markets—public places where they know the babies
will be quickly found. Since what they are doing is illegal,
they often hide and watch in secret, waiting for their babies
to be found and taken safely away. The infants are taken to
the local police station, then to hospitals, and finally to or-
phanages. There they are made available for adoption.

In any given month about six hundred Chinese girls are
adopted by American families. China allows older parents as
well as single mothers to adopt. The program, run centrally
by a branch of the Chinese government, is reliable. Adoptive

parents don't have to deal with the black-market baby-sellers or political turmoil found in some other countries. And the babies available for adoption in China are almost always in good health. Adoptive parents have to travel to China and stay about two weeks, while the adoption is finalized.

Alex and I are sitting here listening to all of this. It's hot in here. Stuffy. The lights go down, and soon a TV up front is flickering with the beginnings of a video. The film is not what you'd call professional quality. There is some Chinese music dubbed over this first part showing a group of Americans roaming the crowded streets of Beijing. The Americans look lost. They're pointing at pigs hanging in market windows, then huddling around a woman selling pearls. They have cameras and good walking shoes just like regular old Americans. Then the scene abruptly switches. No more music. Now it's the echo of people talking, although you can't quite make out the dialogue. The camera settles on the beige carpet, then finds the Americans seated on a sofa, squished onto that sofa, in a hotel room, stark and nondescript. Their eyes are wide and tired, and their ankles appear remarkably pink. Finally, a door opens. And in comes the parade. Chinese woman after Chinese woman, each carrying a baby bundled thick. People point, babble, a translator points, babbles. And one by one the babies are handed to their new parents. "Mama," the Chinese women are saying to the babies, pointing to the American women. "Mmmmaaa—mmma!" And the new mamas, they are stiff as boards, holding those babies. For a moment they are just . . . stiff. And some of the babies are screeching, and some of the babies appear too stunned or too confused to react at all. And then the new mamas, one breaks down into tears, and one giggles uncontrollably, it's laughter and tears and laughter and tears in a jumble of joy beyond dreams.

Watching this, I feel like there's lava in me. Like all my blood has turned to thick hot lava. I cannot imagine. I cannot imagine sitting there and having her handed to me. Finally handed to me. I cannot *imagine*.

But the thing is, I can.

I really can.

The lights go on. The man says, "Let's take a break, folks! There's cookies and coffee and juice." Alex and I wander back to the cookies and the coffee and the juice. We're not saying anything. I'm too hot. My blood is too hot and thick and full. I take my cookie back to my seat and work on breathing. Alex is saying nothing at all.

When the break is over, the woman with the little girl in blue overalls stands up to speak. The woman is about my age, with blond shoulder-length hair. Her daughter is balanced firmly on her hip. "Um, I'm here today to talk a little bit about my trip to China," the woman says, her voice somewhat shaky, her hips swinging her daughter back and forth.

I listen, but I hear little of what the woman actually says. Little beyond the fact that she went to China and picked up her daughter. She may as well be talking about picking her kid up from school.

I sit there leaning into Alex, forgetting all about my maximized personal space, thinking little beyond: So here's a mother, and here she is with her daughter.

The rest of my mind and all of my heart is transfixed by the girl. I don't see her as a child abandoned on a street corner. I don't see her as a child living in an orphanage who has been set free. I don't see her as a child who has been rescued or even as a child who has rescued a mom in need of becoming a mom.

I see her, simply, as a two-year-old girl wildly in love with her mother's hair. "Mommy's pigtails," she is saying, as she grabs each silky hunk and pretends to try on the style. "Mommy's *pigtails!*"

It is nothing so spectacular. I suppose a lot of people could look at this picture and say, "So?"

And yet the picture is everything. It is everything in its inescapability, as is any quiet work of nature. A ladybug on a blade of grass. A tiger on a rock in the afternoon sun. A mother and her daughter. A mother who was born on one side of the Earth, and a daughter who was born on the other. How did it happen? How did they find each other? There can be no earthly answer. There can only be a divine one.

After the meeting Alex and I drive to the restaurant where we've planned to have our birthday dinner. Our conversation about China lasts less than a minute:

"So what do you think?" I say.

"Well, we have to do it," he says.

"Well, we do."

"Okay, then. Happy birthday," he says.

"Back at ya."

CHAPTER NINE

It's a crisp November afternoon, and we are in Philadelphia. My mother has been in the rehab hospital for nearly two months.

And she can walk.

She called me a few days ago, said, "Want to come see me walk?" She said, "Twenty steps! I can walk twenty steps."

The rehab hospital is beautiful, in a country-club sort of way. There are ponds with willows drooping down and arched bridges and long, perfect lawns speckled with bright autumn leaves. It's almost too pretty. It's almost like the designers are working too hard to cheer you up. But you can't really argue with too pretty.

When we get inside, we don't have to look at the directory to find my mom's room. She's zooming down the shiny hall in what appears to be an awfully high gear in her new electric wheelchair. "You're here! You're here!" she is saying, waving to us. My dad is behind her, practically jogging to keep up, his white hair flopping up and down.

She comes to an abrupt halt, throws her arms open wide. "Look at me!" she says. "Don't I look great?"

Well, wow. She looks so . . . upright. I'm not used to seeing her quite this upright. She's wearing a pretty peach top with tidy blue slacks. She's still way too skinny, but she's full of color, her jaw is clenched good and tight again, and her perm is back.

"Look at my eyebrows," she says. "I got them *waxed*. Can you believe that? *Waxed?* Do you think I look like I'm in a constant state of surprise?"

"You look great," I say, bending down for a quick kiss on her cheek. I throw a smile to my dad, who is just as I left him: calm but tired and decorated like a present with his red bow tie. He opens his arms for an embrace, and so I fall inside, comforted by his softness and musty smell.

"Well, I guess I am in a state of surprise," my mother is saying. "Because I'm doing great. This place is great. Isn't this place great?" She puts her hand out for Alex to hold, pulls him gently toward her. "Oh, it's so nice of you to come. Claire and James and the kids were in yesterday. I feel like this is my Broadway debut!" Alex bends down, kisses my mom, and from behind his back brings out a box of dark chocolates from a store near his office, her favorites. "You're such a dear," she says to him, and then to my dad: "Two o'clock! Is it two o'clock yet, John? We are due in the gym at two o'clock."

Okay, then. My mother has never been much for extended pleasantries. My mother is a person who is always on to the next thing. Ever since she contracted GBS, a disease that steals your ability to get on to the next thing, I've thought that it's a particularly insidious one for a person like her to get. Now that she's into the rehab phase, she is starting to process the meaning of all of this. She says the disease has taught her patience; it has forced her to flex her little-used patience muscles, oh, it has given them the workout of their lives. That's the other thing about my mother: She can spin. She can spin misery into a lesson, tragedy into a tool for learning. She has a remarkable knack.

"Well, what does your watch say, John?" she goes on, her

patience muscles apparently having already atrophied a bit. *"Does it say two o'clock?"*

You can tell by the look on my dad's face that he's way sick of the two o'clock question, that indeed it might be beginning to hurt his ears. "We have eight minutes, Claire," he tells her. "You are now eight minutes early."

"I think we should go get in line," she says. "I don't want to miss this. Not when I have an audience."

She tucks the chocolates beside her hip, wheels her chair around, throws it into turbo. "Come on, gang."

"She's gotten a little overly confident with the wheelchair," my dad tells us. "I really think they should give speeding tickets in this place."

And so we head at a brisk pace to the gym for my mother's two o'clock physical therapy appointment.

There are a lot of others already waiting in line. Wheelchair after wheelchair. The people, all ages, are in various stages of paralysis or weakness or without-ness. There is a little girl with no legs. A man whose entire right side has collapsed. A boy with an arm made of metal. And then my mother, with her fan club.

The thing is, we really don't belong.

My mother is not . . . handicapped. I wish I had a sign that I could hold up so people would know. I want everyone in this room to understand this: My mother is not handicapped. Except, well, she is. But she's going to get better. She is getting better. Look at her! So really, can't we just avoid this "handicapped" stage? We are not a family that has ever had to do handicapped. We are not a walker or a wheelchair or an access-ramp family. We are normal! This is the way you have it in the back of your mind if you have never had to put it in the front.

Soon my mother's physical therapist appears. She's a

chunky woman with frizzy hair and brilliant green eyes. She escorts my mother to a corner of the room, and we follow as my mother makes the introductions. "Robin," she says. "I would like you to meet my daughter. She's my baby. And this is her dear husband, Alex. He's a psychologist. They live in Pittsburgh. Well, they did. They live on a farm now, craziest thing. . . . I don't know how I ended up with the kids I ended up with." Robin throws a glance our way, smiles, but is focused on the task at hand. She positions the walker just so in front of my mom.

"Are you ready, Claire?" she asks.

"I'm a little nervous today," my mom says. "I don't want to disappoint my people here. You really think I'm ready for prime time?"

Alex and my dad and I take a few steps back, trying to make ourselves invisible.

Ever so slowly, one jerky movement at a time, my mom slides herself out of the chair and toward the walker. "I'm good at scooching!" she says to us, smiling. She grabs hold of the walker, grabs it with both hands, grips.

"She has a hard time with this part," my dad whispers to me. He's seen this show every day now for a week.

"Okay, Claire," Robin says, putting her hand on my mom's back. "Just like yesterday. I want you to pull with your arms, but I want you to use your legs.

"One," Robin says. "Two."

My mom closes her eyes, scrunches up her face like a kid combing big knots out of her hair.

"Three!"

And with that my mother is standing. Wow! Talk about upright! It is the first time I've seen her stand in nearly six months. Standing! I forgot what she looked like standing. She looks like a stork. A thin bird with even thinner legs that

really should not, as far as the laws of gravity dictate, be holding her up. Did she used to look like a stork? No, I don't
think so. This is my new mom.

She is looking down. She is blowing air out of her
mouth.

"Shhh," my dad whispers to me, even though I'm not
talking. But he seems to want to help her, somehow.

She slides the walker a few inches forward. It has little skis
on the bottom of the front feet and wheels on the back. My
mom has on white Nike AirWalks, giant bulbous gym shoes
intended to impress teenagers. She is looking down at those
Nike AirWalks, staring at them as if she now must have a
word with them. She's concentrating. She barely lifts her
right foot off the ground, moves it forward, flops it back
down like it's a thawed fish. She's holding on to the walker so
tight, her knuckles have whitened. She's holding up most of
her weight with those arms. And she slides her left foot forward.

A step. She has taken a step.

She looks up at me. It is the smallest, quickest glance. A
flash. A checking. I know this look. It's the one I would give
her when I was about six, holding my nose and going under
water for the first or second or third or fourth or twentieth
time. It's the longing for validation that every human being
knows.

I've got my eyebrows raised, trying to support her with
my own constant state of surprise. I'm nodding. I've got the
look that says, "Wow!" The look every mother knows how
to give and this one knows how to receive.

"Pretty good, huh?" my mom says.

"You're doing fine, Claire," my dad says calmly, as if to
say, keep going, you've got quite a ways to go yet.

"Whew," my mother says. "I have to say I think I was

better at this yesterday. Do you know yesterday I made it all the way up to the blue triangle? Tell them, Robin."

"I don't want you to think about the blue triangle," Robin says. "I want you to think about the next step, okay?" She's standing behind my mom, a hand barely touching her back just above her belt.

Soon my mom has her tongue sticking out one side of her face. This is such hard work. This is so heartbreaking. This is so thrilling.

She takes her fifth step, and her sixth. They are more shuffles than steps. And yet now my mother is huffing and puffing. Ninth, tenth. Her eyes are trained on her feet. She is focused on keeping them parallel so she won't trip. Twelfth, thirteenth. "I'm getting tired," she says. "I'm going to need to stop soon." She says this with effort but without embarrassment. Twenty. "That's it," she says. "Okay, I'm done with the torture chamber, Robin. Thank you very much."

Robin brings her the wheelchair, and my mother eases back into it. "Yes, thank you, Robin. Thank you. That is such a pretty name, Robin. That is a name that makes people smile." She looks up at us. "Come on, gang. They have good cookies in the cafeteria."

With that she throws her chair into forward, spins in the direction of the sliding door, which she promptly bashes into. *Thwaaaak!* The door flops inward, the top falls off its tracks, that door is toppling, yes, a giant pane of Plexiglas is headed down, down, down, but then Alex and my dad rush in unison to catch it seconds before it lands on anyone's head.

There is one beat of silence; everyone in this entire gym is frozen in time and perhaps calculating instantly what misery we have all just narrowly averted. My mother has done a 180 to assess the damage. She sees Alex and my dad holding up that door. She looks at me.

My eyebrows are up. Her eyebrows are up.

We crack up laughing.

I throw a glance at Alex, who along with my dad has cracked up, as has Robin and the man with the half-drooping body and the girl with no legs, and so on around the room.

Oh, we are having a great time. All of us. All of us who belong right here. Sometimes I think belonging is a big old game of chance. Sometimes I think we're all just a bunch of helium balloons released into the sky. We belong wherever we find ourselves when the wind dies down.

ALEX AND MY dad have decided to forgo the cafeteria cookies in favor of a trip to the parking lot, where they might discover what the devil is wrong with the latch on the trunk of my dad's Buick.

My mom and I are in the cafeteria, taking in the hum of the lemonade machine. The cookies are huge. Big mushy chocolate chips.

"Now this is what I call a cookie," I'm saying. "You weren't kidding."

"I think we should be outside," my mom says. "You want to sneak out the back door with me?"

"Sneak?"

"Not really. It's a courtyard for the patients. But it's fun to think about escaping, isn't it?"

"I thought you said you liked it here," I say.

"Oh, I do," she says. "In fact, lately I've been feeling like the luckiest person alive."

Lucky? That might be a little strong. "Lucky?" I say.

She shrugs. She chews. She takes a sip from her milk carton, swallows, looks up at me.

"It was like dying," she says. "I felt like I was dying."

Oh?

"That's the thing about this crazy disease, it's like a slow death. One by one the systems go out. I experienced all of that, all of the stripping away. The humiliation."

"I saw."

"And now it's like I'm being reborn, inch by inch. That's the other thing about this disease. And let me tell you, sweetie—you're grateful for every single inch."

We've gathered our cookies, and some napkins, and our milk cartons. She's maneuvering her way out of the cafeteria, toward the back door, and I'm following.

"Gratitude." This, she tells me, has been the overwhelming lesson that her paralysis has taught her. "I just have this overwhelming sense of gratitude," she says.

Lucky. Grateful. Whew. She really does have the knack. "It's a great outlook," I say.

"I'm thankful for every muscle in this old body," she says. "I'm thankful for the ability to swallow, to smell, to hear. I'm thankful I can breathe. I'm thankful that I can pray."

"I see," I say, wishing I could. I wish I had the knack. I wish I could see the God she sees. I wish I could hear the God she hears. I wish I knew how she got where she got, with God. I wish I knew how to ask.

"So you feel like you got God back?" is how it comes out.

She doesn't answer directly. Instead, she goes into an animated lecture about how great "you kids" were during the illness. "I mean, I knew you kids loved me, but *this much*?" she says. We're outside now, parked under an oak tree. It's chilly, but neither of us seems to mind. "The devotion," she says. "It really amazed me. You know, if you're in the hospital for a month or so, a friend will probably come visit. But three months? Six months? And the friends are still coming around? I had no idea I had such a faithful bunch of supporters."

But the attention, she says, had little to do with her winning any popularity contest. "That love was God's love. Where do you think love comes from? It comes from God, and it comes through other people."

I think about this. Usually I walk around thinking of love as a kind of gravity. Just one of those laws of nature, a force that has its way with you. I don't tend to wonder where the law might have come from.

"This crazy disease has taught me so much," my mother says.

"Patience," I say. "You told me about the patience."

"Yeah, but it's so much bigger than that. It's: I am not in charge. Of course, I always knew I wasn't in charge. But— oh, how do I put this? I *surrendered*."

"Surrendered," I say.

"Surrender and serenity," she says. "I never realized how close those two words are. Huh? Think about *that*!"

"The wind," I say, "I think of it as letting go to the wind. You know? Not fighting it. Just kind of allowing yourself to ride along with it."

"That's good," she says, nodding. "I like that."

We sit in silence. There really isn't much wind today. There are some geese overhead making a racket.

"Aren't we having a great time?" she says, finally.

"We are," I say.

"I'm so glad you're going to have a daughter," she says. "Daughters can be such great friends. Aren't we great friends?"

"We are."

It's been only a few days since I told her about our decision to adopt from China. I'm surprised she's so nonchalant about it. You know, just dropping the D-word like that. Daughter. I'm going to have a *daughter*. Whew. Big word.

I was anything but calm telling her and my sisters about the adoption. I don't know why I was so nervous telling them. Maybe it's the whole baby thing. I'm the baby of this family. The baby has a responsibility to stay . . . a baby.

I suppose we all have themes that run our lives, stories that get put on us like tattoos, stories told to us or stories we learn to tell ourselves, stories that become so fused with the self they become *con*fused with the self.

With my announcement about choosing to adopt, well, now I was revealing myself to be someone else: a mom. That pretty much squashes the baby identity. You can't be the mom and the baby. So good-bye, baby. Wasn't this going to disrupt everyone's view of the universe and all the galaxies beyond?

Um, no. In a word. No.

My mom and sisters were happy when I told them. Purely happy. In fact, the general consensus was that this is just what this family needs: a baby. A new life to focus on.

And already, for my mom, motherhood is just part of who I am, just something she can very nonchalantly refer to on an autumn day, under an oak tree and a gaggle of noisy geese.

"When your daughter comes, I think we should have a party," she says. "I could get one of the banquet rooms at Riddle Village. Would that be too weird to have a party for your daughter at the old folks' home?"

At least she's not calling it the funny farm anymore. But "daughter." Okay, that D-word is going to take some getting used to.

"No, Mom," I say. "I don't think that would be weird at all."

★   ★   ★

AND SO ALEX and I have begun to spread the word about our decision to adopt. Not too far, though, and not too wide. Alex has been talking to his kids. How strange this must be for them. Amy and Peter have had their dad to themselves all these years, and even though they're now adults, with their own complicated lives, the idea of a brand-new baby sister has got to be unsettling. But the thing that's great about Amy and Peter is they can say that. They can say, "This is weird for me, Dad." Well, the first thing Peter said was "Whew." He said, "Give me a moment to comprehend this." By now he's had a few weeks of moments, and just yesterday he reported that he may be inching his way toward being excited. It's funny; I would have thought Amy, who is twenty-six and two years older than Peter, would have had the tougher time. She likes being daddy's little girl. But she has demonstrated the most astonishing maturity. "It would be selfish of me not to share you, Dad," she said. "Plus, I'm kind of used to it, you know?" Alex was a surrogate father to many of Amy's high school and college friends. Theirs was the house kids knew they could run to. Alex would take them in, talk to their parents, help smooth things over.

And as for the rest of the story, Alex is telling Peter and Amy everything. But I am not, so far, telling anyone anything. It's a matter of privacy, I suppose. It's different from adoption. With the adoption, there is an actual baby to consider, a baby who has already, at least metaphorically, begun her long journey to her new home.

But, with the rest of the story, well, there really is nothing yet to talk about.

The rest of the story is this: We're doing it. Our one free IVF cycle. Does that seem surprising? Maybe. It's surprising the way you can be so utterly sure in your mind that you are going to make one choice, and then at the last minute the opposite choice swoops in and grabs you by the throat, says, "What are you—*crazy*?"

It's crazy not to. Right? It's sort of like, well, here's a coupon for a free gallon of milk, so why not use it? That's how I'm looking at it when I am thinking clearly and rationally, which is almost never.

The truth is this dream isn't about a gallon of milk. This is about: a baby. A baby that might grow inside me. A baby made out of me and Alex. The most natural dream in the world.

But I am not looking at that. To look at something like that is only to increase the wanting and the hoping, which is only to increase the disappointment if the thing doesn't come true.

So I am looking at it as a free gallon of milk.

The one thing I am seeing clearly, in all of this, is the irony: Were it not for our decision to adopt, we wouldn't be doing the IVF thing at all. It was our decision to adopt that enabled us to pursue the possibility of having a biological child in the first place.

A safety clause, perhaps? Is that what it is? Underneath it all, was I so worried that the pregnancy wouldn't work that I needed to first make sure I had a baby somewhere waiting in the wings?

I don't think so. I really don't think that's it at all.

For me, it's only in the knowledge that I've begun my journey to find my baby that I can even begin to imagine making her a brother or a sister. Maybe it was Alyson, maybe it was a purely romanticized notion that filled my mind like some very lovely cartoon, or maybe it was something else. But

I see the adopted child first. And then a sibling. If possible, a sibling.

If the IVF thing works, then what we will have will be insta-family! Two babies. *Two!* Well, plenty of people have twins. Plenty of people.

But—*two?*

BEFORE WE LEAVE Philadelphia, Alex and I stop at my brother's house. It's high on the hill known as Honey Hill Farm, a farm that is, well, a lot nicer than our farm. It's a manicured farm with a pond large enough to accommodate two zooming Jet Skis. It's a farm of thirty rolling acres featuring a grand stone farmhouse, an actual paved driveway, and flower beds that were modeled after the gardens at Versailles. My brother does things—big. My brother is a streamlined diesel-powered behemoth freight train. In comparison I am but a puny Amtrak commuter.

He and his wife Eileen are happy to hear the news about adopting from China, although their responses differ considerably.

"One?" my brother says. "Why don't you get two or three?"

"Well," I say, not sure where to start on my answer, which is quickly overpowered anyway, by Eileen, the Queen of Gush. "A baby! A baby! A baaaaaaaaaaaaaaaaaby!!!!!!!!!!!" She grabs my arm, tugs it up into the air, and twirls herself under it. "A baby!" See, I love her. She makes such a good Italian, even though she's German, but she's got the mushy, sloppy, kissy, huggy thing down. I have loved her since I was eight years old and my brother brought her home for dinner and she had perfectly wicked dyed-blond streaks in her hair, the first dyed-blond person to ever set foot in our house. I was nine when they married. I couldn't believe my luck. In a way, I suppose I adopted Eileen, and she adopted me. In a way, I suppose most families have plenty of people in them who were adopted.

"I'm going to be your baby's favorite aunt," Eileen announces. "I am going to Toys 'R' Us and get started on my . . . strategy."

It's fitting, after all, seeing as I worked so hard all those years ago to be Alyson's favorite aunt.

She's here. Alyson. I can see her out by the boxwoods, coming inside. Alyson. The one who started it all. The first baby I ever held. The oldest grandchild and so far the only one to be brought into the family through the kind of adoption that gets recorded on paper. She's twenty-four years old now, an artist with long blond hair and about twenty earrings in each ear and a smiley face tattoo on her big toe. She shares my brother's passion for life, specifically his passion for flowers and shrubs and anything that grows. She's working, with his help, on starting her own greenhouse business; she's already secured a loan for a ten-acre spot, and it's a good bet that she'll be landscaping most of Pennsylvania by the time she's thirty.

"Bean!" she says to me when she comes inside. She's called me Bean ever since she was two, trying to pronounce my name. "What are you guys doing here?" She opens her arms wide enough to hug both Alex and me at the same time.

"We came to see Grandmom walk," Alex says.

"How about that, huh?"

"And they have news," Eileen says. "Wait till you hear this one."

"*What?*" Alyson says, looking at me. "About Grandmom?"

"No," I say.

Something in my tone. She gets the shift. "It's [

"Pretty big," I say with a smile.

"Don't tell me," she says. "You're pregnant?"

I shake my head to indicate maybe yes, maybe no, sort of. "We're adopting a baby from China," I tell her.

Her head drops forward, like you do when you're trying to follow a complicated math problem on the blackboard at school. She seems to be computing something in her mind. She's looking at me, squinting.

I don't say anything. Nobody says anything.

Then her face falls. Oh, she seems to have arrived at her answer. She looks at her mother, me, Alex, her dad, back at me. Her eyes have welled up. She's blinking, moving toward me. "Oh my God," she says, wrapping her arms around me. "Thank you."

ON THE LONG drive home, from one end of the Pennsylvania Turnpike to the other, I have plenty of time to think about Alyson, about why she reacted like that and how it caught me off-guard. For her, I suppose my announcement was some kind of validation. My decision to adopt must have in some way said: *Yes. You really do belong.* My decision to adopt must have in some way said: *See? I wasn't kidding.* I wasn't kidding all those years ago when you were in second grade and full of your first doubt; I wasn't kidding when I said how happy I was that you were part of this family, no matter how you came to it. I wasn't kidding when I said the how of coming into a family is as irrelevant as the where. The what and the why are the only things that matter. The what and the why are: love.

I wasn't kidding. In fact, I *so* wasn't kidding that I am

now bringing in another who will travel your same path. A baby born in another woman's body. But a baby that belongs here, with us, in this family.

It makes me feel like a fraud thinking about trying to get pregnant. A fraud. I've been getting all sorts of blood tests taken. The doctors are getting my body ready. I feel like a damn fraud.

We stop at the Blue Mountain rest stop for some coffee refills and a chance to stretch our legs. They have a room with pinball machines. They have one of those machines with the big metal claws. You put your money in, move the joystick around, and try to pluck yourself out a toy.

Fifty cents per chance. I've never actually tried one of these machines before. And here I am with two quarters in my pocket. So what the heck. I put the money in. The claw goes flying toward the back wall like it's alive, and it falls before I can get control of it. It falls with a *thunk*. And when it comes up from the pool of toys, I see I've won, I've snagged myself a toy! The claw glides over to a chute, drops it, and it goes sliding through the chute. When I retrieve it, I see it is a doll. An Asian doll. The character Mulan from the Disney movie. I am standing here looking at it. Alex walks up with our two cups of Maxwell House.

"I just won this," I tell him. "I just won a Mulan doll."

He looks at it. "I guess it's our daughter's first official toy," he says.

Daughter. Yeesh. Why is everyone so nonchalant about using this very big word? And here's her first toy. Well, I guess. But in this moment the doll is a kind of validation all its own. Down the chute. Here comes the girl, down the chute. What difference does the chute make? The chute. My daughter is somewhere, and she'll come to me down a chute;

mine or someone else's, it hardly matters whose. N
are, after all, just mechanics.

I'm standing here wondering how to explain a..
Alex. I have no idea how to explain this.

"You mean I have to *share* my toys?" is what I end up
saying.

"Definitely one of the downsides to parenting," he says.

CHAPTER TEN

I'm standing in a bathroom stall at Wal-Mart, throwing a needle in my stomach like a dart. You're supposed to hold it like a dart. I'm getting pretty good at it. I pinch my stomach with one hand, grab a hunk of flesh, toss the dart in. It's a little needle. It doesn't hurt. I have little red dots all over my belly from two weeks of these injections.

I'm on Lupron, one shot each morning. The hormone is helping my ovaries store all the eggs that the egg-stimulation medication, which I inject at night, is supposedly producing, so I'll have as many chances as possible to get . . . fertilized. It's the middle of January. By Valentine's Day, I could be pregnant. Whew. Is it hot in here? I swear this Lupron is giving me hot flashes.

I feel horrible. I feel like a chicken. I feel like what I think a chicken must feel like every morning before she drops her eggs. Bloat. Major bloat. Actually, this must be much worse than what chickens feel like. No chicken in her right mind would live like this. Then again, most chickens probably don't have a choice.

Whew. See, the Lupron is making me wacky. I'm a big, overstuffed, wacky chicken. I don't know how much longer I can take this. That's what I'm going to say tomorrow morning when I go in for the ultrasound. I'm going to say, "I don't know how much longer I can take this."

Whew. It is really hot in here. And now someone out there by the sink is using that hand blow-dryer thing, which is not helping. And how exactly should I dispose of this used needle? Ordinarily I do these injections at home, but this morning I had to run errands, and the timing of the injections, they said, is critical.

And so I'm here in Wal-Mart. I'm in Wal-Mart to buy little baskets to use to organize my closets with. I'm doing this so that when the social worker comes to our house in a few weeks to decide if Alex and I are acceptable adoptive-parent material—a decision she will then pass on to the folks at the Immigration and Naturalization Service, who will take our fingerprints and send them to the FBI so as to determine whether or not we are criminals—I will at least reveal myself to be a person with organized closets.

Whew.

It is definitely hot in here.

Working on adoption paperwork at the same time as an IVF cycle, it's a lot. The Lupron, the chicken bloat, the needles, the trips to the hospital for blood tests and ultrasounds, plus throw on top of that the FBI and the INS—well, it's just a lot. Putting together a dossier for international adoption is a full-time job, and managing an IVF cycle is another one.

We could have waited, of course. We could have done these sequentially. We could have waited until next year after we get home safe and sound with the baby from China, then tried our luck at the fertility clinic afterward. But the doctors made a fairly good case that it's now or never for me. They said my eggs are just getting older and older. They said for me every month is critical, every month my chances decrease. They definitely turned the panic meter up several notches.

And there was no way I was going to delay the adoption. No way. Nonnegotiable. My baby is waiting. I've got to get to her. I've got to *hurry*.

If all goes as planned and there are no snags, we should have all our paperwork in to the adoption agency by April. These papers will then be sent to the government office in China. About seven months after that we'll receive a letter revealing the identity of the baby who has been chosen for us. We'll get a picture of her, and a medical report. We'll find out what orphanage she's living in. About six weeks after that we'll travel to China to get her. It all adds up to about a year from now. A whole year.

So it's paperwork. It's forms to fill out and get notarized and certified by the Pennsylvania Secretary of State in Harrisburg and then authenticated by the Chinese Consulate in Chicago, and some by the Chinese Consulate in New York. It's a pile of paperwork a foot high so far.

And it's Lupron. It's 0.5 milligrams in my belly each morning. I'm trying not to whine about this, about the chicken bloat, about the little red dots on my stomach. I did, after all, choose this. I chose all of this. The doctors gave me the option of forgetting about my aging eggs. They said I could just take my time and boost my odds considerably by entering the "donor egg program." You know, let someone else grow the eggs, which she would then donate to me. They brought out a book. It listed the characteristics of women willing to donate their eggs. Education. Height. Weight. Hobbies.

I have a few friends who chose this option. I remember them talking about the book. To them, it really did seem to be a quite simple matter of increasing the chances at becoming pregnant. To them, the *pregnancy* was the thing.

To me, it isn't. It's another path toward becoming a mom, a path that has opened up thanks to an insurance company.

And I couldn't imagine another woman's eggs in my body. I just couldn't.

So I said no. I said I am redeeming my one free IVF coupon now, while my chances with my own eggs are best. And that will be that. In truth this is a long shot at best; most women you read about go through half a dozen or more IVF attempts before producing a baby. So my chances are slim. But it's not really about the odds, as I see it. It's about the boost. It's about some sense of obligation I have to give God the boost. I wonder if that makes any sense at all.

This is a maze. You can't really say one way is better than another. You can only say your way is your way. How one woman feels her way through the maze is not a model for another woman. It's just an example. It's a story. It's a story from which to gather courage to move forward on your own path.

And my story, at the moment, is a used needle in a Wal-Mart bathroom. I wrap it in toilet paper, put it in my purse to dispose of later. I find my shopping cart waiting outside the bathroom, right here where I left it in aisle six, Women's Shoes. I've found some pink baskets and also some larger green ones. Yes, these will do fine. I pass a shelf of shelf paper. I think, well, maybe I should get shelf paper and line my pantry shelves. I decide, no. The social worker will just have to see me for who I am: a woman with unlined pantry shelves.

Alex left at the crack of dawn for Little Rock, Arkansas. Just for a few days. He's testifying in court on behalf of one of his former clients, a man in danger of losing custody of his children. The man, Alex says, is a good father, a mechanic with a big heart and little sophistication in matters of being duped—which is probably why he was. The man's ex-wife, a lawyer with a lot of bitterness in her heart, took off with the children abruptly one night, moved to Arkansas, and has exercised her prodigious legal might to keep the children's father out of their lives. The case matters to Alex: It's a kind of crusade for duped fathers everywhere, I think. I'm proud of him. I don't tell him often enough how proud I am of him for being such a heroic father, a father who never even wanted to be a father but who accepted the job with dignity and did it right; a father now fighting for fathers; a father willing to go yet another round and who asks for nothing, really nothing, in return.

Except, okay, a pool table. Right. Well, I've started a little pool table fund, and I'm pleased to report that I'm now accepting donations.

I should put a sign up. I should put a little poster up here on the Wal-Mart bulletin board where they have all these posters of missing kids. Hmm. Maybe not. I roll my cart out the exit door, feel the blast of hot air they throw at you, and think this, yes, this heat is getting ridiculous.

I'm hot. I'm a bloated chicken. I have to hurry home and clean closets.

I forgot to mention Christmas. Forgive me, but my brain is hot and waterlogged and not right. I forgot to say, yes, it happened. My mother. Alex. Christmas. A mere six weeks after that visit to the rehab hospital. We went to my brother's to celebrate Christmas, as we always do. My mom, while getting quite good with the walker, still has a way to go, but she's an outpatient now. Alex asked my brother to put on some music. He put on Elvis singing "Blue Christmas," an odd choice, but my brother was in an Elvis stage. He cranked it loud, as is my brother's way. My mother said, "Oh, John! Do you have to put that music so loud?" as is her way. She had no idea what was about to happen. She has never been through, and will most assuredly never go through, an Elvis stage. Alex walked up to her, tapped her shoulder, and said, "May I have this dance?" My mother tilted her head to one side, smiled. "I don't know if I really can—" But Alex moved her walker aside and held out his arms. And so she hoisted herself up, and Alex took her into his arms, and she leaned on him, and slowly, back and forth, one foot, then the next, they danced. At one point my mother looked over her shoulder at us all huddled in the doorway and said, "He's not holding me up, you know. I'm really doing this on my own." We stood around and took pictures and some of us cried, and by the end of the dance my mom and Alex both had their eyes closed above gentle smiles, like lambs.

I TAKE THE curves on Daniel's Run Road fast; I'm running a little late for the ultrasound appointment. Fortunately, I could drive this road blindfolded.

I see a guy ahead, a guy kneeling on the side of the road. He's waving me over. He's holding something, an animal. Is it dead? Oh God, I don't want to see this. And why is it that you run into men holding roadkill on your way to a very important appointment? Why is life this way?

I pull up slowly next to him, roll down my window. "Everything okay?" But I am not really looking.

"He's fine," he says. "He just likes to lay in the road."

Oh. I look down. It's a little dog. A beagle. It is not dead. It is not even hurt. The man is scratching the dog's ears. The dog looks too tired to care. That is one sleepy dog.

"Do you live around here?" the man says. He's big and square with red hair and a red beard. He has on an orange jacket that says "Road Crew." "Do you recognize this dog?"

I tell him I live around the corner, and no, I don't recognize the dog.

"I've been working on potholes," he says. "This dog has been here every day for the past two weeks."

"Aw," I say. "Well, it's nice to have a companion!" I'm about to roll my window up. I'm late. I don't know the dog. My work here is done.

"He sleeps on the road," the man says. "He seems to like asphalt; I don't know."

I smile politely but without conviction.

"I don't know," the guy repeats, cupping his hand to keep the morning sun out of his eyes. "But I gotta keep him off the damn road or he's gonna get run over."

"Yeah."

"I've stopped every car for six days," he tells me. "Nobody recognizes the dog. I've knocked on doors. I've done all I could."

"How about the post office?" I say. "Did you ask there?"

His face brightens with recognition. "Caroline said she would pass the word," he says.

I smile. Everyone knows Caroline.

"Well, Caroline gets things done," I tell him. "If anybody can find the dog's owner, Caroline can."

"Yeah," he says, leaning back on his knees. "She tell you the post office is moving?" Oh, dear. It appears we're settling in for a . . . chat.

"Yeah," I say politely.

"She tell you about the delay?"

"Um—"

"They had to get bids on the sign."

"Oh," I say. "Right." It's as if we've been watching the same TV show.

"I could have made a damn sign. Did you hear the bid went to a company in Canada?"

"Canada?"

"Canada!" he says. "After all the fuss about it being a U.S. regulation sign."

I laugh. It's as if we've been watching the same TV show, and he's an episode ahead.

"Well, I really have to be heading off . . ."

"Well, what about the dog?"

Um. What about the dog?

"Do you have a pet?" he says. "He would make a great pet."

I look at him, tilt my head sideways with apology. He's looking at the wrong person. Wrong! I don't do the poor-needy-dog thing anymore. I'm way, way out of that racket. I'm in my . . . bloated chicken stage. "You have really, really, really asked the wrong person," I say. "I mean, I'm a sucker for this kind of thing, but . . ."

"I am too," he says. "But I have three cats and two dogs and a wife who would kill me."

"I have three cats and *three* dogs and a husband who would send me to an insane asylum," I say. He flashes a knowing smile. It's a kind smile. A smile that says, *I get you*. Well, it's nice to meet a stranger you like. It's nice to be just driving down the road, minding your own business, and meet someone you can instantly connect with.

"We could take the dog to the Humane Society," I say. It's funny how I'm saying "we."

"But who would adopt a dog like this?" he says. "He's old."

Maybe he's just dirty. He sure is a mangy thing. He's got the longest ears you'll ever see on a dog, and a head much too big for his body. His legs are too short, and his tail is way too long. A child could draw a more convincing dog.

"Well, he's got a collar, so he's somebody's dog," I point out. "Maybe put an ad in the paper?"

"But we have to get him off this road," the man says.

It's funny how he's saying "we."

I think a minute. I tell him, well, I could put the dog in my yard, which is way off the road, until the owner is found. And yeah, I could put an ad in the paper. Yeah. How hard is that? Forgodsakes. It's the least I can do for a lonely old dog who's lost his way.

"How long will you be here?" I ask. "Why don't you keep the dog here until I'm on my way home, and I'll pick him up and put him in my yard."

"I'm off at noon," he says.

Oh. Well, there is no way I'll be back by noon. I tell him okay, here's what we'll do. "When you get off work, just drive the dog to my house, drop him in the yard." I give him directions.

"That'll work," he says. "Thank you. You're the first person who offered to help."

"I'm a sucker for this kind of thing."

"Me, too."

"Just drop him off. And don't worry about my dogs," I say. "They'll bark like crazy, but they'd never hurt a flea."

"Well, should I knock on the door and tell your husband or something?" he says.

"My husband is out of town," I say. "No one's home. But I should be back by two at the latest. You think the dog will stick around?"

"Probably. Did you say it's a left and then a right?" he says, clarifying the directions.

"No, a right and then a left, but not a hard left, just a soft left onto the dirt road," I say. And soon I am drawing him a map on the back of an envelope from an old gasoline bill I find in the glove compartment. "Okay? I really have to go. An appointment, you know."

"No problem," he says, smiling. "Nice doing business with you!"

And so I roll up my window and zoom away. From my rearview mirror I see him waving. Nice guy. I wonder where he lives.

So I'm zooming. I really have to hurry. I zoom onto the highway, floor it.

Finally, and only when I stop zooming, when I enter the city, when I pull into the stinky hospital parking lot, that's where it hits me: I just gave a complete stranger a map to my house. I told him no one is home, that my husband is out of town, and don't worry about the dogs, don't worry about anything until I show up at two by which time I suppose you will have had plenty of time to ransack the place which I have just practically handed over to you.

I can't believe this! How could I have been so stupid?

It's only here, in the city, that this hits me. It's only here, back in my city frame of mind: Don't be stupid! Lock your car and lock your house and shut your stupid big mouth!

And yet in the country, back home, it didn't seem stupid at all. Why would trusting someone be stupid?

"Because," I hear in my head, "because that guy probably does this once a week, probably poses in his road crew outfit with a pathetic dog on some lonely country road and waits for a sucker like you."

I can't believe this. I can't believe it! It's all I can do to not turn around and catch him in the act.

Then again, he did know about Caroline and the post office and everything. Oh, relax. He knew about Canada, for heaven's sake. I shouldn't be so paranoid.

Or I should be more paranoid.

See, I'm stuck not knowing what to think.

But on the other hand, I am a bloated chicken with brain bloat, so I think I should be forgiven.

Blame it on the Lupron. If my house gets ransacked, I'm going to blame it on the Lupron. In some ways, this is a very good drug.

"TWELVE," SAYS THE woman in blue standing over me working the ultrasound machine. "You have twelve follicles."

"Twelve!" I say.

The woman has curly blond hair, and a double chin, and glasses with the kind of oversize frames that were popular in the 1980s. She also has very cold hands. The room is dimly lit, somewhat like the little massage rooms at a spa I once went to, and all you can hear is the whir of machinery. I'm lying here flat on my back, dressed in one of those paper nighties they give you, with the ties in front.

"Twelve," I say. "Well—wow!"

She doesn't say anything. Shouldn't we be happy about this? Twelve potential eggs! "How about that for an old bag like me?" I say.

"I've seen women your age with twenty-five," she says.

"Oh."

"But twelve is good," she says. "It's good. We'll see what we get." She explains that we won't "get" twelve eggs in the actual "harvest." She says usually about half end up being viable.

"Any guess at how much longer they want me to . . .

incubate these puppies?" I say. Perhaps not the most technically precise lingo. I'm nervous.

"If your blood work is okay, you'll probably go Friday,"
she says. "I'd say Friday at the latest."

"Well, that's good," I say. Three more days. "This is getting exciting!"

She doesn't, apparently, think so. Well, she doesn't say
anything one way or the other. She's busy typing on a keyboard, which is connected to the ultrasound machine, which
is connected to me. She is . . . communicating with my follicles? She is sending them some encouraging e-mail, perhaps?
I consider asking, but I don't think I'll get even a smile out of
this woman.

"Well, I suppose I can make it to Friday," I say, looking
into the TV monitor providing a spectacular view of my
ovaries. The overall picture is of black and white swirls, cake
batter before the beaters are turned on. "Okay, ovaries? On
Friday, girls, on Friday you get yourselves a *vacation*."

The woman looks at me.

"They've been begging for a day off," I say.

She pulls her lips back and nods.

"I must say, I've never felt so *close* to my ovaries," I continue. I can't quite seem to stop talking. This is, you have to
admit, an odd situation. How much experience does the average person have with lying on a table while a woman with
a double chin and big glasses looks at your ovaries on a TV
screen? "Yeah, me and the Big O's have really gotten to know
each other over the last few weeks."

Nothing. Not even a smirk. Damn. For a person in the
business of creating people, she sure isn't a people person.
None of the people in this clinic seem to be. What is *with* this
place? Everybody's overworked. Everybody's tired. It's all you
can do to get a phone call returned.

This, I know, is a factory. And I'm a customer. That's the truth of it. I don't know why I just don't give in to that. This is a factory and I'm a customer, and if I'm very, very lucky, I'll get my order filled. My order: for a person.

"Okay, you're done for today," the woman says, hitting the Return key on her keyboard, and with that my ovaries vanish from view. Not even a good-bye. "Someone will be calling you after four with the blood work results," she tells me. "Make sure you're all set for the HCG because that's probably going to be tomorrow."

"HCG?" I say. "Can you refresh me on the HCG?"

She looks at me. Her eyelids fall in a reproving blink. "It's in your manual," she says.

"Right."

My manual. It's a three-ring binder crammed with instructions. I also have a black notebook that I carry with me at all times in which I write down questions and record answers—on the rare occasions that I get to actually speak to one of the doctors in charge of all of this. These doctor moments are actually scheduled talks—sometimes three-minute phone calls—for which my insurance company is dutifully billed. It's all I can do not to slip in a little editorial now and again, you know, *Hey doc, this is quite a racket you're running here.*

But.

Well, I don't.

I don't want to get anyone mad at me or my eggs.

I have *twelve* potential eggs to protect.

Driving home, I'm no longer a bloated chicken. I'm a goose sitting on a nest. The difference is: hope.

I call Alex on his cell phone. He'll have it turned off if he's in court. I don't know what time he's supposed to be in court.

He answers.

"Hey!" I say. "Twelve! I'm hatching twelve eggs!"

"Wow!" he says. "Well, that's . . . great!"

"It's actually pretty average," I say. "Or so I'm told."

"Well, I couldn't hatch twelve eggs," he says.

"True. You are such a sweetie. How are things there?"

"I haven't even gotten to the courthouse yet. I'm in a cab."

"Well, I am thinking of you," I say. "I'm really proud of you."

"Thank you," he says. "So what's next?"

"I'm going home. I have to—well, I really have to get home." I don't say anything about how I have to check to make sure the house wasn't just robbed by a guy posing as a road crew worker with a lost dog. It's just not really something Alex needs to know.

"No, I mean what's next with the eggs?"

"Oh," I say. "Harvest. They said probably Friday."

"Yikes," he says.

"Yikes," I say. "And that means you'll have to do your part Friday, too."

"This is so strange," he says.

"I feel like a goose sitting on a big old nest."

"I feel like a zoo animal—some kind of endangered ape."

"Yeah, but you're *my* ape."

"You're *my* goose."

"Good luck, sweetie. I'm proud of you."

When I get to Daniel's Run Road, I take it slow this time. I'm looking for the dog. Maybe the dog is still on the road. Maybe the guy wasn't a crook, maybe he just didn't really care the way I thought he did. Maybe he simply went home and left the dog here. The disappointment would be better than a robbed house.

The dog isn't here. The dog, I decide, is probably right now snoozing at the guy's feet, while the guy is scratching his beard and congratulating himself on another score.

I make the right and then the left, the soft left onto Wilson Road. I approach my house with doubt and longing and an urge in my blood to rescue trust from the land of the stupid.

It happens. The dog is here. When I pull up, I see him stretched out on the stump of the old willow tree, sound asleep. Betty and Marley and Wilma seem to have long ago accepted his presence and come charging over to greet me. The beagle stays on the stump, lifts his head, looks over at me, and allows his long tail to go *thump, thump, thump* in as much appreciation as he can muster, poor thing.

"Well, hello, dog," I say as I get out of the car. "I'm really glad to see you. Not that you're staying. You do understand that you're not staying, don't you?"

Thump, thump, thump.

I feel nothing for the dog. But I am glad he is here because I am glad to know I am not stupid and I am glad to know that trust is still a commodity worth investing in.

The dog slowly lowers his head and, with a deep sigh, resumes his nap in the sun.

MAYBE IT SEEMS early for this, but we've picked out a name for the baby we are adopting from China. In a way, you could say the name picked us; it took nearly a hundred years to get to us.

Alex's grandmother, my grandmother. Both were named Anna. Which is a nice enough coincidence. But his grandmother and my grandmother, both of the Annas—they lived in the same town. Which would be a nice enough coincidence if it were just Detroit or Minneapolis or some other place people have actually heard of. But no. His grandmother and my grandmother, both of the Annas—they lived in Šiauliai, a tiny village on the northern tip of Lithuania, a town nobody has heard of, at least nobody who lives very far outside of Šiauliai.

So, Anna.

It's another one of the coincidences, like the birthday. Anna.

We'll name her after the grandmothers. We'll name her after all the coincidences. We'll name her Anna.

Just saying the name brings me comfort.

Today I need comfort.

It's Sunday. Five days after I learned about my twelve eggs, five days after a dog helped rescue trust from the land of the stupid, five days after Alex testified for a father who now has the court-ordered right to once again see his children.

Sunday. A day most people are in church. Instead I am here in this doctor's office in a large medical complex, with the lights low, and Alex holding my hand, and I have to pee. I have to pee so bad.

Anna. The thing is, if I just keep saying "Anna" in my head, I don't have to pee quite so bad.

They said to please make sure I had a full bladder. They said the doctor can see better if the bladder is full. And I am a good girl. I drank those glasses of water this morning. And I drank two extra ones just to make sure. I am a good girl! I am going to wet my pants. I am going to explode.

Anna.

Pee psychosis! I am having hafta-pee psychosis. I am not prepared for this. I was not prepared for Friday, either. Friday, the day of harvest, yes, it happened on Friday, just as the woman with big glasses predicted. Harvest. I wish I had been prepared. I wasn't expecting any of what happened. None of it was in my IVF manual. They gave me something, then put a needle in, they put me under, but not really under, because I could feel yanking, I could feel tugging and twisting, and at one point I dreamed, but it was more real than a dream, that I was being attacked by a shark. The shark, to his credit, wasn't biting. He was more just a spearing shark. Spearing me in the stomach. I was glad he wasn't eating me but confused that he was spearing me that way. But then I realized: Oh. I'm in the sea! But I don't live in the sea. . . . I live where there's *air*. I need *air*.

I awoke and my first thought was: air.

They said, "Six. We got six."

Six viable eggs.

Into each of the six the lab technicians then injected one of Alex's big manly hunkatomic-power sperms. They sent us home. They said they would call us and let us know. I don't remember going home, I only remember waking up, really waking up finally, in my bed, and learning that it was now Saturday afternoon and the phone was ringing. They said, "Four." They said, "You have four embryos here. They look good."

Four.

Okay. Four.

It was a number. It was just—a number.

And the thing that got me, and still gets me, is that Alex and I seemed to be the only ones talking about anything beyond the number.

"You need to decide how many to transfer," the nurse said on the phone. "Okay? Because you have four. Are you going to transfer all four?"

Um . . .

She said another option was to put in two now and freeze two, to be transferred later. She said it was up to us.

"Um."

She offered no advice. The most I could get out of her was, "The more you put in, the better your chances of having one stick."

Stick.

The goal was to now get one of these embryos to stick onto my uterine wall, where it could then grow into a baby. Getting an embryo to stick is the one remaining mysterious piece of the whole IVF equation. They don't know why some stick and some don't. They don't really have any science to help that process along. They don't know why embryos made out of older eggs tend to have much lower sticking power. They don't know why, in some women, you can put in four and have all four stick, while in others you can put in six and have zero stick.

Lying here on this table, having to pee, I'm glad of that. I'm glad that there is no way to control the sticking. I'm glad there's one piece of this puzzle that is still fully—and only—in God's hands.

But mostly I am not glad. Mostly I just have to pee so bad. Where is the doctor? Why is this taking so long? The nurse was in about a half hour ago to apologize for the delay—but that was a *half hour* ago.

And the urgency of having to pee, the actual pain now in my bladder, the immediacy of all of this, creates panic. Hafta-pee psychosis. Well, it certainly contributes to the panic. How many embryos do we put in?

I can't believe we are receiving no guidance on this question. This enormous question. Where is the guidance? This was not in the manual.

Well, to be fair, they gave us a chart. Age of woman along one side, number of embryos on the other, and in between little percentage markers indicating chances of pregnancy.

But I'm not talking about numbers.

I'm talking: embryos.

What *are* they? What is my responsibility to them? Do I have any? And what if I put four in and all four stick? What am I to do as a forty-year-old woman with four babies growing in me?

"Selective reduction," they say. Just get rid of a few of them.

See, now wait a second.

I don't know! I don't know where I stand on these matters! And shouldn't someone be asking me? Shouldn't there be something in that big three-ring binder that helps guide me through some of these questions?

There is nothing. That's what gets me. There is *nothing*.

This is an industry. This is the fertility industry. This is the business of making humans. And there is nothing, absolutely nothing *human* about it.

This is what gets me.

And I have to pee so bad.

Anna.

The only thing that calms me down is thinking: *Anna*. And the feel of Alex's hand. I am lying on this table, and he is seated here up by my head, and he is holding my hand. I am so glad for this hand. And I am so glad for Anna. My baby. Wherever she is, somewhere in China, most likely not even born yet, which is quite beside the point. I feel her. I know her. She's waiting for me. Well, I'm coming! I'm coming, sweetheart!

Sweetheart.

A baby.

It's so human.

It's: air.

Anna.

The doctor comes in, finally. "Hello," he says. "I am so sorry to keep you waiting."

Well, that was nice. That was . . . human.

He is a puffy man with a full head of jet-black hair and a small ruby-red mouth. He wastes no time. Without pausing to chat or even to look at my face, he walks directly to the end of the table opposite my head, takes the chart from the nurse, lowers himself out of sight behind the sheets with which my knees are draped. "So, four," he says. "We are transferring four."

"Actually, we had some questions," Alex says, craning his neck to be seen.

"Yeah, we're not sure about—" I say.

"Oh, you have to put in four," the doctor says. "Oh my, yes. I would highly recommend—I mean, you didn't go through all of this to . . . dispose of them."

"Dispose," I say. "No, but there's the option to freeze—"

"Oh," he says. "I can't recommend that. We don't know how many will survive the freeze. You could easily lose two in a thaw. I'm telling you, you have to put in four."

"But—" I say.

"We don't want—" Alex says.

And the doctor stands up, looks at Alex, and then looks over at the clock on the wall. *He looks at the clock?!* He's got, what, a lunch date or something?

We're here trying to figure out what in God's name we're supposed to do, and we really mean in God's name, and this guy is looking at the damn clock, and I have to pee so bad I may vomit.

"So, okay, four?" the doctor says.

I think, *If I just say four, can I then go pee?*

We say four.

The procedure takes seconds.

I feel nothing.

Afterward the nurse prints out a picture of my uterus with the four embryos allegedly in it, which are not visible to the human eye. She says we should call in ten days for the pregnancy test. She types "GOOD LUCK!" on the bottom of the page and hands it to me as I rip it out of her hands and bolt off the table and race toward the bathroom door.

But it isn't the bathroom door. It's a closet. A damn closet. I am lost in The Land of My Own Wrong Turns.

CHAPTER ELEVEN

A-roo! A-roo! A-roo!"

That is one distinctive bark, that beagle bark. The beagle is off in the woods, chasing a scent again. Maybe a turkey? A fox? The point is, he's come to life. For his first few days and nights all he did was sleep soundly on that willow tree stump. Then, suddenly, he sprang to his feet, looked around and stretched, first his stubby front legs, then his back ones. There he stood, his tail wagging, his nose in the air as if sampling the smells of the wind, his little legs happy and free. It was like watching a wind-up toy that just got wound.

"A-roo! A-roo!"

"That is one enormously weird bark," I'm saying to Skippy. I'm down at the barn, brushing my dear mule on this cold January afternoon.

"A-roo! A-roo!"

If you didn't know that noise was coming from a dog you might wonder if it was coming from an animal at all. It sounds almost mechanical, industrial, like maybe the shrill sounds of a rig pumping oil from the ground, or the squeaking brakes of a runaway train.

It's been weeks and I have not yet found the dog's owner. No answers to my ad in the paper. I took his picture and gave it to Caroline. She had Sammy post it on the bulletin board. So far, no one recognizes the dog.

Wendy, one of my friends from the city, called to say she might be interested in adopting him if his owners are not located—she's always wanted a beagle, a beagle she imagined naming Fletch. But then when she came down to meet the dog, you could see the disappointment in her eyes. She liked him just fine, thought he was one adorable dog, but he was not, she said, Fletch. She stood on my porch smiling, but shaking her head. I said I understood. He's a hunting dog. Clearly, he's lived his life in the great outdoors. He's not even house-trained. He's just not a dog you'd see on the end of a leash prancing down a city street.

One thing Wendy did before she left, though, she came up with a name for the dog. It came to her, an inspiration. She said, "Sparky!" This was before he had finished with his rejuvenation sleep, this was when he was still just lying there, a snoozing lump.

"Sparky," I said. It was a good name, full of irony and mystery. And it stuck.

Sparky, Skippy, Sassy. It's getting a little hard to keep all these names straight. Too many "S" names on this farm. Definitely. Not that Sparky is staying.

I'm not opening my heart to Sparky. No. At least not any further than it's already opened. (Barely a crack.) Because I already have three dogs. So forget it. I'll find his owner or I'll find him a good home. That's the least and that's the most I can do.

There is not enough of me to go around. Not now, anyway. I mean, let's review. Four embryos. One baby on her way home from China.

Five. I am now, potentially, the mother of five. I am the

old woman who lives in the shoe with so many kids she doesn't know what to do.

"Five," I say to Skippy. His winter coat is like a luxurious tan blanket. It covers a stocky body that is pure power. I've got the brush just along the ridge under his mane, one of his sweet spots. He has a lot of sweet spots. What a sweet mule.

"Next year at this time, Skip, next year I may have five children so I probably won't have time to do this." Skippy appears to be listening, but I'm not sure the comprehension is there. He's staring straight ahead, blinking his huge, soft eyes slowly, sort of like a child does when his mother is breaking the bad news about going to the dentist.

Four embryos. I can't believe this.

Chances are slim, of course. But I shouldn't have let them put in four. I agreed to four only so I could go pee. That's no way to make a decision. That's like a sleep-deprived prisoner; pretty soon he'll agree to anything.

Right now I am filled with regret. Right now I think I made the wrong decision—all of it. I shouldn't have bothered redeeming my one-free-IVF coupon. I should have just said, "No thanks." Why didn't I just say, "No thanks"? I am not, after all, a woman who has spent her life longing to become pregnant. I am a mom in need of a child. And I can love any child. And I came to this motherhood role late, and so I came to it with what Mother Nature has to offer: an adopted child, or two, or three. Why didn't I just stay on that path, the path that felt so right? Why did I veer off onto this path?

Why?

Well, why *not*? What's so unusual about this? What's so unusual about wanting to have a baby?

I want to have a baby. That's the truth of it. I want to make a baby with Alex. Of course I do. Is that so abnormal?

Is that so wrong? Is that not the most natural thing in the world to want?

That is the most natural thing in the world to want. It's the whole reason the world is still even here. All those babies being born, all those species keeping themselves going.

Except mules. See, mules are sterile. "Skippy, I don't know if you can possibly understand any of this," I'm saying. Skippy will never father a child. Is he bothered by this? I suppose not. But I'm really not sure the comprehension is there.

"I just shouldn't have put in four," I say to him. "But I had to pee, Skip," I say. *"I was having hafta-pee psychosis."*

What do you do when you think you may have made a wrong turn and there is no chance to right it? What on earth do you do?

You brush a mule, that's what you do.

You get grounded back in the here-and-now.

You say to God, "Whoops." You say, "I think I may have taken a wrong turn." You hope He is a loving God. You hope He is listening. You hope the comprehension is there.

You pull at your mule's mane, untangle, and comb. You think: *Four.* And your heart goes *thump, thump, thump* with fear. And so you try, you force yourself back to your mule, back to the here-and-now, a time and a place that exist like a blip, like a soaring sparrow there is no way to climb aboard.

Chances are less than slim, of course. In fact, given my age, and fertility history, the odds are that none of the embryos have stuck. Zero. But the thing is, *four.* It is actually possible I am pregnant with quadruplets. I'll find out something tomorrow. Tomorrow I take the pregnancy test.

"The thing is," I'm saying, flipping Skippy's mane over. "If the choice is between having zero or four, I'm praying for zero." Because I can't . . . selectively reduce. I know myself, and I know I can't. Nor am I likely to be physically capable of carrying four babies. "If the choice is between having all of them stick, or none of them stick, then please let it be none."

It's good to talk to God through a mule. It takes the pressure off somehow.

"Please," I say into the crisp winter air. "Please don't let this happen." Please let me be a normal person, pregnant with just one.

Skippy's leaning his big head toward me. It's his way of saying "My ear, please. It is now time to scratch my ear." Mules are famous for their big ears, of course, and their ears are extremely sensitive, their ears are the key to their hearts. Earn the right to scratch a mule's ear, and you have really gotten somewhere.

Skippy likes it when I gently grab his ear with the tips of my fingers and rub it up and down, inside and out. See, he's lowering his head now, showing his trust. His head is now down by my knees.

Aroo! Aroo! Aroo!

Skippy doesn't even take note of the odd bark in the distance. Like the rest of us here at Sweetwater Farm, he's grown accustomed to it.

"Well, thanks for listening, Skippy. You want me to pick your hooves?" It's not his favorite grooming event, but it needs to be done. Our horses and mules have the run of perhaps twenty acres, and we always have to make sure that their feet don't pick up stones or thorns.

Just then Marley appears, prancing up and popping his nose through the barn gate. "Hey, Marley boy, what's up?" I say to him, even though I already know the answer. He's usually a few steps ahead of Alex. He has a way of announcing

Alex, like a bugle blaring, da-da da-da *dum*! Nothing like having a husband with a poodle heralding him.

"Sorry I didn't join you sooner, sweetie," Alex says, popping his head in. "Did you brush Maggie?"

"Nope. She's waiting for you."

"Good," he says. "I was talking to George on the phone."

"Oh?"

"Actually, it was Pat who called. She's stuck on the Food Network again."

"Oh, jeez." Ever since George and Pat redeemed the certificate we gave them for a free Dish Network satellite system, they've had problems. And every time they have a problem, they call me, which I don't mind, of course. It's just, well, what happened was, shortly after George got his system going, he got a certificate in the mail for a free satellite dish he might give to a friend (and it wasn't even his birthday), so George did, he gave it to a friend on Daniel's Run Road. And then, guess what? The guy on Daniel's Run Road got a certificate in the mail for a free satellite dish he might give to a friend, and let's just say this thing is catching on. Problem is, any time any of these people have a satellite dish question, they call the person who gave them the certificate for the free dish, and that person calls the person who gave it to him, and mostly it all funnels back to George or Pat, at which time George or Pat calls me for troubleshooting advice. Which I don't mind, of course. But I have to say the potential here is starting to scare me.

I'm "TV Girl." One of Pat's friends put it that way, she said, "Can you call that TV Girl for me?" And see, I don't want to be TV Girl. It's bad enough that I'm the one who brought the gift of Dish Network to Scenery Hill. This is not the reputation I had hoped for.

"Well, did you tell Pat I'd stop over later?" I say to Alex.

"Yep—and then George got on the phone and wanted to know if I saw *Who Wants to Be a Millionaire?* last night."

"Oh, God."

"I know."

"What have we done to George?"

"I know."

"He's turning into a couch potato!" Pretty soon he won't have any stories to tell. "I feel like I've brought a *disease* to Scenery Hill. I've ruined the place with TV!"

"I don't think it's that bad."

"Well, I feel bad," I say, bending over and tapping Skippy's front hoof. He surrenders it quickly, lifting it into my awaiting hand. "But Pat is not, I want you to know, stuck on the Food Network."

"No?"

"No, she just keeps setting up her Favorites menu wrong, to where all she puts on it is the Food Network."

"Well, I'm sure you'll set her straight."

"Yeah." I'm carving the mud out of Skippy's hoof, careful not to disturb the fleshy "frog" area. Who knew such big animals required such tender care? It makes you wonder how they did in the wild. Hmm.

"You nervous about tomorrow?" Alex asks.

"I was just talking to Skippy here about that," I say.

"Oh?"

"Skippy does not, for his part, want me to be a mother of five."

"Well, Skippy usually gets what he wants."

"I do want to be pregnant, though."

Alex looks at me. He's standing here picking out burrs from Maggie's tail. "That's the first time I've ever heard you actually say that out loud."

"I think it's the first time I ever did."

"Well, good for you."

"Well, I don't feel pregnant."

"I don't think you're supposed to feel anything yet."

"I think I should feel *something*. Maybe a craving for pickles. Or ice cream with anchovies."

"I think that only happens on TV," he says, as if TV Girl could possibly need any pointers. I'm finished with Skippy's hooves, so now I'm giving his rump a good scratch. His sweetest spot of all. His reward. He'd be drooling now, if mules drooled.

"I was wondering," Alex says. "Do you think we should have told that social worker you might be pregnant?"

"There was really nothing to tell," I say. "If the test is positive, I'll call and tell her then."

"It probably won't change anything."

"Well, if there's *four*—"

"There's not going to be four," he says.

"No."

"And I'm sure plenty of people get pregnant while doing adoption paperwork," he says. "I'm sure it happens all the time."

"I suppose. But probably a lot of people then stall the adoption, which we're not doing."

"No."

"Anna," I say.

"Anna," he says.

It's become a kind of password. A way of showing our commitment to bringing this baby home, no matter what happens.

Even so, I can't say I'd advise pursuing adoption and pregnancy at the same time. This is not a frenzy I would recommend to anyone. Right after we did the embryo transfer, I had to rush home and start organizing closets. The social worker was due for the first of our three home-study visits, and I was determined to have a clean house.

The morning of the visit, I cooked applesauce, I chopped up apples and added sugar and cinnamon in an attempt to fill the kitchen with the smell of Home. Then I worried that the smell might not make it all the way back to the family room, where we were going to sit for our little chat, so I went down to the basement and got a fan. I was plugging in the fan in the kitchen, aiming it at the back of the house, when Alex came in and said, "What in the world are you doing?" And I explained about the smell, about the *reach,* and he told me to sit down and he unplugged the fan and he rolled up the cord and he took the fan back downstairs.

I was nervous! I'd never been visited by a social worker before. I'd never had to put my domestic self out for review. It is not my most developed self. My inner Martha Stewart is not what you'd call a fully actualized identity.

And I had the cosmic complexity of four embryos inside me to worry about.

And it was raining.

And so the social worker pulled up in her white car, and that white car was covered in mud from our driveway, and I sat there looking out the window, filled with mud regret like gravy on top of my embryo regret, and I watched her walk up the walk through the rain, watched her feet dance around the puddles. She had short hair and a bright blue coat and friendly shoulders, and the moment she got in the house I began my apologies. For the rain. For the gray sky. For the ruts on Wilson Road. For the way the kitchen is not yet renovated. For the lightbulb that is out on the porch. For the way the cat sleeps on the satellite dish receiver despite the fact that I have provided him with a perfectly good cat bed.

"You seem nervous," she said. "Please don't be. This is

not an investigation. This is a . . . warm-and-fuzzy. You know? I'm just here to help you bring your daughter home."

And right then and there I calmed down.

"Anna," I said. "We're going to name her Anna."

"Let's sit down and talk about Anna, shall we?" she said.

And everything, all the worry and regret and anxiety, it all went away in an instant, if only for an afternoon. Anna. Anna has been my air. Anna has been my rock. The social worker stayed for a few hours, asking us questions about everything from our childhoods to our views on parenting. Afterward Alex said I did great, and I told him he did great, too. Well, we passed.

Back here in the barn, as we begin to put away our mule- and horse-grooming stuff, I tell Alex that I'm taking Sparky to the Humane Society tomorrow.

"Oh?"

"The one up in Washington," I say. "I called. It's a no-kill shelter. They said they'd take him. He'll have a much better chance of finding a home from there."

"Oh," Alex says, looking off into the woods, where the beagle's odd bark is still filling the valley. He seems almost disappointed. But I could very well be projecting that.

A-roo! A-roo! A-roo!

The squeaking brakes of a runaway train. Definitely.

IT'S FRIDAY. THEY said they'd call with the results of the pregnancy test sometime after three o'clock.

It's noon now. Three o'clock. Then it will be official.

In the meantime I figured I'd get the unofficial results. On the box it says this home pregnancy test is ninety-nine percent accurate, so I'm giving it a try, I'm going for the sneak preview, I'm peeing on a stick, I'm peeing for five seconds on the Wide Absorbent Tip.

Blue line means no, blue line plus pink line means yes. In three minutes. The directions say wait three minutes.

I go into the other room to put on the TV, because three minutes is a long time to wait, and you'll see a pink line in anything if you look hard enough at it.

On TV a man is cooking eggs. That's funny. That's funny for a number of reasons. First of all, how come my TV is on the Food Network? I never watch the Food Network. It's Pat's favorite channel. Could her remote somehow be in cahoots with my receiver? No. For heaven's sake. Come on, TV Girl, don't get paranoid.

But—*eggs*? Oh, for heaven's sake. He's whipping up an omelet. Poor eggs. Poor chickens. All those poor chickens. I am glad I'm not a chicken. Eggs. This is my year of eggs.

Has it been three minutes? Probably. But maybe not. Let's just sit here patiently and see what he's going to do with these sautéed mushrooms.

Duh.

He's going to throw them in the eggs.

I don't really know why the Food Network is so popular. Seems like a lot of predictable story lines to me. Then again, maybe it's not a very popular channel. Maybe it's just Pat. And she has George with all those stories to entertain her. Or she did. I've ruined George. He's probably discovered *Wheel of Fortune* by now.

My brain is kind of idling in neutral here. Is it three minutes? I'm sure it's three minutes. What-*ever*. Well, I have to go look. I've given my ovaries one good fighting chance. I've given God all the help I could muster. Maybe too much help.

But I want the pink line to be there. I want it just like all those people in the waiting room at the fertility clinic wanted it, the waiting room with the big fish tank with all those beautiful, bored fish.

So here we go.

Okay.

Um . . .

The pink line isn't there. But the blue line isn't either. What the hell does that mean? Blue line in square window means no, blue line plus pink line in round window means yes. But what about no lines in no windows?

Blank. Just . . . blank. That's all I'm left with.

I can't believe this.

I go back to the Food Network. I plop myself on the couch and watch the man drop parsley sprigs on his omelet. What a fine omelet. Yes, indeed.

I could run out and get another home pregnancy test. Maybe that one was defective? Maybe the Wide Absorbent Tip didn't absorb? Well, never mind. The clinic is going to call me after three. I can wait until three. Three hours. No big deal.

I have work to do. I have a lot of adoption paperwork to do. I have bills to pay. I have an awful lot to do. I have to take Sparky to the Humane Society. Is he even around? I look outside. Oh, that is so cute. He's curled up with Wilma on the porch. He's got his beagle head resting on Wilma's substantial hip. That is so cute. I go out to the porch.

"Hey, Spark," I say. "Maybe I should give you a bath before you go."

He looks at me. He looks at me with his droopy eyes as if to say, "Well, that's profoundly stupid." And "You don't think I'm going to get pretty stinked up pretty fast at the pound?"

Yeah, but. "If you start out smelling clean and looking

good, you'll have a better chance," I say. Oh, he'll make someone a fine pet. I wonder if I have to disclose the fact that he's not house-trained.

"Come on, Spark. Let's get you all cleaned up, okay?"

I lead him to the basement and lift him, ugh, into the laundry tub. God, for a little beagle he weighs a ton. "Looks can be deceiving, Spark. You are one densely muscled canine."

I wonder if this dog has ever had a bath. He doesn't seem to mind the water. He's got his tongue out, trying to lap it up as it pours out of the faucet.

"Pee-you!" I'm saying. "You stink, Spark. Whew! Just what is it that you roll around in out there in those woods?"

I hope this shampoo is strong enough to de-stink a dog that stinks this bad. I'll bet his coat will come up shiny, though. I'm scrubbing. I'm getting a good lather here. Sparky has his eyes closed, he's limp as a water balloon here in this tub, totally surrendering to the beauty treatment. "Good for you, boy. Good for you."

What a sweet dog. You can learn a lot from a dog like this. This is one serene dog. This is a dog that has surrendered.

I wonder why surrender is so difficult. I wonder why we have to yank and pull and push at life to behave *our* way. Maybe we can't help it. Maybe it's the essence of our human-ness. It's the little bit of God in all of us.

I'm standing here fighting it. I'm standing here fighting my own human-ness.

Well, I suppose surrender isn't surrender if it's a fight.

This is so messed up.

It's better to be dumb. It's better to be a dumb dog limp as a water balloon in a laundry tub. It's a more honest life.

I've rinsed Sparky about six times here, and I guess this is as good as he's going to get. He'll smell better once he's dry, I'm sure. Wet-dog smell is not good under the best of circumstances. "Pee-you!" I've got him out of the tub, on the floor, and I'm trying to get as much of this water out of him as possible because I know as soon as I let go, he's gonna do a dog shake.

"Okay, boy," I say. "Feel better?" I take the towel away. He looks around, moves one step forward and then . . . *wap, wap, wap, wap!* His long ears fly back and forth as he shakes, flying like he's some kind of doggy helicopter readying for takeoff.

When he stops, he stands here with his shoulders hunched up and his tail between his legs and an expression that says, "What in God's name just happened to me?" or maybe "Where are all those good smells I collected?"

"Down the drain, Sparky," I say. "A lot of you just went down the drain. But trust me on this one, okay? It's better. It's better."

It's cold out so I'm not about to put him back on the porch, plus I don't want to risk him rolling in more stinky stuff, so I find Marley's old dog crate. I bring it upstairs to my office, throw a blanket in. "Here you go, boy," I say. "You stay here." He enters the crate with little fuss. He curls up on the blanket. He seems to like it just fine.

EVEN THOUGH THEY said "after three," I was sort of expecting the phone to ring at three o'clock on the dot. Which it did not. It's now four o'clock. This is ridiculous. How long does it take to read a damn pregnancy test? I get out my three-ring binder, look up the number, and call.

I am put on hold.

I am on hold for several minutes.

"Well, we have nothing here," the nurse says when she finally gets back on the phone. "The lab was supposed to fax us, but it looks like they didn't."

"Well, why not?"

"Well, I have no idea," she says. "Why don't you call them and ask?"

Jeez.

She gives me the number. I dial. I get a recording saying the lab is out to lunch. At four o'clock? I call the clinic back.

"Oh, they must be closed for the day," she says. "I guess we won't know till Monday then. They're not there on weekends."

Hang on a second. Everyone just hang the hell on. I tell the woman. I tell her, woman-to-woman, I say, Look, *I really need to know.*

She gives me another phone number for the lab.

So I call that number. A woman answers. I let out a big sigh. I ask her if she has my test results. I can hear her rustling through papers. "Oh, here you are," she says. "Yes, this is you."

I ask her to please tell me what the results say.

"Oh, I can't do that," she says. "It has to go to the doctor."

I am now sweating. I am actually sweating.

"Fax it," I say. "Fax it to the clinic, please."

"We already did," she says. "I don't know why they're saying they don't have it."

"Fax it again," I say. "Please fax it again."

I call the clinic back. "They will fax it again," I say. "Please call me with the results as soon as you get them, okay? Could you do that for me? Could you please?"

"There is something coming through right now," she says. "There is a fax coming through right now."

"Oh."

"This is you," she says. "Yes, I think this is you."

"Oh."

"And it's . . ."

"Yes?"

"No," she says. "It's—well, it's, I mean that's a very low number. Very low."

"Well—maybe I just need to stay on the progesterone for a few more days," I say meekly.

"No," she says. "If the number is this low by day fourteen, I'm afraid it's no. Definitely no."

I hang up.

My stomach is big and hollow and low.

I sit down.

I look at Sparky. He's sound asleep. In fact, he's snoring.

"It's no," I say to him. "The answer is no."

I call Alex. I tell him it's no.

"No, as in zero?" he says.

"Zero," I say.

"Oh, I'm so sorry."

"At least it's not four. I've been saying for days now that zero is better than four."

"Right."

"It's okay. I'm okay. Really. It's no big deal." I tell him I have to go.

"I'm coming home," he says. "I'll be home in about an hour."

"Good, then."

"Would you like to go out to dinner?"

"We'll see. I'm going to go take Sparky to the pound now. I could use the drive."

"Oh, sweetie, I don't think—"

"I gave him a bath," I say. "He really looks great."

"I don't think you should take him today—"

"You think I should put a red bow on him or something?"

"Honey, I really don't think—"

"I'm not putting that dirty collar back on, if that's what you're suggesting. I gotta go. Hurry home, okay?"

"All right."

"Bye-bye. I love you."

I put a red bow on Sparky. Oh, he looks divine! He looks like he's going to a red tie event! You know, now that he's all cleaned up, he looks a lot younger. I don't think he's nearly as old as we thought he was.

He rides in the front seat, beside me. He's a remarkably calm car dog. He really does not seem to mind much in life.

"Sparky, I think I am going to have to disclose the information about your not being house-trained," I'm saying as we head together down Route 40. "Because if your new owners don't know, and then you pee on their carpet, it won't go well for you, you know. It just won't."

He doesn't, naturally, say anything.

And I am, naturally, okay. Unnaturally? I am remarkably okay. Zero is better than four. I am a thousand times relieved that it's zero instead of four. I really am. I am so . . . okay!

"But I'm sorry, Anna," I'm saying. "I was thinking perhaps I could make you a brother or sister. I was really thinking I could. But it appears I can't. And I'm sorry, sweetie."

Sweetie.

And why is everything getting so blurry?

The thing is, I am not *one hundred* percent okay. But I am like my mother. I have the knack. Don't I? I can spin misery into a lesson, tragedy into a tool for learning.

The knack. I should have asked my mother about the knack. Where did she get it? Um, I thought I had it.

I don't think I have it.

No, I'm quite sure I don't.

I need to pull over. I need to pull over right now. I am looking for a place to pull over. I skid into the entrance of an old coal mine, feel the car drop into a pothole, then another, and then, finally, stop. Stop.

I just need to breathe. I just need to know. I just need to breathe. I just need to ask: *Why?* Why didn't they stick? Why didn't *any* of them stick? What's the *matter* with me?

I lower my head onto the steering wheel. And it's here, outside an abandoned coal mine, sitting in a car next to a beagle wearing a bright red bow, that I sob the sob of a lifetime.

In the end, I turn the car around and take Sparky home. It's too much good-bye for one person. It just is. I am taking Sparky home.

III

HUGGING THE WIND

Chapter Twelve

One thing I think is: Don't look back. I get this from my mother. Growing up I'd hear her say, "Who has *time* for yesterday?" with a wave of her arm. "I'm too busy with today."

I don't know what yesterdays she was trying to forget. But in general I'm pro-forgetting. I mean, if what you're trying to do is learn how to be present in the moment, one of the easiest things you can do is just dump history.

It's November, more than a year and a half since my mom succumbed to GBS, and so naturally I'm hearing a lot of her don't-look-back rhetoric these days. She's mostly recovered, still receives outpatient therapy; they say she may always have some degree of numbness and tingling in her toes. Her walk is not, and never will again be, the forceful *clip* CLOP it once was. It's more of a *plop, plop* now, over the white carpet of Riddle Village. Her feet, she says, sometimes feel like dead flounders. But with a cane she can get around just fine. She's already accumulated a small collection of canes, including a colorful cloisonné one my dad got her from the Smithsonian catalog. The knack: She can turn canes from symbols of disability into a hobby.

And so she is not looking back. Last night on the phone she told me, she said, "Just because I survived this stupid disease doesn't mean I have to define myself in terms of it." She said, "I am not going to keep reliving the darn thing."

"No," I said.

"I am not a re-liver," she said.

"No, you are not," I said.

She said she's done with GBS. Just . . . done. "Nothing more to say. It's time to go *forward*. That's me, I'm a moving-forward kind of person."

"Yes, you are," I said, because I believe her. Or I want to.

And I'm a here-and-now kind of person. Or I'm trying to be. My mother is a help. A mother's example is a kind of permission. A mother's example gets hardwired into you. My mother's example, I think, virtually assured that I wouldn't end up an emotional lingerer, a pouter, a moper.

But I don't think it was just her indelible sway that helped me let go of the events of last spring—the sadness over the discovery that I probably would never carry a child. There was, of course, now another influence. Anna. I had a baby to think about, a little girl somewhere in China to pray for and shop for and worry a mother's worry over.

I love the bookend effect of all this. My mother on one side, my daughter on the other. The two of them holding me in their embrace while I grieved what I had to grieve.

Eventually, the fact that a baby wasn't growing inside me became just that: a fact. A fact that came to separate itself from emotion, like a moth after the light goes out. A fact of my life. But not a fact that would define my life.

We are, each of us, managers of our own memory. There really are choices we make.

But I am making this sound too simple. There is, of course, more to the story. There is probably always more to the story.

The truth is, you can't just dump history. You can't. History leaves scars. History is what moved you from then and there to here-and-now. History leaves skid marks.

I can see them in my mother's story—the leftover stuff she doesn't talk about. You know, before GBS, she knew herself to be an artist. She had worked and worked at becoming an accomplished painter. The paralysis hit, and so of course she couldn't paint. And as she struggled to regain control of her body, painting hardly seemed to matter. But now her body is back. So . . . where is the painter? She hasn't even taken her brushes out of the boxes we put them in when we helped move my parents to Riddle Village. Her easel sits collapsed in the corner of the spare bedroom.

Collapsed.

When I broached the subject recently, she said, "Forget it." She said she's probably done with painting. She said it's just not important to her anymore.

The disease robbed her of her art?

That seems like a pretty serious scar. Why is she not struggling with this? Is she struggling with it? Perhaps, for her, it's something that comes up only briefly, in those moments between sleep and wake, those tiny blasts of consciousness you do your best to ignore.

As for me, I suppose my recent history has left plenty of skid marks worth noting and tracking and calculating. And I suppose one day I may recognize them. But right now, in these moments, I can't see any at all. I am not looking back.

Right now, in this moment, I think: Hey, I got a dog out of the deal. Sparky. He's doing great. Almost too great, actually. He's house-trained now, although he's having some trouble understanding house rules. He sleeps on the bed, on the couch, anywhere he feels like—just the other day I found that he had figured out a way to climb up, and was now sleeping on, Alex's brand-new, beautiful mahogany pool table.

(Indeed, the pool table has moved out of the realm of abstract notion and into, well, pool table.) Sparky was curled up right there by the eleven ball, poised as it was to drop into the corner pocket. "Spark!" I screamed, waking him, and he jumped down. I said, "The *pool table*?" And he had a look of "Well, I didn't *know*." Pretty much the same look he had when I found him sitting *on* the dining room table eating a hamburger—a hamburger I had let out of my sight only so as to locate some pickles, and I came back with the pickles and there was Sparky. "Spark!" He had that same look. A look of "What? You mean, *I'm wrong*?"

See, he really doesn't know. How is a dog that has spent his entire life thus far roaming the great outdoors supposed to understand boundaries and ownership and entitlement?

More to the point: How is it that Sparky ended up belonging, really belonging, here at Sweetwater Farm? I mean, isn't that strange? *Here?* He's part of this family? Sometimes I just sit around and wonder just how exactly that happened.

Sometimes I think this whole thing, this whole journey to motherhood I'm on, it's all about belonging. The formation of a family—however you define the family unit. It's all about belonging. And the more I figure out about belonging, the more I realize I can't figure it out at all. How does anybody end up belonging where they belong? Is it really all a random mess? Are we really just a bunch of helium balloons floating in the wind, waiting to land? Do we belong nowhere until we simply land somewhere?

Okay, let's say we do. Let's say that's how it works. Well then, who or what controls the wind?

I need to get to the bottom of this. Or the top of it. The truth is, I don't want to be a helium balloon floating in the wind, and I don't want Alex to be a helium balloon floating in the wind, and mostly I don't want Anna to be a helium balloon floating in the wind. I want to know that this family that is about to happen is about to happen for a reason. That it is inevitable. Maybe anyone who adopts a baby has this question, in some form, at her core. How will you know that this baby really belongs to you?

Okay, this may be a stupid example. Well, I suppose holding a beagle up as an example is no more stupid than holding a Chihuahua up. But I have to say, I don't think Sparky was a random accident. I think of Sparky as a kind of bumbling, stinky angel. You know, just a dog. But a dog that ended up filling a most urgent vacancy in my heart. He came into my life when I didn't need him, couldn't even deal with him, and then he turned out to be right there in the seat beside me, with a red bow around his neck, when my heart was breaking. I needed him more than I knew.

I suppose the stinky-angel identity is another reason Sparky tends to get preferred treatment around here. But still, you can't let your dog sleep on your husband's pool table. You just can't. There are limits.

The pool table arrived on September 22. It was Alex's birthday present. Of course it was. Why was he so surprised? I really don't think he was expecting it; we'd been living on a tight budget, saving every extra nickel for the adoption. But I figured, well, what are credit cards *for*? So of course I did it. I wanted to make Alex the happiest man alive, seeing as he was making me the happiest woman alive by agreeing to parent a child with me.

That's the thing about love. The more you get, the more you have to give, and the more you give, the more you get. It is just a straight get-give-get-give equation. No subtraction necessary, no division. Love is particularly easy on those of us who are bad at math.

For my forty-first birthday, Alex surprised me with a

stroller. A fancy model with thick-treaded tires designed for use over rough terrain such as our dirt road. The SUV of strollers. How thrilling it was. What a symbol of motherhood! I put Sparky in it, just to try it out. He seemed to like it. Maybe too much. I think he believes that part of what it is to live in a family is you get to ride in a cushioned chariot.

For now, I let him believe. I can use the strolling practice anyway. Once each day we stroll, me and Sparky, down the driveway. Sometimes we go left to the mailbox, and sometimes we go right to visit the old lady. The old lady greets us as if there is nothing at all unusual about taking a beagle for a walk in a stroller. See why I like her? It doesn't even occur to her to comment.

I've grown to love this new version of my walks in the country. I love the feel of pushing a baby down a bumpy road. I love being . . . attached to something. It's somewhat like holding hands with the love of your life, only with more responsibility. You're not just attached, you're steering, you're watching out for ruts and puddles and worms.

"I think I'm going to like this parenthood thing," I said to Sparky the other day as we avoided a rut or a puddle or a worm. He was sound asleep, his chin resting on the front tray. I had the most profound urge to pick him up and burp him.

See, that's not good. It's definitely not good to get an urge to burp your beagle. And I made a mental note to go home and start working on remembering that you burp babies, not beagles.

And so. There you have pretty much the sum total of my parenting thoughts thus far. Burping is for babies, not beagles. And see, that's not good. Definitely not good. I should be . . . preparing for parenthood. Why am I not preparing? I haven't much thought about what kind of parent I'll be. I haven't thought once about what my philosophy of discipline might be, nor have I taken a firm stance on sugar consumption. I haven't, for that matter, thought about what will happen to my marriage when Alex and I become parents together. How will our little love fest change with the presence of a new, constant companion? I haven't even begun to plan for the larger, most serious challenges of raising a child born of another ethnic heritage, raising her with an awareness of a cultural identity I know so little about.

Then again, I haven't thought about what I'm going to have for dinner three weeks from now, or how I'm going to digest it.

You can get too far ahead of yourself. That's what I think. The future is a place inhabited mostly by dragons that have as good a chance of being friendly as foe—so why slay them now? That's the way I look at it. You know: Don't look forward. Anti-anticipation, that's me. Yep. Pro-forgetting and anti-anticipation. Wedge yourself in the here-and-now. At least this is what I'm trying to do.

Coping with the idea of something really huge looming on the horizon of your life is often just a matter of turning off that imagination. Off!

Anna. Must go get Anna. Must go to China and get Anna. I've been containing most of my anxiety right here in that thought, which is plenty big.

We're expecting to hear from the adoption agency any day. If all goes as planned, this next call will be one hundred percent good news: "Congratulations! Here she is! Here is Anna!" Something like that. In adoption lingo, it's called the referral. It's the big moment of truth. You find out who your baby is, where she is living. You get a medical report and a photo. You can reject a referral, but people almost never do. Most people see the picture, and they're goners. The adoptive parents I've spoken to describe receiving the referral in similar terms to those that a woman giving birth might. A baby is handed to you. You fall in love. There's a pull no one can possibly understand until they feel it. That's what they say. I can only go by what they say.

Many people adopting from China like to speculate about what happens in the Matching Room, the actual office where all the files are: a pile of paperwork about prospective adoptive parents over here, a pile of paperwork about babies available for adoption over there. Who goes with whom? How do they decide? And how is it that these matches end up being so utterly perfect? That's what everyone ends up saying: "This is the perfect child for me!"

How can it happen over and over again? Is there some Chinese mystic on hand in the Matching Room, a skinny old wizard with a long beard rubbing sacred stones, receiving messages from the ancestors? Or is it just some clerk blindly filling out forms, matching the baby on top of one pile with the parents on top of another? Or something else?

As I sit and wait for Anna, wait for the call in which her identity will be revealed, I find that no matter what stance I take, no matter how anti-this or pro-that I become, no matter how good I am at containing my anxiety, I really can't stop doubt from slipping in. I wonder about belonging. I wonder: How does it happen? How does the bond between mother and daughter happen?

And what if it doesn't.

THIS MORNING, UNLIKE most recent mornings, I am not sitting by the phone waiting for the call. This morning we are having some technical difficulties here at Sweetwater Farm.

Skippy.

Where is Skippy?

Alex and I are standing high on the ridge overlooking George's farm, and we have our hands on our brows so as to help with long-distance viewing, and all I can say is, it's a good thing I put an orange scarf on Skippy. It will be easier to spot a mule dressed in orange.

We see sheep. We see cows. No mule.

"I can't believe this," I say.

"This is not good," Alex agrees.

"You think he's been shot, don't you?"

"I did not say that."

Today is Monday, the first Monday after Thanksgiving. Translation: Today is opening day of hunting season. Around here it's a *holiday*. Kids get the day off from school. This is a day for the family to be together, load their rifles, and— *pow!*—kill remarkably beautiful animals.

What a day for your mule to run away.

When I awoke this morning, I looked outside and did my usual equine roll call: "Horse, horse, mule, mule." Except this morning I said, "Horse, horse, mule . . . mule?" So then I got Alex up, and we put on our mud boots and the blaze-orange hats we have learned to always wear during hunting season, and we headed out to see where Skippy might have wandered off to. Apparently, a frightened deer came bounding through our fields and ripped down the electric fence, and Skippy took advantage of the opportunity. Cricket, Maggie, and Sassy are not intelligent enough to figure something like this out. But Skippy, as I may have mentioned, is gifted.

"Well, it looks like he didn't head north," Alex says, squinting in the morning sun.

"Not unless he went *really* north," I say.

I cup my mouth, yell, "Heeeey, SKIP!" into the hills. "Mama's here! Heeeey, SKIP! Come to Mama!"

Nothing.

"See, we should have made sure he had a cell phone," I say to Alex.

"Or at least a beeper," he says.

We are decidedly and uncomfortably low-tech. We are up on this ridge, high above civilization, and with little use for what civilization has to offer. We are two people with a lead rope and a bag of carrots.

We've never lost a mule before, and we don't know what to do.

"Well, it's a good thing you put the orange scarf on," Alex says.

"Yeah," I say. "And see, you thought that was crazy of me."

"I did not!"

"Well, you were *laughing*."

"I was laughing at *Skippy*," he says. "It was the first time I'd ever seen him in a . . . babushka."

"Yeah. He seemed to like it, though."

"Yeah."

"You think someone shot him?"

"No," Alex says. "No, I do not."

Skippy is, vaguely, the color of a deer. But he's the size of a moose. I put the orange scarf on so as to offer a helpful hint to any confused hunter walking by our property. (Hey, George put orange tape on his llamas one year.) We don't allow hunting—we have signs posted everywhere—but some hunters do get confused.

"See, now I think maybe he took it as some kind of permission," I say to Alex.

"Huh?"

"Maybe Skippy thought I was putting the orange on him

so he could go and hang out with the hunters. Do you think that's possible?"

Alex looks at me with the uncomfortable look you reserve for, say, a lunatic. "No," he says. "No, I do not think that's possible."

I let out a big sigh.

"Honey, he's safe," he says. "No hunter is going to aim at something with blaze orange on it. You know that."

"Yeah, I know."

I cup my mouth, yell, "Hey, SKIP!"

"Heeeey, SKIP!"

Nothing.

Nothing except two hunters waving at us from up over the rise on George's side of the fence. Hello! Hello! It's like seeing the rescue team arrive.

It's orange and, wow, *orange*. Sometimes the orange on these orange outfits is so bright, it's hard to make out any of the details of the person wearing them. But soon enough I recognize them: Joe and his son Joey. We know them well. In fact, Joe and Joey were the first people I met the day we moved to the farm three years ago. As it happened, moving day was opening day of hunting season. There I was just innocently walking with Betty to the mailbox, hum dee dum. And then, just like today, I came upon two guys all done up in bright orange. They introduced themselves. They were nice enough. Mostly they were concerned that I was wandering around without an orange hat on. They were pretty adamant about the hat thing.

"Um," I said. "I don't have an orange hat."

"You don't *have* one?" Joe asked.

But I was busy with my own culture shock. I'm supposed to have an orange hat? Here I was moving to the country, to the land of fresh air and sunshine, and I had to be wary of gunfire? I couldn't wander around on my own property without worrying about getting shot? Wasn't this more of an urban-type worry?

I remember going home and telling Alex. He was busy talking to a man about how to stop the driveway from washing away, and also how to save the barn from collapsing. I remember we sat and talked about the gunfire. Oh, there were so many facts of country living smacking us in the face in just our very first few hours of country living. "How hard can it be?" That had been our motto. Now it was more like: "Help!"

A few days later Joe and Joey showed up at our house bearing gifts: two orange hats and a package of fresh venison. Well, that was . . . sweet. The hats were big, foamy polyester caps bearing the insignia of Hoss's Family Restaurant. These are the hats we still wear for two weeks each year, beginning with the Monday after Thanksgiving. These are the hats we are wearing today, as we greet Joe and Joey on our hill.

"Hey!" I say to them.

Joe is all smiles. He's tall and handsome in a boxy Eastern European way, with a square head and chiseled features I've always found to be particularly beautiful. Like if you were a sculptor, you probably couldn't resist doing a sculpture of that head.

"What are you two doing out here?" Joe says.

"Oh, we just shot a twelve point!" I say.

He laughs. He knows me well enough by now to know how preposterous the claim is. "And I suppose you sighted him from five hundred yards," he says.

"A *thousand,*" Alex says. See, it would be good if he could spit some tobacco juice at this moment. But, well, he can't.

"Amazing," says Joey with a wide grin. He looks nothing

like his father. He's smaller, and tidier, with the neat black beard of an Englishman.

That's the thing about Joe and Joey; I like them. I consider them friends. And isn't that amazing? I've befriended two . . . hunters?

One day a few years ago I got the nerve to say, "I really don't get the whole dead deer thing, guys." I told them about my experiences as a teenager with the deer at Springton Lake. I told them about how I took it upon myself to scare the deer, to teach them to never trust a human, thanks to humans like them. I told them I felt angry about the rift they had created between man and animal. I was prepared for a debate.

Joe and Joey tried to explain. About meat. About being out in the woods. About the thrill of the hunt. But I still didn't get it.

So I told them, I said, "I'll never get it." And that was when Joe invited me to go hunting with him. "Maybe you'll appreciate it," he said. I told him I doubted it. But at the same time I was curious. No, of course I didn't want to shoot anything. I didn't even want to hold a gun. But I wanted to understand. And I didn't want to be accused of being judgmental about something I really knew nothing about. So last year I did it. I went through an entire hunting season with Joe and Joey. I sat in the woods with them for two freezing cold weeks, waiting for a deer to come by, trying to understand. It felt like an enormous personal challenge. Like a Muslim taking Holy Communion maybe, or a cat deciding to learn how to swim.

The pleasure of killing. I didn't get how two gentle people like Joe and Joey, two kind-hearted characters with nothing but goodwill on their minds—two guys I had really come to like—could aim a gun at one of God's innocent creatures and steal its life.

So I sat there in the woods, mostly with Joe. Joey would often be on foot, walking the trails and driving the deer toward his father. At least that was the plan. After two weeks of this, Joe and Joey killed not one deer. "This is ridiculous!" Joe said. They are avid hunters; they had killed antelope in Montana and bear in Alaska and elk in Canada. And here at home, during deer season, they always got at least one deer each.

But this. This was an off year.

It was weird the way I felt bad for them on that last day. Even though I felt good for the deer. It was hard to reconcile all of this. But I told them, I said, "I'm really sorry you didn't get anything."

"Well, that's deer season," Joe said, with a shake of his head. "It's really not about killing."

Now I really didn't get it.

He was rubbing a rag over his rifle. "It's more about loving the deer," he said.

"Loving?" I said. "Killing something you love?"

He tried to explain, but the words fell flat.

Like so many words you hear, only the echo made sense. Some words you have to just sit and wonder and wonder about before you can hear. Killing something you love? Joe said it was about nature, about loving nature, a most primitive form of love.

I came to understand that the hunter, through the act of killing, becomes a part of nature. He becomes a hawk or a mountain lion or a robin yanking a worm out of the ground. He becomes the animal side of man. He is bound by a covenant between man and animal that is as old as man and animal itself. Killing the animal is not a personal act. It's a ritual act. You participate in the death of the animal whose meat becomes your life and whose death you have brought about. The ritual links you to the larger truth, the larger organism. The ritual allows you to recognize that you are of nature, an organ of the larger organism.

I came to understand. The understanding did not, of course, make me want to hunt. It didn't convert me. But it was understanding, all the same.

The thing about understanding is, it opens the floodgate of forgiveness. I felt so much easier about my friendship with Joe and Joey after that.

So now here we are, with Joe and Joey on this hill. "Either of you get your deer yet?" Alex says to them.

"We saw a six point," says Joey. "Couldn't get a shot at it."

"Aw," I say. But see, they know I'm still rooting for the deer.

"So what the heck are you doing out here?" Joe says again. "Is there a problem?"

"Funny you should ask," I say.

"You seen a mule around?" Alex asks.

"He's wearing an orange scarf," I say.

"You know, I did see something peculiar this morning," Joe says. "It was like around daybreak." He says it was foggy, far away, hard to see. But it looked to him like a man in orange chasing a school bus. "But then I noticed that it couldn't have been a man, because it had four legs."

"A mule wearing an orange scarf perhaps?" I say.

"Could be!" he says. And then he points. "He went that-away."

So Alex and I say good-bye to Joe and Joey, wish them luck, and head back home. We get in our truck, head that-away on Spring Valley Road, which is where we spot Debbie, the mail lady, coming toward us in her little white car with the flashing yellow strobe light on top. Her car is roaring loud as a Harley. We wave her down, tell her our problem. "They were just talking about that up at the hardware store!" she yells over the motor, explaining that she was in the hardware store to get some wire to hold up her muffler. She's looking up at us from her car, holding her hand raised to block out the morning sun. "The guys in the store were talking about a mule wearing orange," she says. "I didn't get the whole story."

We thank Debbie and head to the hardware store. We wonder why on earth Skippy would go to the hardware store, let alone chase a school bus.

When we get to the store, Jim, the hardware guy, says, "Oh, is that your mule?" He says Joe the trapper, no relation to Joe and Joey the hunters, was just in buying parts for his coyote traps, and he talked about seeing a loose mule down at Sam's sheep farm. Sam has the farm just over the ridge from George's. "Those coyotes killed two more of Sam's ewes this week," Jim says. "Hard to know why they pick on Sam the most of anybody around."

We thank Jim and then head to Sam's, and we are beginning to feel like characters in a Winnie the Pooh story, yanked this way and that. When we pull up to the sheep farm, we see Skippy standing there with Sam, a skinny man in a cowboy hat, who has him on a rope. "That's our mule," I say.

"Well, here you go," Sam says. "He was eating the corn I had stored up."

"Sorry about that."

"He might have a bellyache," he says.

"Oh, Skip," I say. He appears neither happy nor sad to see me. He appears to be processing some important mule matters in his head. He's smacking his lips, looking left.

I walk up, stroke his soft pink nose. "We're going home, boy," I say. "Adventure's over."

It's funny to think about how circular all of this is. If it weren't for the hunters scaring the deer, the deer wouldn't have knocked a hole in the fence, and Skippy wouldn't have gotten out. And if it weren't for the coyotes, which were introduced into the area to control the deer population, Joe the trapper wouldn't have been up at the hardware store buying traps on behalf of Sam. Well, if it weren't for the fact that the coyotes long ago figured out that sheep are a heck of a lot easier to catch than deer, which is why we still have so many deer, which is why the hunters are allowed to hunt. And if it weren't for Debbie's muffler dropping off . . .

"It's probably easier to send a satellite into space than to work all that out on purpose," I say to Alex.

"It's probably easier to teach a mule how to use a cell phone," he says.

"Come on, Skip," I say, snapping the lead rope on his halter. Alex gets into the truck. "I'll see you back at the house," I say to him, and we both say good-bye to Sam, thanking him for his kindness.

And so Skippy and I head across Spring Valley Road, then onto George's field. It's pretty muddy, and Skippy's hooves pierce the ground like giant pencils in clay. "Watch your step, Skip," I say, and soon enough I am reviewing with him matters of the hunter being connected to the deer connected to the coyote connected to the trapper connected to the hardware store connected to Debbie the mail lady. "It's like the knee bone is connected to the thigh bone and the thigh bone is connected to the hip bone," I say to him.

"You know what, Skip," I say. "Maybe that's it. Maybe everything is connected."

Maybe it's not all random. It's not just some wind blowing. Everything's connected. You just don't get to see the blueprint most of the time.

★   ★   ★

OUT MY WINDOW I now see: horse, horse, mule, mule. And I see that the birch tree has finally let go of its last leaves; winter is closing in.

In these ways, everything is back to normal—again. Boy, normal sure doesn't stick around long. Normal, I think, is like a series of blips. Or normal is like a string of stepping-stones. I think some people create lives with the stones all nice and close together, barely any weeds or briars to negotiate as they walk. And then there are the rest of us. We could perhaps use some assistance with our landscape design.

I'm at my desk, trying to get some work done. Sparky is my footstool. Lying down, curled up like this, he's just the right height for a footstool. He is, however, snoring. It's the snore of an old man, sophisticated and confident.

The phone rings.

"Hello?"

"Hello!" says a woman in the cheerful tone of a friend. I'm not sure I recognize the voice. "This is Lori from Great Wall China Adoption?"

"Oh?" I say.

"Are you sitting down?"

Oh! This is it? But—I'm not prepared! I should be prepared! This is not how this is supposed to happen. Um. I was going to be . . . prepared! How was I going to be prepared? Um. I was going to have a pen, and a piece of paper. I grab a pen. And a piece of paper.

"I'm prepared!" I say.

"Well, I'm calling to let you know you have a daughter," she says.

I swallow. The D-word. More real than ever now. Good God! I feel it in my throat like a shot of whiskey.

But then the words, they just keep spilling out of her, like a river is flowing, which of course a river is supposed to do, but whew, her words are just flowing and flowing and flowing so fast. "Oh, she is just gorgeous . . . She is eight months old . . . She's in a pink dress . . . She's bald! . . . She's living in the Jiangsu Province, that's J-i-a-n-g-s-u . . . We'll send the package tomorrow . . . Oh, she's lovely . . . Her name is G-u Y-u Q-i-a-n . . . That's Goo Oo Chin . . . It means Pretty Like Jade . . . Do you have an e-mail address? . . . Would you like me to e-mail her picture right now?"

Right now? Daughter-right-now? But . . . um. *I am not prepared!*

"Yes, I have an e-mail address," I say.

"Great," she says. "I'll send you her photo now, and then when you get the package, just give me a call and we can go over everything, okay?"

Um. Lots of words. Huh? And, um, daughter-right-now?

"Hello?" she says. "Okay?"

"Daughter-right-now?" I say.

"I'm sending it right now," she says.

I hang up. I call Alex at his office in Pittsburgh. *Emergency! Emergency! Dr. Bombay! Come right away!* Oh jeez, I'm doing *Bewitched*-talk. I am lapsing in my terror and excitement into old sitcom lingo.

I wish Alex was here with me. I can't believe this! This is not at all how I imagined it would be. I imagined the two of us, sitting by the fire on a Friday night, popping open a bottle of champagne. I imagined sitting on the fluffy flowered couch with the dogs curled up by the fireplace. I imagined a big white envelope on the table. The package that would just have arrived from the agency. The package that would contain our first glimpses of a little girl in China who had been chosen to be ours. We would take a deep breath. We would open the envelope. We would reach inside, and we would see her, fall in love with her, fall into each other's arms, fall all over ourselves with joy and promise and possibility.

Instead . . .

When Alex answers, I tell him to turn on his laptop because the picture is on its way. "Oh?" he says. *"Oh!"* He is processing this information at approximately my same rate. "Oh, my . . ." I can hear him fumbling with his computer. I am fumbling with my computer. "Okay, I am downloading," he tells me. "Okay, I am getting . . . numbers. Just lots of . . . numbers. Something is wrong."

I'm getting a screen full of numbers, too. Apparently our computers can't convert this kind of file.

"Well, I guess this is what she looks like in numeric code," he says.

"Right."

But—I don't want to see her in code. I want to see her! Oh, this is not at all how I imagined it would be.

I sit down, take a breath. Collect myself. Okay. She isn't here yet. She is just a string of numbers. There is a piece of me, a string of my own numerical code, that is relieved. She isn't here yet. I still have more time. I still have a few more moments as my old self. My nonmother self. *(Inhale.)* My free self. *(Exhale.)* I haven't thought too much about parenting, and I haven't thought too much about this either: turning into a parent.

When Anna comes, I will become a whole new self. Is that correct? A mother self, fully actualized. A self, they say, who will never again sleep. A self, they say, whose career could go belly up. A self who won't have time to take a shower, let alone brush a mule. A nonself?

A baby is a beginning, but a baby is also an end. This is what I find myself thinking. This is not what I imagined thinking. This is not at all how I imagined it would be.

Alex suggests I call the agency back, ask someone to please send the file in a different format. So this is what I do. "Of course!" the woman says. "Oh, she's such a cutie . . . She is living in the Kunshan Welfare Institute . . . That's K-u-n-s-h-a-n."

I call Alex back, say here it comes. I click download. And before I know it, I see a flash of pink. I close my eyes tight. A picture. Yes, definitely a picture came through. I don't want to see it until he does.

Alex says he sees pink coming through, too.

"Close your eyes!" I tell him.

"Okay," he says. "On the count of three, let's look."

"Okay," I say. "But how about the count of ten instead?"

"Okay."

"Well, you count," I say.

"No, you!"

I am actually trembling. I am digging my feet into Sparky's armpits, poor dog, but he is sleeping through all of this.

Five, four, three, two . . .

I open my eyes.

"Oh," I say, and feel my spine turn to rubber.

"Oh!"

I can't seem to get the rest of the words out.

"Oh!"

I feel it in my stomach like a punch. "Oh!"

The rest of the words?

The rest of the words are these: I know *her*. I just . . . know her. Those enormous cheeks. Those fiercely focused eyes. That funny arch of her left eyebrow. *I know her!* She is she and I am I, and just like that, in the blink of an eye, we belong.

I can't believe this.

I stop trembling. I am instantly and thoroughly . . . calm. This is not at all how I imagined it would be.

Alex finally speaks. "I just see little pink dots everywhere," he says. "Just speckles everywhere."

Oh. There is something wrong with the screen resolution on that old laptop. Oh, poor Alex. "She is beautiful," I tell him. "She is bald! She is frowning. She has chipmunk cheeks. I don't know how to tell you . . . This is so weird, honey, but *I know her*."

He says he's getting in the car. He says he'll be home in an hour.

I tell him hurry home. I tell him: "Pretty Like Jade." I tell him hurry home, I'm waiting.

And I better get used to waiting. It's going to be six or eight weeks before we'll be allowed entry into China to go get her.

I think: How can I wait?

Well, I can't.

That's all there is to it.

I'm a mom. Here's my baby. What do you mean I can't hold her? What do you mean I have to wait? I'm a mom. Here's my baby. I have to get to her. I have to take care of my baby.

I sit here staring at her picture, my feet digging into a snoring beagle, and I start calculating. I think about digging to China. I think about getting Billy in here with a backhoe. I think of packing myself in a big wooden box and mailing myself to China. I think of the satellite dish on my roof, beaming TV in from outer space. Couldn't I rig it to somehow beam me up, and then down to China? I think of *Bewitched*.

I think of Samantha and *I Dream of Jeannie* and *My Fav*
Martian and so many of the friends I grew up with who could
just click and go.

I think of the moon. I wonder if anyone has even shown
her the moon. I think of writing her a letter immediately and
telling her about the moon.

I sit here overwhelmed with thoughts, stupid and huge. I
sit here discovering everything and yet only the tip of all there
is to know. A mother's love doesn't begin with the mother, or
the child, or anything having to do with the mind. A mother's love doesn't begin with a smell or even a touch. A mother's
love comes on like a thunderstorm. You may or may not hear
the rumble as it approaches, you may or may not have time to
close your windows and call in your cat. But when the storm
comes, the storm is all there is. The sky opens and weeps and
howls and devours.

CHAPTER THIRTEEN

And don't I feel like a gym teacher, holding this clipboard. I should have a whistle. *Tweet, tweet!* "I want to see you kids *hustle!*"

But I am not a gym teacher. No, I am a mother. I am a train. I am the mother of all trains. I am packing to go to China.

On this clipboard I have a color-coded packing list: my stuff written in green, Alex's in blue, Anna's in purple.

The purple thrills me. "Diapers." "Formula." "Bottles." "Bottle Liners." How exhilarating it is to have baby-gear words in your life.

"Anyway, I'd love to stay and chat," I say to Alex, apropos of nothing—and everything. "But I have to go pick up Anna."

Alex is on the floor, hunched over the suitcase. "You're just going to keep saying that?" he asks.

"Apparently."

I just keep saying it. "I'd love to stay and chat, but I have to go pick up Anna." I love these words. Words I'll probably be saying years from now, when she's at school, or at piano lessons, or over at her best friend's house. But words that I now get to say for the first and second and third and fourth times as I run around like a gym teacher with a clipboard but no whistle.

But I am not a gym teacher. No, I am a mother. I am a train. I am the mother of all trains.

We leave for China in the morning.

It's already February, three months since we got the referral. Three months! It wasn't supposed to take this long. But between the backlog of paperwork at the U.S. Consulate's office in China, and the astounding number of government holidays the Chinese government seems to have, and all the complicated scheduling of appointments at all the various government offices we'll need to visit in order to adopt Anna—well, it took three months.

But it's over now. The wait is just about over.

I hand Alex a bag full of toothbrushes.

He looks at them. "You want me to pack the whole bag?"

I nod.

"You really think we need, like, twenty toothbrushes?"

"Twelve," I say.

"You really think we need twelve toothbrushes?"

Sigh. Surely he knows I've already worked this through. "Sweetie," I say. "You can't drink the tap water in China. So what if you forget? You just absentmindedly wave your toothbrush under the faucet . . . That toothbrush is a goner."

"We're going to do that twelve times?"

"Six times for each of us," I say.

He holds his lips tight. "Well, you sure are thinking of . . . everything."

"I am," I say smugly.

"Everything and beyond."

I flop my head to one side. "Honey, I'd love to stay and chat, but—"

He throws in the toothbrushes.

I look down at my clipboard. Check.

It's now eight o'clock. And the thing is, it's snowing out-side. This, if I allow myself to think about it, bothers me. Snow is not on my checklist of something I would have to deal with. I have decided that this means I don't have to deal with it.

Well, I am not dealing with it for other reasons, too. There is, of course, the thing about snow as it pertains to air-ports and airplane runways with too much of it on them. But this is a gentle snow. So far just a dusting over the barn roof. So the airplane worry has barely even kicked in.

Mostly, the snow I am not dealing with puts a sadness in my heart. The more I work on not dealing with it, the more I drift toward a barely iced-over sorrow.

Damn it.

Snow.

Snow means: cold. Snow means: freezing cold. And no matter what your feelings of winter and cold blasts may be, this is just not the kind of environment you like to imagine when you imagine a missing dog.

Sparky.

He's missing.

What was that I said? Everything is connected. Everything fits. From a distance you can sometimes see the blueprint, or at least the traces of one.

It helps to try and see the blueprint. It helps when enough of the pieces of a puzzle fit together and the picture starts to reveal itself and you can just sit and think about the picture.

Well, it's easier. *Keep your brain working!* Put all your en-ergy into brain work! Forget about the snow and think about the picture, or think about your packing list, or just keep *thinking*. I'm telling you, if you can accomplish this, you dra-matically decrease your chances of feeling anything.

So here is what I think. I think that it makes a kind of

beautifully sad sense that Sparky would go—go right when he did.

It was the day after we got the referral.

Yeah, the day after.

It was a normal enough morning—as normal as anything seems to get these days. I'd had a fitful sleep; all night I kept having to turn on the light to look once again at Anna's picture, to remind myself that it was real, that she was real. My heart was like a big happy frog, hopping and bopping with abandon.

But in every other way, it was a morning like every other morning. I woke up. I pulled my feet out from underneath Sparky, who was stretched out like a log on the bed. I brushed my teeth. I put the coffee on. I went back into the bedroom to see if any of the snoozing lump of mammals known as my family was even beginning to stir.

"Good morning, gang!" I said. And Marley, first Marley woke up. He stood, did his dog shake, which woke Sparky up. Sparky jumped off the bed, did his dog shake, which woke Betty up. I swear dogs have a whole dialogue going on with those dog shakes. I opened the door to the yard just as I always do, and the dogs filed out.

Ten minutes later Alex was getting up, and I called the dogs in for breakfast. Marley came in, Betty came in, but Sparky did not. On the face of it, this was not a giant worry. This, I figured, could be one of those days he'd spend sniffing through the great outdoors. It had happened plenty of other times. I'd always hear his *A-roo! A-roo!* in the distance, and I'd feel comforted by the knowledge that he was probably onto something good.

But on that day last November I didn't hear any *A-roo! A-roo!* All day I was listening for it, and I never heard it.

The next day I went out looking for him. I went to all his

favorite places. I hiked clear over to the cedar-shake house on Needmore Road with the collie mix that Sparky had taken a shine to. I saw no signs of Sparky. As the days progressed, so did my heartache and so did my understanding.

I called every animal shelter from here to Pittsburgh and down to West Virginia. I posted signs everywhere, in the post office and the hardware store and even up at the Wal-Mart.

Nobody called.

Sparky, it seemed, had vanished.

As the weeks turned into months, my heartache softened with thanks and forgiveness. Sparky. A bumbling, stinky angel. He'd shown up when I needed him. And then, the day after I got the photo of Anna, well, I guess his work here was done.

It was the only way I could find to think about it. I needed to find a way of thinking about it. Not that the thinking has made it all that much easier. This, of course, is the main problem with thinking: You just can't keep it up. Sooner or later your brain needs a break and then, BAM. Your heart takes over.

I'm probably way off the charts with this missing I feel. He is, after all, just a dog. But a dog that for a time filled the shoes—well, the stroller—of my baby. A dog escorting me from sorrow to joy.

"He's moved on to his next home," I tell people who ask about him. "He wandered off just as he wandered in."

I try to make it sound like I've let it go. I don't mention the fact that I still drive to our local animal shelter once each week, just in case. I do this in lieu of calling them on the phone. Because nearly every time I call they say yes, they say, "We have a male beagle, just came in this morning!" And so I hop in the car with all my hope, and then I get there and it's not Sparky. There are, I've discovered, a lot of male beagles that wander off. And none of them is Sparky.

He isn't coming back. I really do know this. I really need to let this go. I've got a baby to go get. And I've got to pack.

But you know, it's snowing.

Snow must be one of worry's most efficient fuels.

Damn it.

I put down my clipboard. "I'll be right back," I say to Alex. I head into the hall, find my coat. I open the door, step out onto the porch.

The snow has poured a hush over the farm. The moon is hiding. The sky is dark as ink.

I cup my hands, yell "Heeey, Spark!" into the darkness, as I have been doing for the past three months, since he first left.

"Heey, Spark!"

Nothing.

And to think not long ago I was calling Skippy in from his big adventure. At least I found Skippy. I'm starting to think of scaling back on pets. On love. The more you have, the more you just have to lose.

"Heey, Spark!"

I imagine Sparky trapped somewhere, shivering, too cold to let out an *A-roo!* for help.

But snow is a blank canvas on which any imagination can run wild.

So give me a second. I mean, let me work on this. I fold my arms, hug my chest.

Okay, here we go: Instead of outside shivering, at this moment Sparky is warm and snug inside someone's house. That's it. Right now Sparky is doing a happy dog shake in the bedroom of some otherwise sad little girl, or in the kitchen of some otherwise sad old man, or in the basement beside a TV being watched by an otherwise sad and pimply teenager. Stinky Bumbling Angel does it again. Stinky Bumbling Angel to the rescue!

He's working on someone else's heart.

Good for you, Spark. Good for you.

We are, each of us, managers of our own imagination. There really are choices we make.

But still.

"Heeeeey, Spark!" I yell, one last time, just in case I'm wrong about this.

OKAY, NOW LISTEN up, team! *Tweet! Tweet!* This packing list is five pages long. There is still so much to do.

Let me just say it is not easy getting two weeks' worth of clothes for three people—plus two weeks' worth of baby formula and diapers and toys; plus a dozen gifts for orphanage personnel, MADE IN USA, individually wrapped in red paper; plus piles of clothes and toys to donate to the orphanage; plus pounds of official paperwork, and, well, a living room's worth of STUFF—into two checkable bags measuring no more than sixty-two linear inches apiece and two carry-ons of no more than forty-five linear inches apiece.

Whew. Okay. I have Ziploc bags. No, not the kind with the little slide thingy. I tried those. I need a *tight* seal. Because air, I am discovering, takes up too much room. So I put Anna's little PJs into a one-quart bag, then seal it all the way up except for a little space to stick a straw in, then, *fwooop,* I suck out as much air as I can, and then I quickly finish the seal. *Voilà!* Vacuum-packed clothes! This is really working. I wonder if I can fit my sweater and Alex's jeans into this one-gallon bag. And these little dresses, oh, look at this outfit

Kristin got for Anna, the one with the rabbit on it, oh, I can really see her in this one.

Anna is waiting. She is sitting there in the Kunshan Welfare Institute in Jiangsu Province, wondering where I am. Well, maybe not. She is only eleven months old. She is too young to know she even has a mom over here grieving a beagle, a mom posing as a gym teacher, the mother of all trains, or the train of all mothers, trying to condense a family-to-be into two suitcases and two carry-on bags.

I'm stuffing. I'm cramming. I'm *fwooping*. I'm zipping. I'm thinking of all the things I've forgotten to pack. The things I have no idea how to pack.

I'm thinking of the baby shower that Eileen and Kristin and Claire threw for me and the generosity of spirit that energized that day. My sisters, sitting there eating cake, sipping punch, armed with presents and eagerness and acceptance for this baby born on the other side of the globe, a baby they regard instantly, simply, impossibly, as one of us.

There is Alyson in the center of the crowd, wearing a velvet pantsuit, understanding everything.

There is Amy, who could very easily have freaked out at the idea of a new baby sister coming into her father's arms, but who was at that shower with bells on, bringing so many presents for Anna, we had to take a *break* after I was finished opening them.

I'm thinking of Peter, who might also have simply fled but who is taking a week off from work so he can be at the airport waiting for Anna.

I'm thinking of my mom and my dad, the two of them taking the picture of Anna all through Riddle Village, bragging about their new grandchild.

I'm thinking of George and Pat who came over one

night with storybooks, gifts for Anna. I'm thinking of the old lady who made a wreath of dried flowers—a gift for Anna. Then she gave us a pillowcase with pink and blue flowers embroidered on it. She told us she embroidered it herself, back when she was grieving the loss of her own daughter in the house fire. She told us embroidery was what helped keep her sane. "But I didn't know I was making something for a girl from China," she said. "But why not?" A gift that grew out of a mother's tears. How perfect that seemed.

I'm thinking of my Pittsburgh friends who threw the most wonderful "Anna is coming soon!" party. I'm thinking of Wendy making those invitations on rice paper, stamping each with Chinese characters. And Beth making a gourmet meal of Chinese food. And Nancy, who is normally so *not* the kitchen type, spending days making homemade fortune cookies, each with a fortune she had written herself. *"Look!"* read mine. *"There are baby-sitters all around you!"*

I wonder how I will ever explain any of this to Anna. I wonder: Just how do you pack this stuff? I wish there were a Ziploc bag that could hold the world's welcome.

But there is not. No, when it comes to Ziploc bags, you just have your quart size, your two-quart size, your gallon size, your two-gallon size. I've used boxes and boxes of these miraculous bags. It's nearly midnight, and I am finally zipping the suitcase. Alex is sitting on it. We've got just about an inch of zipping here to go. This is unbelievable! I should go on TV and teach people how to cram stuff into a suitcase. Of course, it helps to have a clipboard, and pens with colored ink. And a sturdy new suitcase, a fancy schmancy number with exterior fabric that's practically bulletproof. We bought the top of the line.

"Voilà!" I say to Alex, finishing the zip. He's happy. I'm happy. We're done.

"Let's practice," he says. "Let's see how it will be to wheel this monster."

"Good idea." I push the button, and the handle flies up like magic. Then I tilt the suitcase, I tilt it so it can rest on the wheels, which is how you pull it, I am tilting down on the handle, down, down, and the suitcase is not budging. The handle, it goes: *snap.*

Snap.

The snap is echoing through our heads as we try to process the reality of that snap.

The handle. It just snapped off like a toothpick.

"Oh, dear," I'm saying, holding the handle that used to be part of the suitcase.

Alex is glaring. I think I see steam coming out of his nose. Or maybe from his ears? *"How much did we pay for this thing!?"*

A lot. But—well. "We put too much stuff in!" I say. "It's too heavy!"

"Why are you defending the suitcase?" he says.

Right.

Peace. I need there to be peace. No tension! NO TENSION! It is, okay, it is midnight and we are, okay, we are leaving for Beijing in the morning. Eight in the morning, to be exact. Our flight leaves at eight. And—we have a broken suitcase. We do not have another suitcase in this house, at least not one even close to this size.

Um.

"Wal-Mart!" I say. "Wal-Mart is open twenty-four hours! I'll run to Wal-Mart, get a new suitcase."

"They're not going to have good-quality suitcases at Wal-Mart," Alex says, all defeated. "This is the top-of-the-line suitcase!"

"Maybe the middle-of-the-line suitcases work better?" I venture.

"I can't believe this," he says.

"Right."

"Let's go," he says, grabbing his keys. "We need a suit-case."

Well, if he's going to go to the store for a new suitcase, shouldn't I stay here? I should stay here and clean up and organize. But this is how he deals with anxiety—he needs a lot of *togetherness*. And his times of anxiety, I have to say it's not when I most want his togetherness. But I've learned. I've learned to GO WITH THE FLOW. I've learned to STAY CALM. I've learned to NOT GET WORKED UP WHEN I FEEL LIKE I AM A TRAIN WITH TOO MUCH STEAM BUILT UP AND ABOUT TO EXPLODE. Yes indeedy, GO WITH THE FLOW.

We trudge out. Trudge out in the snow. We have to clean off the car from all the snow. It's, wow. A lot of snow.

It takes us a good ten minutes to drive as far as Daniel's Run Road, which is technically just around the corner. The snow is surprisingly deep. When did all this snow fall? And why hasn't the township plowed? We have to drive maybe fifteen miles an hour, it's so hard to see, the snow is blowing in fits.

"This is ridiculous," Alex says.

"It is," I say.

"At this rate it's going to take us an hour to get to Wal-Mart," he says.

"And an hour back," I say.

"Forget it," he says. He's right. We turn around. It's funny how neither of us is saying anything about the snow as it might pertain to our ride in the morning to the airport. No, we are just talking about how to use a broken suitcase. It still has wheels, just no handle. We'll concoct something. When we get home, we concoct something. We concoct a theory that the only way we can take this suitcase, which neither of us can lift, is if we remove forty pounds of stuff. All my Ziploc bags that I sucked down to Ziploc bricks. I am too good at packing. See, you can be overprepared.

We open the suitcase, reach in, pull out, pitch. We pitch out bricks of clothes. Pitch and pitch and pitch, reconfigure, pitch, pack, repack, zip. It goes on and on. I mean, *on and on*. It is three in the morning by the time we are finished. Our flight is at eight. They say to check in two hours early for a transatlantic flight, so that means we should be at the terminal by six. It takes an hour to get there. We have to leave at five.

We have to hurry up and sleep with our remaining two hours.

We can't sleep.

We lie here with our eyes wide open, holding hands, wondering what it is that just happened and what-all is about to happen. Is this, I wonder, what it feels like to begin giving birth, to lie waiting for that first contraction that signals the end of the waiting and the end of the planning and the beginning of being an actual mom?

Outside our window, where the moon is still hidden, I can see the glow of the porch light. And I can see that the snow is now falling in sheets. And it's funny the way the word *blizzard* has not even once occurred to me.

HUGE TRANSITIONS IN your life never go the way you think they will. Huge transitions are like tunnels you walk through in which, for a time, you are not quite you and your mind is not quite yours and your heart is definitely experiencing some serious reformatting. You can never predict any of this, and while you are in it, you can't begin to understand it. I am in it. I am stuck in it. I am in . . . Chicago? Well, look at that, we made it as far as Chicago. We got on one of the very few planes to leave Pittsburgh and one of the very few planes to actually land in Chicago during this blizzard. Yeah, blizzard. Everyone you meet is using the word: *blizzard*.

We are in Chicago, but we aren't going to Beijing today. No more planes leaving Chicago. *Hello? This is a blizzard. This is a blizzard in Chicago.* And all the nearby hotels are filled with other stranded passengers. So we find a spot, somewhere between Gates 71 and 72. We find a spot on the floor to curl up. To stretch out. To curl, stretch, curl.

That would be: night number two of no sleep.

AND SO NOW it is tomorrow. Or maybe yesterday. When you travel over the international date line, there is no telling. We are just now coming out of the vacuum-packed tube that flung us for fourteen hours through the air and over the sea to this, the other side of the world.

So, then. Here we are. Does this mean it's time to sleep? We have not slept for days.

Here, anyway, is how it was supposed to go: We were supposed to have a day to sleep. The adoption agency schedules a day of rest in Beijing. We were supposed to have a whole day. Then after that we were to fly to Nanjing and meet Anna.

But no. We are here in Beijing a full day behind schedule. The blizzard that now seems light-years away has stolen our day of rest.

This is becoming an increasingly hideous reality. If we don't soon get sleep, we may, in fact, start screaming and spitting and foaming at the mouth.

In the Beijing airport we are met by a representative from our agency, a very sympathetic woman who nonetheless whisks us ruthlessly onto a plane to Nanjing. In Nanjing we are greeted by another guide, Sophie, who will be in charge of us the rest of the time, poor woman; she kindly makes no mention of the foam coming out of our mouths. She is in charge of us and five other families traveling to get their babies, five other American families who apparently have come from states well west of that blizzard. They had their day of rest in Beijing; they are looking so rested, I feel the urge to put my head in their laps and cry. I am delirious. Or I might be. China, from the window of the van we are now riding in, is not real. It is a sunny, tiny place on the other end of a tunnel. Barely visible from behind my blurred eyes. It is, I think, Planet Bicycle. Swarms of bicycles weave in and out of the congested traffic with a graceful assurance that defies logic and good sense and everything that ever flashed through your mind the first time you decided to wear a bicycle helmet. Some bicycles carry more than one passenger; some appear to carry entire families. Some balance crates stacked six high, all of them brimming with fruit. The man pedaling beside our van is dressed in a business suit, and strapped to his handlebars is what appears to be a seventeen-inch television set.

I elbow Alex to show him the man with the TV. Alex has his head tilted back, his mouth hanging open like melted cheese. His head is jiggling. I think he may have passed out.

"Gu Yu Qian?" says Sophie, from the front of the van. "Whose baby is Gu Yu Qian?"

Alex pops into consciousness. "Our baby!" he says to me. "Isn't that our baby?"

"PRETTY LIKE JADE?" I shout.

Sophie smiles. "Pretty Like Jade," she says. "She is yours?"

"She is ours!" I say.

Sophie is holding a cell phone. Um. Anna is on the phone?

"I just got word she is waiting for you in the hotel lobby," Sophie tells us. "She is there right now."

Oh.

There right now.

Right up the road.

Oh?

BUT WE HAVEN'T SLEPT IN FOUR HUNDRED DAYS AND WE ARE FOAMING AT THE MOUTH. Doesn't she realize this? Doesn't anyone realize this?

And, um, couldn't we change our clothes or something first? At least brush our teeth with one of our twelve toothbrushes?

"Camera!" Alex says to me. "Film in camera? Battery?" He has stopped speaking in complete sentences, having discovered several time zones ago that verbs are a waste of energy.

The van stops. We are . . . at the hotel? Yes, we are told, this is the hotel. There are big banners outside, and golden dragons climbing a pillar as if slithering toward Heaven. Everyone is jumping out of the van, jumping out as if, ho-hum, here we go into a hotel, jumping out as if this were not the most important hotel anyone in the history of mankind ever was about to enter. Anna is in that hotel. Anna is in that hotel even as we speak, waiting. Waiting for her foamy-mouth parents to appear.

Alex and I lag behind. We are trying to load our cameras. Plus, I am somewhat frozen with the knowledge that we are about to do it, we are about to enter the most important hotel anyone in the history of mankind ever entered.

We enter the hotel.

We don't see anybody.

It's a huge lobby, shiny and gleaming. Glorious cascading water spits out of fountains beneath enormous ficus trees.

There are big fish tanks. Fish tanks? There is a sign pointing the way to the bowling alley on the second floor. A bowling alley?

"I'm pretty sure I saw Sophie and the group go right," I say to Alex. He's got the video camera rolling. He wants all this on tape.

"They must be just around this corner," I'm saying to Alex, as I go right, wander through the lobby, and he follows like an Action News Cameraman who still believes in truth.

What a huge lobby. And what huge legs I have. My legs are heavy with exhaustion. I do not feel entirely human. I may, in fact, have turned into an ape.

"They must be just around this next corner," I'm saying to Alex. We keep going around corners. No Sophie. No group. Soon we are entering a coatroom. Lots of hangers everywhere. No Sophie. No group. Just a woman with a mop, mopping the coatroom. She is looking at Alex, who has the video camera rolling.

"Um—cut," I say to him.

"Oh," he says to me. "Sorry," he says to her.

"We took a wrong turn?" I say to her.

She stares at us, her mop still going back and forth, sloshing. We leave the coatroom.

We are lost. We are apes. We are lost apes in the land before time. We may soon start grunting.

Just then Sophie appears. She grabs my arm. "This way! This way!" she is saying, pulling me. (The group had gone left.) Soon she is running. We run behind her. Alex is rolling again.

"Your baby!" Sophie is saying. "Your baby!"

I see a baby. I see a baby in the arms of a Chinese woman. The woman has on a black leather coat with a brown fur collar. She has wide cheekbones. And yes, she is holding a baby.

Anna.

Pretty Like Jade.

Oh my God.

I can't hear anything. I can't feel my feet or my legs or my toes. I am an ape. I'm an ape just barely smart enough to have made it through a maze.

Anna.

She's in a big orange snowsuit with stripes and little cats all over it. She has the same intense eyes she had in the picture, the same gigantic cheeks, and her hair has grown full and rich.

Oh, Anna.

I approach her. I am actually tiptoeing. I don't want to . . . charge her. I don't want to scare her.

I am a giant, awkward, exhausted ape. I am her mother. She is looking at me. It is not a look of "Well, hi, Mom!" No, it is not. It is more a look of "What the heck?" It is a look of "Can I help you?"

Alex is rolling. I wish he would turn the camera off. I wish he would get over here. But behind the lens seems to be his safe zone, and Anna is in hers, and it seems that it is up to me now to make the introductions, to make this family . . . happen.

"Hi, baby," I say, finally. And I reach out with my index finger and touch her hand.

She has no reaction.

The woman jiggles her.

Nothing.

I look at Alex. "She's afraid," I say to him, to the camera, to all the folks back home, to Anna at age twelve seeing this video. "Give her a minute."

"Hi, baby," I say again. And again. I am not sure what else

to say. "Um. I usually look a lot better than this," I say. "You know, I haven't slept . . . And my hair is, well, I have a lot better hair days than this. But your hair, well, honey, wow!"

Oh my God. *I'm doing hair talk?*

"A toy!" says Mary, one of our fellow travelers. She and the others have formed a circle around me and Anna and the fur-collar woman and Alex with the video camera. She and the others are still waiting for their babies to arrive. "Give her a toy!" Mary urges.

A toy! Of course, a toy! The toys I brought, which, yes, were most certainly *on my packing list,* the toys are all in Ziploc bags deep in the suitcase.

Um.

Mary passes me a pink rattle. I offer it to Anna. She takes it into her hand and studies it quietly. She's so . . . gentle. She's so peaceful. She's a lamb on George's hill, distant and unknown.

The fur-collar woman lifts Anna higher, holds her out to me.

I look at the woman. I look back at Alex. Right. I know what to do. Of course I do. Here goes. This is what a mother does. I open my arms, and she falls in.

Oh, Anna. Her body is soft, light, calm as the breeze that holds all quiet answers.

Oh, Anna, so this is it. So this is what it feels like to hug the wind.

"She's so . . . calm . . . ," I'm saying to Alex, to the camera, to all the folks back home, to Anna at age sixteen or eighteen or twenty-one. "She's so calm she's calming me down." Maybe that was the whole idea anyway. Or half of it.

"Come meet your daughter," I say to Alex. "Come hold your baby girl."

He takes the camera away from his face. He is white as paste. I'm handing her to him. "Here you go," I say. "Here's your baby girl."

He opens his arms, and she eases right in. His eyes are wet and full. His chin is quivering.

She glares at him. She grabs his nose. She strokes his chin stubble. They are just barely getting acquainted—but then Sophie interrupts.

"Please," she says. "We must move upstairs."

Move? I don't want to move, ever.

"We must hurry," Sophie says. There are others with her. A man and two women with pleading eyes.

We follow blindly. We are led up to our hotel room. The man and the women chatter excitedly. They give us pens. They ask us to sign things. We sign blindly. Alex does not let go of Anna. Then they lead us outside. We follow blindly. What-ever. Nothing matters now that we have Anna. We take turns carrying her. We complain that our turns don't last long enough. They whisk us to a notary or some such place, then to a store for a photo to be taken, then to another notary or some such place, it is one blur beyond the blur I'm already in, circles and more circles, deep into a whole new tunnel, but now with Anna in my arms, a person to protect and guide through.

Night falls. My exhaustion now beyond exhaustion, something so very far beyond. Back in our hotel room at last, I put Anna into the crib beside our bed, a blue metal crib with crisp white sheets lovingly pressed.

I turn to find that Alex has flopped on top of the bed and is already asleep—still in his clothes. I take his shoes off. I pull at his big toe. Does he really want to sleep in his clothes? I pull his toe again. Nothing. I kiss his cheek and put a blanket over him.

I climb into bed. My head falls onto the pillow like an anchor dropping into a most willing sea.

The weight of the world, off for now. Off.

Anna is watching me. Her head is just inches away from mine. It's just the two of us now, for the first time just us. Her cheeks are flushed, her hair slightly moist from her hat. I want to tell her about hat hair. I want to tell her that her father gets hat hair, too. But I suppose there will be time for that. Instead, I tell her she smells like rain. Summer rain on the porch at Sweetwater Farm.

"Well, good night, baby," I say. "We've earned a good sleep." I turn off the light and darkness comes, and she doesn't cry.

I close my eyes.

In a moment I peek, just to make sure it's all true.

It is. She is. She has closed her eyes.

In a moment she peeks, catching me peeking. Or I've caught her.

We do this again. And again, back and forth. In the darkness we are playing an eye game, we are doing a first-you-blink-then-I-blink dance.

Eventually, I break the rhythm with a double blink. And this is when, for the first time, I see my daughter smile.

CHAPTER FOURTEEN

They are taking us somewhere. They are taking us to the orphanage, Kunshan Welfare Institute, so we can see how Anna lived and so we can meet some of the people who cared for her.

Everyone in the van is eerily quiet on this ride. We are down to three families now—our original group has splintered and splintered again, according to the regions where our babies are from and where each family is required to travel and complete paperwork with local officials. And so we are with Ken and Debbie, from Buffalo, New York, and their baby Emily, who, like Anna, is from Kunshan. And we're with Mary and John, from Austin, Texas, and their baby Amy from the orphanage in Suzhou, just east of Kunshan. We've just spent a few days in Suzhou, a small city known for its gardens and silk. Sophie toured us through some of the gardens and took us to a silk factory where we watched four women in white hats take seventy cocoons from seventy worms and stretch them and stretch them and stretch them into one layer of silk, adding it to seventy such layers, and thus creating one heavenly quilt.

And now we are back in our rickety white van. It smells of diesel fumes and doesn't take bumps too well; with each of the road's considerable wallops, it squeaks as if complaining of arthritis.

Anna is on my lap, limp as a rag doll. We're eating Cheerios. I give one to her, one to me, one to her, one to me. The Cheerios help counteract the diesel fume smell, which, if left unchecked, would make me carsick.

"You sure you don't want some?" I say to Alex, offering him a handful.

"No thanks," he says. He's looking rested, finally. We've been here five days, and I think both of us are on China time now.

"Then how about some of those pretzels I lovingly packed?"

He shakes his head no.

"You sure are not a car eater," I say.

"A car eater?"

"You know what I mean."

He's not a snacker, like Anna and I are. Nor does he go for nibble food, as Anna and I do. Well, you can see already how this family is dividing up. There are things Anna does that remind you of her mother and there are things she does that remind you of her father. We've been her parents for just five days, and already there are these things.

She burps like her father. The burps come out like little jokes, each followed by an expectation, a quick scan to see who in her audience appreciates how terribly funny that noise is. (She laughs, like her father, at her own jokes.)

She sleeps like her father. Out like a light, instantly. You can open all the windows, play loud music, you could probably bring in a tuba player, and like Alex, she'll lie motionless.

She sings like her mother. Off-key, and with abandon. As we walked the streets of Nanjing last week, she hung off the front of me in a blue corduroy sling singing "Laa-waaa-waaa-laaa!" in a voice so loud, it turned heads.

She is a happy-go-lucky baby. She is cheerful. In the morning she lies in her crib and plays with her toes.

Just as I did as a baby.

How does it work? It makes you wonder. All that business of character and personality, all those tendencies we see in our children that remind us of us. How much of it is the passing on of genetic material and how much of it is plain, ordinary old searching for ourselves to make a connection? It makes you wonder how much of what our children become is us seeing what we want to see, or us seeing what we're afraid to see, or in any case it's the parents seeing, and then saying, and seeing and saying until the image and child are one.

Alex and I have been sending e-mails once a day to family and friends back home. Last night, in my e-mail to my mom, I told her about Anna playing with her toes in the morning; I told her, "She's such a cheerful child."

"Just like you!" my mother wrote back. Just as I expected. I loved reading that. I loved the confirmation. "And you know, I was like that, too," my mother went on to write. I knew she would add this, too. (This was a set-up.) I loved the confirmation; I loved thinking of my mother, me, Anna as a continuum.

You might think: But really, now. How can Anna be a cheerful child? She was abandoned at the gate of a hospital at just two weeks old and then lived for ten and a half months in an institution, for heaven's sake. She should be . . . traumatized. She should be angry. She should be spending her infant mental energy brewing up a lifelong feeling of victimization, a "Why, God, *why me*?!"

I suppose you could project any of that onto her, if that

was the theme you had to bring. But that is not my theme. And so I don't see it in her. I just don't.

Out my window I see the streets of Kunshan bounce by. It's a peaceful, modern city, not too far from Shanghai. China is so much more colorful than I had imagined. I don't know what I was expecting. Something . . . Soviet, perhaps? I spent a lot of time in the Soviet Union, back in the early 1990s when I covered its demise for *Life* magazine. The bread lines, the milk lines, the vodka lines that inevitably erupted into riots—it was all so difficult and exciting and depressing. It was like being in the brain of a very miserable teenager. I remember rows and rows of drab cement apartment houses, as far as the eye could see. I remember a cab driver secretly selling me a sausage. Mostly, though, I remember an absence of color, an absence of joy.

The China I've seen bears no resemblance to those sad and surreal images. In the China I've seen there is music in the streets, and performers doing yo-yo tricks, and while many of the buildings appear flimsy as paper, the rooftops with the ubiquitous curlicues on either end signal a playfulness that seems a mixture of tradition and hope. That design element is said to symbolize the tails of the dragons sitting on those roofs, dragons bringing good luck to all those who enter beneath.

The China in which I've become immersed in the last five days has been all play and hope and color and peekaboo. Ah, yes. Did I mention that Anna plays a mean game of peekaboo? And not just on command. She'll actually start the game. She'll be in her crib playing with her toes, and when she sees you looking at her, she will grab her blanket and pull it up, then down, doing the whole peekaboo deal all by herself. This is a particularly fetching routine. This is the sort of thing a parent sees that helps her make the determination that her

child is the most brilliant creature to set foot on this Earth—
a tendency that all new parents seem to have, no matter what
else they are bringing to the table in terms of projection. The
thing about your child is, she is more amazing than other
children, she is truly a genius, she is so-smart-she-scares-you,
she is more special than special, she is an angel, a heavenly
creature who, due to her own vastly generous spirit, has agreed
to lower herself and appear before us mere mortals.

This, I am discovering, is just how it works.

Alex must have been noting this, too. I mean, this must
be exactly why he said what he said a few days ago in the van
when we were still in Nanjing, when our group was still quite
large. It was just two days after our babies were placed in our
arms. And you could tell everyone in that van was in love.
There was this continued, prolonged hush of . . . love. And I
guess that's why Alex said it. Shouted it, actually. *"So,"* he
said. *"Does everyone think they got the best one?"*

He got a good laugh. Oh, it was so crude and so true. We
could each acknowledge that the other babies were . . . cute.
But none of them was quite as special as our own.

"The best one," I whisper in Anna's ear, as I give her another Cheerio. "I still can't believe I got the best one."

She has come a long way in just five days. When we first
got her, on that first day, she couldn't sit up. She couldn't roll
over. She had virtually no muscle tone. That's not something
a regular old American is used to seeing. At eleven months
old many of your basic Gerber babies are already standing, or
even walking, and here was this baby, belly-bound. I gave her
a set of stacking cups to play with, and rather than sit up and
stack them, or clickety-clack them together as most babies
her age would, she would merely examine them, lying on her
back, holding them up to her eyes, turning them around and
around with a kind of glee. It broke my heart, watching her

play like that. It was . . . odd. It was not the sort of animated play you'd see a blubbery baby in a Pampers commercial do.

If I hadn't read so much about what to expect, I suppose I would have been alarmed. But many babies coming out of institutionalized care are delayed in some way. Babies who don't get "floor time"—the opportunity to simply play on the floor, reaching for toys and squirming around under the watchful eye of amazed and delighted and cooing parents— are going to be way behind their peers who grew up with families since day one.

What's amazing is how quickly they can catch up. In less than a week Anna has gained muscle tone in her torso. She is able to sit up now, and roll over. It has been the most remarkable thing to watch, like seeing a flower opening in time-lapse photography.

We're stalled here in traffic, and I'm watching a swarm of businessmen on bicycles overtake us, and I'm thinking that Alex and Anna and I, as a family just forming, we probably look like a flower opening in time-lapse photography, too. As a family, we've gone from bud to bloom in no time at all.

Those first few days, I was so tentative. I wasn't quite sure how to hold Anna, how to feed her, how to most comfortably change her shirt, and when she would poop, I would have to leave the room and turn the parenting over to Alex. He was remarkably good about this. He seemed to have something of a hero thing going on with the poopy-diaper deal. Like he was being a hero in my eyes and a hero in Anna's eyes. Which, I have to tell you, he was. And that wasn't a bad role for him in my eyes, and probably not in Anna's either. And so as long as the hero thing was *working* for him, well, a dad on diaper duty was working for all of us.

I love watching him play with her. They'll roll around on the floor, and she'll tug his nose and poke his eyes, giggling like *Hey, this guy, this guy here puts on a helluva show.* And he'll laugh a laugh I'd hardly ever heard before, a deep, low guffaw. Before my eyes I've watched Alex get . . . young. It's as if he's shedding years right there on the floor, like a snake slithering out of a too-tight skin. But I guess that's one of the things love does to people.

Alex and Anna go to breakfast together; that's their thing. I sleep in. That's my thing. Later, after a morning of some sight-seeing, we usually come back to the hotel, and I curl up with Anna on the bed for a nap. That's our thing. (I am doing an awful lot of sleeping.) And Cheerios in the van, that's our thing, too. We've already figured so many things out. I know exactly how she likes to be held; I fling her around like an old pro, and I can change her clothes with my eyes closed, and while I have not yet changed one poopy diaper thanks to a heroic husband (enabler?), I've got the feeding thing down, the spoon at the right angle so I can shovel in and wipe with one efficient motion, no mess, no fuss, I'm a mom.

"You okay?" Alex says to me, elbowing me out of my mom reverie.

"Huh?" I say. "Oh, I'm about a six," I say. "Maybe a seven."

"Huh?"

"Carsick quotient."

"Oh. Well, actually, I meant are you okay with what we're about to do?"

"I'm okay," I say. "I'm thrilled, in a way."

"Yeah."

"I mean, I want to see it, and I don't want to see it."

"Yeah," he says.

We have no reason to believe that visiting the orphanage is going to be some horrific experience. Quite the contrary.

We've met with the orphanage director, Chen Wei Guo, several times already, and when he spoke about the orphanage, it was with pride. I get the sense that Kunshan Welfare Institute, a brand-new facility, is one of the jewels of China's orphanage system. While many families who request a visit to their child's orphanage are politely declined, our request was met with eagerness.

Mr. Chen has been a constant surprise to us. I don't know what I was expecting an orphanage director to be like, but I'm sure it wasn't him. During one of our meetings to go over some documents, he handed me a large green box. Inside, wrapped in delicate tissue paper, was a framed silk tapestry. The image embroidered on it was of a panda and her cub. "My gift to your family," Mr. Chen said.

I didn't know what to say. This was not at all how I imagined it would be.

Then he handed me a small red box. This gift, he said, was for Anna.

I opened the box and found in there a pendant, a rabbit carved of jade. A rabbit because Anna was born in the Chinese year of the rabbit, he said. And jade because of the name she had at the orphanage. Pretty Like Jade.

I looked at him. Through Sophie, who was translating, he said, "She will take this home to America from me."

He said, "I would like to request that you take good care of this precious girl."

I had no words. Or the words I had seemed so tiny compared with this man's gesture. This was not at all how I imagined it would be. I pictured a lot of things, but I never pictured a loving orphanage director handing me a prayer in a red box.

"Thank you," Alex said finally. "We are honored to accept this. We feel embraced."

That was a good way of saying it.

Embraced. By him and by the Chinese people in general. They have been as welcoming as they have been inquisitive. Strangers selling oranges, or hats, or teapots, tend to stare at us, at our babies, back at us. I wonder what they know, what they understand of our stories. I think of what we know, what little we understand of theirs. I can only conclude that there must be quite a legend passed among these people. People who have learned to live with the notion that every family is entitled to one, just one, child. People who perhaps all know of at least one woman whose only choice was to leave her baby on a street corner. People who seem to want to believe in some happily-ever-after story, because these people, when they see us, when they see these westerners carrying their babies as we tour their cities and their gardens and their silk factories, these people don't look at us with disdain or spite or indignation. Instead, these people cry out, in English: "Lucky baby! Lucky baby!"

And it's funny. I mean, each time it happens, I must have the oddest look on my face. I think, lucky? You mean Anna? Oh, well, wait a second. You've got it backward. We're the lucky ones.

It has barely begun to hit me how monumental this task is going to be. This privilege and this challenge of raising a girl born in a culture that I can never understand. Raising her with respect for a heritage that, at best, I can know only as an onlooker. Raising her with a consciousness that I can't, myself, ever have. Quite apart from the issues any child who was adopted will have to one day face, there will be all of this.

And there is me. I'm just a . . . mom. And there is Alex. He's just a . . . dad. We're just two people, making a family, longing for belonging just like anyone else. And I suppose just like anyone else who gets the prize, who is lucky enough to get the gift of a child, we have what comes with that gift, a responsibility as wide as the world. Responsibility looks different from parent to parent. And this, so far, is one thing I know about ours.

Someone once told me that being adopted outside of your native culture means forever holding the contradiction of belonging and not belonging, of feeling at home and wondering where home is. I thought that was such an interesting observation, especially since it is the very contradiction I believe myself to be walking around with. *Belonging. Where do I belong? How do I know if I really belong?* And I grew up with my biological parents right there in the next room. And I never got yanked out of one culture and plopped into another. So I don't know. Perhaps I'm not alone. Perhaps the contradiction of belonging and not belonging, of feeling at home and wondering where home is, perhaps that is the contradiction of being human.

So, all right. So Anna spent nearly a year of her little life in an orphanage. So that's her story. Let's see it. Bring it on. It's a memory we need to go get, for her. It's a memory we'll need to hold and protect and figure out what to do with, how to give it to her when the time is right.

The van has stopped outside of a large complex of buildings, white with green tile roofs.

I recognize it from the photographs that our agency sent.

The orphanage is huge, brand new, so new the trees' trunks are still wrapped, as if they were planted just last week. Come to think of it, it reminds me of my parents' retirement village. Well, that's weird. That's oddly circular.

"And so this is our destination," says Sophie, standing up.

She's a petite woman with serious eyes and a fierceness about her. The actual orphanage, she explains, is just a small part of this campus, which also includes a home for the elderly and a hospital.

As we climb out of our van, I see Mr. Chen waiting for us in the driveway. He's standing in front of the facility with his hands behind his back, a polite and important stance. He's young, maybe thirty-five, a compact man with a wide brow and a suit and a tie and a yellow sweater vest. When he sees me, he becomes animated. He is saying something to me. He is pointing to the sky.

Sophie is listening to him, saying "Oh?" and "Oh!" And then to me: "He is telling you that this mountain behind us, this is Jade Mountain." Mr. Chen is smiling, bowing, smiling. "This is the mountain she was named after."

It's a small mountain, really just the peak of one rising like a pyramid out of the flat earth, and it has a pagoda on top.

"Oh!" I say, unsure what to make of this.

"Anna," Alex says. "Your mountain!" But she is sound asleep, hanging here in the blue corduroy sling.

I pick up her hand, wave to the mountain. "Hi, mountain," I say, trying to figure out what Anna might have to say to this mountain. "You're very pretty, mountain."

"Pretty Like Anna," Alex says.

We are toured through the campus, which is eerily peaceful. It could be a movie set. It's hard to figure out where all the people are. The "baby house" is the smallest of the buildings, way off in a corner, and it has a swing set out front. As we enter, we are told to put our cameras away.

It smells like kindergarten. That's the first thing that bowls me over. It smells exactly as I remember kindergarten. Perhaps they use the same cleaning solution? In the foyer there's a bulletin board decorated with paper snowflakes, and photos of children that I scan until I find, yes, I find Anna. There she is! I pick up Anna's hand, wave to the photo of Anna, the old Anna, the Anna who used to live here. In the photo she's with a group of other babies, all of them in little walkers, kind of clogged there in the corner, like bumper cars in an amusement park. She appears to be studying the feet of the baby next to her, studying them as if to say, "You mind giving me some room here?"

How strange to see her life before Alex and I entered it. How fantastic and unexpected to see her honored on a bulletin board. "Hi, Anna!" I say again, waving her little hand at the picture. But she is sleeping through all of this.

We are moved along quickly, up the steps, down a hallway lined with pictures, the sort of artwork made by children that teachers hang to impress parents. Except there are no parents. Except, well—us. We are told that there are about sixty children living here now, and two dozen "nannies" to care for them. We are escorted into a play area.

Anna pops awake. Maybe it is the smell? Maybe the sounds? There are four nannies in the room, all of them dressed in white. They see Anna in my arms, and Emily in Debbie's arms, and they come rushing toward us. One of them reaches out, pleading with me. "Of course, of course," I say, and I hand Anna to her.

Of course?

Anna goes without resistance, and the woman carries her away, to a corner, to a toy bear. Perhaps it is a favorite toy, perhaps it is something special they shared. When the nanny returns, she is jiggling Anna, singing a song. Then she points to me. "Mmaa!" she says. "Mmmaaa!"

She is trying to get Anna to say it.

"Mmmaa!"

Anna does not say it. She looks at the woman. She looks at me, like "What, you two expect me to perform on command?"

The nanny is laughing. I am laughing. By the time we leave that room, the nanny is saying good-bye through tears.

Mr. Chen, who at this point is starting to remind me of a kinder, gentler Ghost of Christmas Past, leads us next to a room prepared with a banquet.

This is not at all how I imagined it to be.

Soon we are seated around a grand round table elegantly set with fine china. Before the delicacies are presented, Mr. Chen stands to speak. He speaks for a long time, while Sophie bows her head. Finally, she translates:

"It is a privilege for us at this orphanage to treat you all from far away in America. We are very happy now all the babies have a family. Before they were adopted, we treated them like our own children here at this orphanage. Now it is your responsibility to take care of them. We hope that when you go back, you will always offer us information and pictures of the baby. And we also hope your families will stay in contact with each other. Let us make a net, a net of love to make the baby grow up happily and healthily. It's not only the friendship between your family and this orphanage, but it is also the friendship between China and the American government. Thank you."

We sit for a moment in silence. We smile politely at Mr. Chen, bowing our heads in thanks.

It is getting harder and harder to make sense of all of this. This is not at all how I imagined it to be. Somehow when you think *orphanage in China,* you just don't think of yourself being welcomed, really welcomed, into a family. No, it's fair to say the only way you might imagine it is quite the other way around.

I didn't know about the net. I didn't know about the net of love being woven.

Alex nudges me. "Shouldn't one of us say something in response?" he whispers.

"Um . . ." But of course we aren't prepared. And looking around this table at all of the blank stares, it would seem that none of us is really the speech *type*. None of us except . . . Alex? All eyes on him now.

He stands. He clears his throat.

"We have come very far to collect our children," he says slowly, deliberately. "We are so grateful to you for the excellent care and love and attention they have received for so long. And we hold you and this orphanage and the people of China in the highest regard. We feel an enormous gratitude that we will teach to our children as they grow into young adults. Thank you very much."

Well, good for him! And good for us! And come on, family, let's eat!

We heap our plates with delicacies of fish and chicken and rice and noodles. And as we eat, Mr. Chen offers us one last gift. He would like to escort us to the places where our babies were found. Perhaps it would interest us, he says.

And so when the meal is over, we pile back into our rickety white van. And Mr. Chen climbs into a red van parked in front. We follow him out the gate and onward into the heart of Kunshan city. As we drive, I look out my window, and it is hard not to look at the faces, especially the women, it is hard not to think: *Is that her?* Or maybe that one over there. I see familiar cheekbones in that one, and a chin over there. Perhaps that one, perhaps she is Anna's birth-mother? It is hard not to wonder how she's doing. It is hard not to imagine her sobbing. It is so very hard to curb my imagination. It feels like my imagination has never been so invasive. And so I close my eyes and pray. I pray that she'll somehow know that Anna is doing beautifully, that this cheerful child is on her way to a good life with loving parents, not to mention a mule wearing an orange scarf and some horses and more pets than a kid could ever dream of, and a sheep farm next door, and a community of characters to sing songs about, and half of suburban Philadelphia sitting there with bated breath waiting for her, and a large fan club in Pittsburgh that, no doubt, is planning a party at the airport for her arrival—a family so giant, a net of love that extends from here to there and back again.

I sit here praying that somehow she'll know. I put in a request for an angel, her own Sparky or her own Chihuahua or whatever her equivalent may be.

I sit here full of wishes and prayers and special orders, and I sit here with a perfect baby on my lap, humbled.

The van stops. Mr. Chen comes running toward us, pops his head in the door. This, he says, must be quick. I don't understand why this must be quick. Perhaps we are double-parked? He's full of urgency. I get the sense that this is not a government-approved activity, that it's some kind of dangerous favor.

Through Sophie, he tells us this is the place, yes, this is the gate of the hospital where Anna was found. It doesn't look like a hospital, except there is a sign with a red cross outside of it. It could be a storefront. There is a bicycle leaning against it. I think, *Now wait a second.* How could someone have left a bicycle here, at this sacred spot? "We must hurry," Sophie says. We are afraid of getting in some sort of trouble? Alex grabs the camera, hops out to take a picture.

"Um," I say to Anna, holding her face to the window. "Say bye-bye." I pick up her little hand and wave to the spot, the bicycle, the red cross. "Say thank you." And: "Say I love you."

But now I am starting to feel like a ventriloquist. And I think if there is one thing a mom shouldn't be, it's a ventriloquist. But I am new at this.

Our driver revs the engine as if to provide the hint, and Alex pops back into the van with the camera, and we are whisked away from that spot, whisked away forever.

Or not. Maybe Anna will want to come back here someday. I wouldn't mind bringing her back. She'll be a genius, she'll be an astronaut, she'll be the first woman to walk on the moon. And I'll be a tired old lady with fulfilled if ancient dreams, and Alex will be a very old man learning all-new burp tricks. We could eat Cheerios in a van that doesn't take bumps too well. We could stare together at this spot, we could be cheerful or we could cry. We could sit together in a mystery in which we've long since learned we belong.

IV

UNCOMMON LOVE

CHAPTER FIFTEEN

This earth is so dry. You would think the spading fork would work better, but no. I have to use the shovel. I place it about eight inches from the base of the plant. Ready. Aim. I hop and then, *stomp!*

Anna erupts with laughter. She is with me in the garden, sitting on a large ripe pumpkin. Over her windbreaker she's wearing a tutu. A white tutu. And she has her tap shoes on. Indoors, outdoors, this is what she likes to wear.

It's November. We've been back home here at Sweetwater Farm for nine months. Anna is not quite two years old yet, but the thing is, she's already such a . . . person. A person with interests and words and laughter and everything.

Strange how that happens. My baby is a *person*. I don't know why this is taking me so long to get used to. Then again, I'm the one who almost tried to burp a beagle. Maybe, like a lot of people who come late to parenting—and who spend so many years accumulating pets to fill the void—well, maybe we just get confused.

Sometimes in the morning I'll find myself saying, "Anna, do you need to go out?" or, "Come on, Betty, time for your bottle."

I am still new at this.

And so, for that matter, is Betty. My poor little mutt went

through quite the grieving period, hiding under the bed, apparently quite depressed to have lost her alpha status to a goo-coated kid. She's doing better now, thanks in no small part to the bits of cheese dropping like glorious presents from a sky commanded by Anna.

The pumpkin Anna is sitting on should probably be picked. But really, what do we need with yet one more pumpkin? We had quite a harvest this year, and we've now got jack-o'-lanterns everywhere, up the steps, on the picnic tables, atop fenceposts. The place has never looked so festive. And it's funny; Alex and I never bothered carving pumpkins when it was just the two of us. But with Anna it's, *Hey, let's make jack-o'-lanterns!* This is one of the things kids do: They give you your youth back. No one told me about that part. What a spectacular bonus.

Anna's hair is wispy and chocolate brown, and it's almost down to her shoulders already. Well, her neck is short, so . . . Her cheeks aren't as giant as they once were, but there's a fullness to her face that is welcoming and, in its own way, thrilling. I often find that I can't stop looking at her. She is, I'm quite sure, the prettiest girl on Earth.

And joyful. Her personality is easy, braced by a backbone of curiosity, and loaded with laughter. She laughs with her mouth wide open, a crackling AH, AH, AH! I love that laugh.

Ready, aim, hop, *stomp*!

AH, AH, AH!

She really seems to get a kick out of the sight of her mother jumping up, then down, on the blade of a shovel. I can't say I get the joke, but hey, entertainment is entertainment.

I am taking to motherhood. Taking to it with a mixture of ease and enthusiasm. In the end I find myself glad I waited as long as I did to become a mom; I don't think I would have been any good at this in my twenties or my thirties. One of the first things you learn about motherhood is that motherhood means never, ever getting any of your own stuff done. All the things you used to do for yourself—out the window. Hobbies, interests, personal grooming, the nightly news— out the window. The child is the center of your universe, as she should be. She is all that matters.

And so the *you* that you took so long to become is, for at least a time, irrelevant.

I would have resented this, in my twenties and in my thirties. I don't think my maturing *me, me, me* could have taken the competition. I would have been a terrible mother.

And now? Well, I think I've at least got the capacity to get good at this. *Capacity,* I say. I am, you know, making some notable motherhood mistakes.

Take yesterday, for example. Okay, that was a doozy.

I was frying up some pork chops, feeling a little cocky, like maybe I had this motherhood thing all worked out— oh, I was a regular old mom in a Stove Top Stuffing commercial. Anna, dressed in a tutu (pink) and tap shoes, was in her high chair enjoying a cheese-and-peas appetizer. "Cheeeze!" she was saying, because *cheeeze* is about her favorite word.

I heard something behind me. A swooping sound. I turned, and there was nothing there. Nothing except Stevie, the cat, sitting on the piano with his head ducked low. Okay, he knew something I didn't know . . .

I heard a scratching sound, then a fluttering. It was coming from the pot rack. *Swoop. Swoop.* A bird? A little bird! A sparrow?

No, not a bird. No, not a sparrow.

"A BAT! A BAT! A BAT!"

I said this many times, running in circles on my tiptoes, as if somehow I was safer up there. "A BAT! A BAT!" I ducked for cover and went charging out the door.

See, you never know how you're going to react when you see an actual bat in your house. It isn't like seeing a little field mouse. It isn't even like seeing a slithering snake. It is, okay, A BAT.

Out on the porch, breathing in, breathing out, I realized: Wait a second. I just ran out of my house, leaving my child alone in there.

I just left my child in the house with a bat swooping around her.

Mother of the Year.

I dashed back in. Which was no small psychological feat, let me assure you. Every bad bat movie I ever saw was racing through my mind.

Anna was mashing a pea with her right index finger. She was oblivious to the bat, which struck me instantly as kind of *unfair*. But the bat. The bat was hanging, yes, upside down off a pot on the pot rack.

Slowly, stealthily, I scooped Anna up. "We are going outside," I whispered. "We are-going-to-very-quickly-and-quietly-go-outside so Mommy has a chance to THINK."

We dashed out to the porch. "Whew," I said. "I'm fine." It was imperative that she not see my fear. Because motherhood is at least in part about image. Of course! You present a certain portrait of control, of proficiency, like that Stove Top Stuffing lady.

Speaking of which. "Pork chops," I said to Anna. The pork chops were still on the stove. Sizzling. Smoking. Soon to be burning. I had to go back in that house and turn the stove off.

Back in that house where the bat was.

I put Anna down. I took a giant deep breath. In one hasty motion I flung open the door and darted toward the stove. The bat came swooping as the cat went flying after it and the bat landed *on the stove,* right next to the sizzling pork chops. "A BAT! A BAT! A BAT!" I yelled yet again, from a place inside my gut that seemed connected to hell itself. I grabbed the pan and flung it into the sink and ran outside and grabbed Anna, all the while yelling "A BAT! A BAT! A BAT!" and together we charged this way down the driveway.

Well, that went well.

And why was Anna looking at me in the way she was looking at me? She was looking at me in such a way as to say "Who *are* you?"

See, this was bad. My daughter had just discovered that I was not, in fact, the Stove Top Stuffing lady. Not even close.

"A bat, honey," I said to her. "A bat." I wanted her to forgive me. I wanted her to know that some situations are extreme and that a mother should be given some slack.

Just then, I heard a car coming up Wilson Road. Oh, thank the Lord in Heaven.

Alex pulled up, saw us, came leaping out of that car. And I could tell by the look on his face that he thought we were out there to greet him. Like Samantha and Tabitha on *Bewitched.* Oh, he seemed consumed with sweet, mushy thoughts about how nice it was of us to do that. Fatherhood has its own expectations of motherhood.

"A BAT!" I howled at him. "BAT IN HOUSE!"

He said, "Oh." Like his feelings were hurt. Like he was feeling used or something. He trudged inside, got a big empty coffee can. He put it over the bat. He slid the lid on, came outside, let the bat go. No big deal whatsoever.

"Wow!" I said. "Our hero!" I told him how amazed I was. Oh, I pumped him up nice and high to compensate for the part where we weren't really out on the driveway to greet him like Samantha and Tabitha. "Daddy saved the day!" I said to Anna. "Daddy saved us from the *bat*!" Her mother's reputation may have been shattered, but her father's was intact.

Or was it? She was looking at us. First him, then me. She was looking at us with all the wisdom of the world in her eyes. *(So these are my parents?)* It appeared she was about to render her verdict.

"Peeeas!" she said. It is, well, her second most favorite word.

SO THIS BASICALLY brings us up to date. I am, as you may have noted, no longer craving family noise. I barely remember aching for it in that way that once made my teeth hurt. I have no idea what sound my kitchen clock makes. No idea on this earth.

As for the other folks around here, let's see. George and Pat are doing well. Pat has not been stuck on the Food Network for months now. George continues to show Alex the ways of the country. They've been going to a lot of tractor auctions lately. After the last one Alex came home with an ancient, rickety manure spreader George talked him into bidding on. You could tell Alex was trying to look really happy about winning it. Also, George went with Alex to this year's Equine Clinic. Alex told me that the partitions are still the same at the Ramada, but this time he sat up front.

As for the old lady who lives down the road, she broke her hip. She slipped on the ice on her way to the mailbox and nearly froze to death. A guy in a township truck driving by spotted her, saved her; she's doing fine now. We were down at her house recently (no, we still haven't asked her about buying that piece of land), and the township guy stopped in to see how she was doing—and lo and behold, it turned out to be the same road crew guy who found Sparky way back when. We had a nice reunion. I told him everything. I asked him to please keep an eye out for Sparky. He knew I was serious, and he promised he would.

The Scenery Hill Post Office finally moved. Oh, it seemed to take forever for that to happen. You know, the sign finally came in from that company in Canada. Well, it had gotten lost for a while. Lost *in the mail*. Caroline got a real kick out of that one. But then the U.S. Post Office sent out the request for bids to install the sign, and by the time they accepted a bid, the company they had accepted it from had gone out of business. Caroline said, "Isn't this getting *fun*?" The bid finally went, for reasons never to be explained, to an undertaker.

"When I told my husband about the undertaker," Caroline said to me, "he said, 'Oh, don't tell me any more. Because now I don't believe you.' "

But the sign went up and moving day came, and opening day was a pretty gala one here in the 15360 ZIP Code area. Everyone went up to see. "Can you believe this!" Caroline was saying, laughing. "I feel like I work in a shopping mall!" The place is huge, shiny, and clean. There are big bright signs everywhere announcing Express Mail services and inviting you to use your debit card. For opening day Caroline kept the door to the walled-off area open, so we could all see Debbie and Kathy back there with all that *room* to sort mail. And light! And climate control! It was surprising to see how joyful everyone was. It was as if they'd all just won the lottery. In that moment it really did seem about as good as happily-ever-after gets, for a post office.

As for Sammy, the mentally retarded man who had come to depend on Caroline to do his laundry, he's bought his own washer and dryer.

SO THIS IS all that's left. Just me and Anna, a pumpkin, and a shovel.

My foot. My aim. Hop. And: *stomp!*

"AH, AH, AH!"

"Oh, Anna, I'm so glad you're enjoying the show."

The earth opens with its satisfied crunch. A little air in those joints. I'm able to free the roots of the plant with a gentle rocking motion, and soon I'm able to lift it. A daylily. Whew, one whopper of a daylily. It could be the Hyperion variety, or maybe Happy Returns, or Uncommon Love. See, my mother would be able to tell you. She would be able to tell you the botanical name, and what height to expect it to reach, and when.

These are the daylilies I dug up at her house at Springton Lake. These are my mother's daylilies.

When I first brought them to the farm, I didn't know where to put them. Things were, you know, a bit complicated that horrible, paralyzing spring. So in my haste and confusion, I plunked the daylilies into a temporary spot, here in the corner of the vegetable garden.

"Just—stay alive," I said to them. "Do you hear me? That's all you have to do."

I think back now on how driven I was to rescue my mother's flowers. Her garden, her passion. Her lime-green explosion of hope every spring and her wilted brown exercise in faith each fall.

These plants held my mother's wisdom, that's how I looked at it. Wasn't it my responsibility to care for them and it? My mother is, after all, the reason I turned into a gardener. Oh, she's directly responsible for my addiction to dirt and indirectly, I suppose, to my turn finally to become the tiller of one giant fifty-acre garden. But she knows she did this. She says she turned me into a gardener by doing precisely nothing. She never pushed, never made me garden as a kid, never allowed hoeing or tilling to be categorized as chores. She would just quietly go about it all, a shadowy figure in the background of my summers, weeding and singing. "I never wanted you to resent flowers" is the way she says it now.

Nowadays my parents are the only people at Riddle Village who actually have a garden. Well, it's really just lots of pots they put out. They'd made sure to get one of the apartments that opened onto the courtyard, and even though everything at Riddle Village is regulation this and regulation that—with a team of groundskeepers responsible for keeping the place in constant bloom six months of the year—my mom befriended one of the bulb-digger guys, and he quietly let her put out pots of impatiens, and then more pots, and more, and pretty soon people got used to seeing that one corner of the courtyard blooming its own special blooms.

So they have a little garden. My dad waters, my mom pinches and prunes. The two of them are doing beautifully, easing into old age with a kind of dignity I can only hope to one day earn.

About a month or so ago my mom got bothered by something. It occurred to her that she had, over the years, painted pictures of all of her grandchildren. And now there was a new one. Anna. A girl with no picture.

That was her inspiration. That's what sent her charging to her paints. That's what catapulted her through the blank-canvas fear. "I have to do a portrait of her before I kick off!" she said. "She musn't feel left out!"

So she began painting a picture of Anna sitting on the grass, examining a daisy. "And you know what," she said to me on the phone last night, reporting that it's nearly finished, "it's not bad. I am really not too bad at this, sweetie."

"No, you are not," I said. I didn't want to get into it with her. I didn't want to jinx the whole thing by saying "Duh, you're an *artist!*" I reminded her that I had a barn full of her practice canvases, should she ever want to see them.

"Oh, throw those old things away," she said.

"We'll see," I said, even though I already saw. Then I told her that my garden had finally gotten around to letting me know where her daylilies belong: down by the barn, on a bank leaning into the afternoon sun. I told her I was going to go out in the morning and start digging them out of the vegetable garden and transplant them there.

"That sounds lovely," she said.

And so this is what I'm doing.

"As you know, we are running out of transplant weather," I say to Anna as I lift this one plant out of the earth and drop it onto the ground nearby. *Thud.* This thing has more than quadrupled in size since I planted it. "Talk about Happy Returns," I say to her. "We'll have to divide." She sees me aiming the shovel and cracks up before the joke is even told.

Ready, aim, hop, *stomp!*

"Again!" she says. All right, then. Because I do need to divide my divisions.

Ready, aim, hop, *stomp!*

"Again!"

Okay, now she's applauding, the show has gotten so good.

I don't remember laughing at the sight of my mother dividing daylilies. Is this the sort of gardening wisdom I'm going to pass on to Anna? Gardening is . . . funny? I was hoping for something more. I was hoping to be the kind of mother who knew botanical names or at least the kind who could inspire a gardening obsession in her kid.

"Someday maybe you'll take some of these daylilies to your garden," I tell Anna. What a testament to a mother, to want to bring a chunk of her hope, her faith, into your own garden. How do you get to be that kind of mother?

I look at the daylilies, dry and tired and ready to curl up for winter, and wonder how my mother would answer. She would probably tell me to not bother getting all twisted up trying to be the kind of mother she was, but to let loose and be the kind of mother I am. Talk about Uncommon Love.

Ready, aim, hop, *stomp*!

"Again!"

Oh, we are having a wonderful time. We are dividing the past. We are preparing the future. We are rooted in the here and now.

And we are working up a sweat. Whew. Each of these whopper daylilies is yielding about eight plants. And I've got nine, ten, eleven, I've got twelve rows of these things. Why did I take so many? Did I really need *that* much of my mother's wisdom? Twelve times ten is one hundred and twenty. If I get eight plants out of each clump, that's almost *a thousand* daylilies I have to plant. This is exhausting, horrible news.

I wipe my brow, look at Anna. "Never, ever do math while you're gardening," I tell her. "Remember that."

Ready, aim, hop, *stomp*!

"AH, AH, AH!"

And so we spend the next few hours like this, hopping and stomping and laughing into Hyperion, or Happy Returns, or Uncommon Love, our perfectly complete unknown.

ACKNOWLEDGMENTS

I wish to thank my mother, who has lovingly endured my use of her life and wisdom as material for my stories.

Portions of this book first appeared in different form in *The Washington Post Magazine* and *Esquire*. My thanks to the editors of those magazines for helping to bring this project to life.

I am grateful to my agent, Andrew Blauner, for his continued support and friendship; to my devoted reader and friend, Robin Michaelson, who conceived of this book and rallied behind it; and to Kate Miciak, my spirited editor at Bantam, for the infectious enthusiasm she brought to the project.

My thanks to the people of Scenery Hill, for passing on their wondrous stories. To the babes and my family, for sticking around while I locked myself away in the attic at the farm to write this.

To Anna, for the dream and the dancing. To her new sister, Sasha, whose promise motivated me once again to the moon and back.

And to Alex, who by joining me on this journey, made it happen.

ABOUT THE AUTHOR

Jeanne Marie Laskas is a columnist for *The Washington Post Magazine,* where her "Significant Others" essays appear weekly. A "writer at large" at *GQ,* she writes for numerous national magazines, and her work has been selected for Best American Sports Writing and other anthologies. She is the author of *The Balloon Lady and Other People I Know; We Remember: Women Born at the Turn of the Century Tell Their Lives in Words and Pictures,* and *Fifty Acres and a Poodle,* available in trade paperback from Bantam Books and featured on Animal Planet's "A Pet Story."

A professor in the creative nonfiction program at the University of Pittsburgh, she lives and farms with her husband and daughters, along with their animals, at Sweetwater Farm in Scenery Hill, Pennsylvania.